BLACKOUT

BLACKOUT

*Reinventing Women for
Wartime British Cinema*

ANTONIA LANT

PRINCETON UNIVERSITY PRESS

PRINCETON, NEW JERSEY

Library of Congress Cataloging-in-Publication Data

Lant, Antonia
Blackout : reinventing women for wartime British cinema /
Antonia Lant.
p. cm.
Includes bibliographical references and index.
ISBN 0-691-05540-8 — ISBN 0-691-00828-0 (pbk.)
1. Women in motion pictures. 2. World War, 1939–1945—Motion
pictures and the war. 3. Motion pictures—Great Britain—History.
4. Sex role in motion pictures. 5. Feminism and motion pictures.
6. National characteristics, British, in motion pictures.
7. Motion pictures—Social aspects—Great Britain. I. Title.
PN1995.9.W6L36   1991
791.43′652042—dc20   90-25290

This book has been composed in Linotron Times Roman

Princeton University Press books are printed on
acid-free paper, and meet the guidelines for permanence
and durability of the Committee on Production
Guidelines for Book Longevity of the
Council on Library Resources

Printed in the United States of America by
Princeton University Press,
Princeton, New Jersey

2 4 6 8 10 9 7 5 3 1
(Pbk.)
2 4 6 8 10 9 7 5 3 1

For

B. S., T.P.R.,

and

R.P.D.

CONTENTS

LIST OF ILLUSTRATIONS   ix

ACKNOWLEDGMENTS   xiii

LIST OF ABBREVIATIONS   xv

INTRODUCTION Cinema *in Extremis*   3

CHAPTER 1 Projecting National Identity   19

CHAPTER 2 The Mobile Woman: Femininity in Wartime Cinema   59

CHAPTER 3 The Blackout   114

CHAPTER 4 Processing History: The Timing of a *Brief Encounter*   153

CONCLUSION From Mufti to Civvies: *A Canterbury Tale*   197

APPENDIX I Bogart or Bacon: The British Film Industry during
    World War II   221

APPENDIX II British Box Office Information, 1940–1950   231

SELECT FILMOGRAPHY   235

SELECT BIBLIOGRAPHY   243

INDEX   253

LIST OF ILLUSTRATIONS

1.1 Blitzed BFI Doorway, *Sight and Sound* 9, no. 35 (Autumn 1940), front cover.   27

1.2 Cartoon on the impermanence of wartime's shifted class boundaries, *Everybody's Weekly*, 3 February 1945, p. 13.   42

1.3 Macleans toothpaste advertisement, *Picture Post*, 20 June 1942.   54

1.4 Ministry of Food information bulletin, *Time and Tide*, 20 November 1943, p. 957.   55

1.5 Advertisement for Weetabix, *Picture Post*, 6 June 1942.   56

1.6 Hollywood femininity, cartoon, *Colliers*, 5 March 1949, p. 18.   58

2.1 Advertisement for Clarks shoes, *Picture Post*, 17 February 1940, p. 3.   64

2.2 "Will She Have a Chance to Wear It?" *Picture Post*, 6 January 1945, front cover.   67

2.3 Fougasse cartoon, "Joan and John," *Punch*, 2 September 1942, p. 183.   70

2.4 "Keep Mum, She's Not So Dumb!" Wartime poster, courtesy of the Trustees of the Imperial War Museum, London.   71

2.5 G. Lacoste poster, "Don't Tell Aunty and Uncle," courtesy of the Trustees of the Imperial War Museum, London.   77

2.6 Reginald Mount anti-VD poster, 1943–44, courtesy of the Trustees of the Imperial War Museum, London.   78

2.7 Poster artwork for *Next of Kin* (1942), courtesy of the Museum of Modern Art, New York.   79

2.8 Advertisement for Evan Williams shampoo, *Picture Post*, 16 December 1939.   80

2.9 Advertisement for Palmolive soap, *Picture Post*, 18 April 1942.   81

2.10 Advertisement for Potter and Moore's Powder-Cream, *Picture Post*, 19 October 1940.   82

2.11 Advertisement for Kemt hair spray, *Picture Post*, 2 March 1940.   82

2.12 "La Donna è Mobile," cartoon in *Time and Tide*, 16 October 1943, p. 841.   87

2.13 Howard looks down from the parapet. Frame enlargement from *The Gentle Sex*, courtesy of the National Film Archive, London.   91

2.14 First title image from *The Gentle Sex*. Frame enlargement, courtesy of the National Film Archive, London.   95

2.15 Title image from *The Gentle Sex*. Frame enlargement, courtesy of the National Film Archive, London.   95

2.16 Title image from *The Gentle Sex*. Frame enlargement, courtesy of the National Film Archive, London.   95

2.17 Cartoon, *Everybody's Weekly*, 20 March 1943, p. 13.   98

2.18 Cartoon by John, *Everybody's Weekly*, 24 July 1943, p. 13.   99

ix

LIST OF ILLUSTRATIONS

2.19 Poster by Jonathan Fosse for the Air Ministry, 1941–43. Courtesy of the Trustees of the Imperial War Museum, London. 100

2.20 J. W. Taylor cartoon, *Punch*, 23 June 1943, p. 524. 102

2.21 Cartoon of tattooing, *Everybody's Weekly*, 9 January 1943, p. 13. 103

2.22 Cartoon of an A.T.S. supply room, *Everybody's Weekly*, 24 July 1943, p. 13. 104

2.23 Cartoon about barrage balloon duty, *Everybody's Weekly*, 16 January 1943, p. 13. 105

2.24 David Langdon cartoon, *Punch*, 9 September 1942, p. 216. 106

2.25 Supply room scene. Frame enlargement from *The Gentle Sex*, courtesy of the National Film Archive, London. 107

2.26 Good-time Dot. Frame enlargement from *The Gentle Sex*, courtesy of the National Film Archive, London. 108

2.27 Frank Reynolds cartoon, "The Recruit," *Punch*, 19 September 1942, p. 241. 109

2.28 Article illustration on wartime corsets, *Picture Post*, 2 March 1940, p. 26. 110

3.1 Cathy sees Robert off at the troop train. *Perfect Strangers*, 1945, production still, courtesy of the Museum of Modern Art, New York. 120

3.2 Robert and Cathy admire each other's new star image after three years apart in the forces. *Perfect Strangers*, production still, courtesy of the National Film Archive, London. 122

3.3 Advertisement for Mazda lamps, *Time and Tide*, 23 October 1943, p. 867. 131

3.4 Advertisement for Osram light bulbs, *Picture Post*, 2 March 1940, p. 6. 132

3.5 Advertisement for Ediswan lamps, *Picture Post*, 10 February 1940, p. 10. 133

3.6 Ghilchik cartoon, "The Light is Let In," *Time and Tide*, 28 April 1945, p. 353. 134

3.7 The doomed couple of *Piccadilly Incident*. Production still, courtesy of the National Film Archive, London. 136

3.8 The new international family of *Piccadilly Incident*. Production still, courtesy of the National Film Archive, London. 137

3.9 Lady Barbara Skelton (Margaret Lockwood) brandishing her gun. Production still from *The Wicked Lady*, courtesy of the Museum of Modern Art, New York. 139

3.10 Fougasse cartoon, *Punch*, 27 August 1941, p. 183. 143

3.11 "Wait! Count 15 Slowly." Poster designed by G. R. Morris around 1940 for the National Safety First Association, which in 1941 became the Royal Society for the Prevention of Accidents. Courtesy of the Trustees of the Imperial War Museum, London. 145

3.12 Illustration from an article on shelter life, *Picture Post*, 26 October 1940. 147

3.13 Soap advertisement, *Picture Post*, 2 November 1940, p. 40. 149

4.1 Mervyn Wilson cartoon, *Punch*, 17 October 1945, p. 329. 160

4.2 The Ketchworth fireside. Still from *Brief Encounter*, courtesy of the Museum of Modern Art, New York. 186

4.3 The underground romance. Still from *Brief Encounter*, courtesy of the
    Museum of Modern Art, New York.   188
4.4 The ramshackle boathouse. Still from *Brief Encounter*, courtesy of the
    Museum of Modern Art, New York.   189
4.5 The realist woman: Laura Jesson. Still from *Brief Encounter*, courtesy of
    the Museum of Modern Art, New York.   190
5.1 Allison at the station. Frame enlargement from *A Canterbury Tale*,
    courtesy of the National Film Archive, London.   200
5.2 Thomas Culpepper. Frame enlargement from *A Canterbury Tale*, courtesy
    of the National Film Archive, London.   201
5.3 Allison and Bob in Canterbury Cathedral. Still from *A Canterbury Tale*,
    courtesy of the Museum of Modern Art, New York.   202
5.4 "Mary Jenkins," cartoon on the Women's Land Army, *Punch*, 26 August
    1942, p. 163.   203
5.5 J. W. Taylor cartoon on the Women's Land Army, *Punch*, 18 July 1945,
    p. 51.   204
5.6 John cartoon on the Women's Land Army, *Punch*, 13 August 1941, p.
    139.   205
5.7 Prudence Honeywood and a W.L.A. worker. Frame enlargement from *A
    Canterbury Tale*, courtesy of the National Film Archive, London.   206
5.8 Allison listens to Culpepper's local history lecture. Frame enlargement
    from *A Canterbury Tale*, courtesy of the National Film Archive, London. 209
5.9 Cartoon on the nylon stocking supply, *Punch*, 14 November 1945, p. 409. 212
5.10 Allison investigates the crime, by interviewing a fellow W.L.A. worker.
    Frame enlargement from *A Canterbury Tale*, courtesy of the National
    Film Archive, London.   215

ACKNOWLEDGMENTS

THE RESEARCH for this book was made possible by fellowships from the Fulbright Foundation, the Yale Center for British Art, the Lehman Foundation, and the Center for International and Area Studies.

Many thanks are due to William K. Everson for giving me access to his superb collection of British films, and for his suggestions for the manuscript. Dudley Andrew at the University of Iowa, Elaine Burrows at the British National Film Archive, Scott Wilcox at the Yale Center for British Art, Bill Ford at Cornell University's Olin Library, and the staff of the British Film Institute Library, the Lincoln Center Library for the Performing Arts, the New York Museum of Modern Art, the Sterling Memorial Library, Yale University, the Imperial War Museum, London, the Library of Congress (Motion Picture, Broadcasting, and Recorded Sound Division), and the Sussex University Mass Observation Archive were all most helpful in making sources available.

I thank the many friends and colleagues who freely and willingly discussed, reacted, and contributed to the work at its various stages, especially Andy Brower, Leslie Camhi, Lynn Siefert, Karen Lucic, Charles Musser, and the gardeners of North Triphammer Road. Paul Chedlow helped wherever and whenever he could, and I thank him warmly. I owe much to my former teachers at Leeds University, T. J. Clark and Griselda Pollock, and to colleagues and teachers at Yale, particularly Jennifer Wicke and David Rodowick. I am grateful for the contribution of students in my seminar on Powell and Pressburger at New York University, especially Doug Riblet, Ingrid Periz, David Lugowski, and Graham Fuller, and for discussions I had with Wolfgang Schivelbusch about the blackout. I thank Joanna Hitchcock, Carolyn Fox, and Laura Ward at Princeton University Press, and John Belton, Linda Williams, Christine Gledhill, Robert Herbert, Richard Allen, and Robert Sklar for their careful readings of the manuscript; I am particularly grateful to Donald Crafton, who gave his generous support, both scholarly and practical, all the way through the project.

LIST OF ABBREVIATIONS

Ack-Ack	Antiaircraft fire
A.C.T.	Association of Ciné-Technicians
A.F.S.	Auxiliary Fire Service
A.R.P.	Air Raid Precaution
A.T.C.	Air Training Corps
A.T.S.	Auxiliary Territorial Service
B.B.C.	British Broadcasting Corporation
C.E.A.	Cinema Exhibitors' Association
G.I.	General Issue (or Government Issue)
G.P.O.	General Post Office
L.D.V.	Local Defence Volunteers (later Home Guard)
L.M.S.	London, Midland, and Scottish Railways
M.O.I.	Ministry of Information
M.O.L.	Ministry of Labour
R.A.F.	Royal Air Force
U.S.A.F.	United States Air Force
W.A.A.C.	Women's Army Auxiliary Corps (U.K., World War I)
W.A.A.F.	Women's Auxiliary Air Force
W.A.C.	Women's Army Corps (U.S.A.)
W.L.A.	Women's Land Army
W.R.A.F.	Women's Royal Air Force (World War I)
W.R.N.S.	Women's Royal Naval Service ("Wrens")
W.V.S.	Women's Volunteer Service

BLACKOUT

Cinema *in Extremis*

I T I S H A R D to think of a cinema less celebrated than the British. Accused of being too talky and long-winded, too indebted to theater, bereft of a distinct visual style, and altogether lacking in verve and pace, this cinema has been written off as dull, odd, or at best marginal. While the uneasy alliance between British cinema and the enormously influential British theatrical tradition, in both its upper- and lower-class manifestations, may justify this reaction, there has also been a conspicuous countermaneuver by critics who commemorate British cinema's dismal reputation by lovingly repeating epithets redolent of the pity and disdain felt by others toward its products. This activity represents, in part, the need to cast coherence upon a country's cinema, a need particularly experienced by critics working during World War II. The specification of consistent stylistic failure builds, in a convoluted way, the possibility of an identity. Expressions of disparagement and disinterest provide the wherewithal to clump together films emanating from Britain. Indeed, Truffaut's pronouncement on the fundamental incompatibility between "cinema" and "Britain" has by now been used to distinguish the very cinema it set out to dispense with.[1] The Frenchman's observation becomes the hallowed ground on which the British cinema can be made to coalesce as a national product.

We should not be surprised. National identity is nothing if not internationally defined. No cinema *has* national identity; rather, it is secured cross-culturally, by comparison with other national outputs, formed as part of a circuit of reciprocated exchange. Within this international matrix,

---

[1] I refer to Truffaut's "Well, to put it bluntly, isn't there a certain incompatibility between the terms cinema and Britain?"; Alan Lovell's paper, "The British Cinema: The Unknown Cinema"; and Peter Wollen's comment, "The English cinema . . . is still utterly amorphous, unclassified, unperceived." See François Truffaut, *Hitchcock: The Definitive Study of Alfred Hitchcock by François Truffaut* (New York: Simon and Schuster, 1984), p. 124; Alan Lovell, "The British Cinema: The Unknown Cinema," seminar paper (British Film Institute Education Department, 1969); Peter Wollen, *Signs and Meaning in the Cinema* (London: Secker and Warburg, 1972), p. 115. Charles Barr provides an extensive survey of this discourse in *All Our Yesterdays: Ninety Years of British Cinema* (London: British Film Institute Publishing, 1986), pp. 1–7.

British cinema inhabits an embattled but uniquely interesting space. Here is a film industry whose history has been more entangled with, not to say strangled by, Hollywood's than that of any other country: domination has been economic, stylistic, linguistic, and political.[2] But the space of British cinema still remains distinct, if only geographically, or discursively, and if only at particular historical moments. One of these was World War II.

The desire for a distinct national style has always been part of the British cinema endeavor, but at no time was this project more urgent, nor the existence of British cinema more imperiled, than during that war. Under conditions of "total war," or "The People's War," as it was then termed, both the cinema and its audience were threatened with extinction. The very possibility of film production and projection withered away. Cinemas and studios were requisitioned, technicians were conscripted, and even light was rationed. Familiar conditions of film-viewing vanished: screenings were punctuated with air raid sirens and evacuations, and were held in canteens, newly formed Army and Navy Camp Film Societies, factory halls, and mobile vans as often as in the "ideal" surroundings of the motion picture auditorium.

These changes in the technology, exhibition, and reception of cinema took place within a wider context of social transformation. Families were disbanded and children were transported. Consumable items were rationed. Blacked-out nights begot a new sensibility of both fear and excitement in everyone who had occasion to maneuver about in them. Classed compartments, always an integral part of the British railway journey, were partially abolished to facilitate troop and passenger movement. Women were compulsorily drafted, and they became almost entirely responsible for running Britain's antiaircraft defenses, and radar stations in Southern England. As the most familiar daily routines disappeared, those surviving acquired a peculiar, symbolic glow: rearing a champion marrow became an act of patriotism; sighting an orange, a precious glimpse of peace. Domestic life lurched from being the epitome of the ordinary to the quintessence of the extraordinary. It became a central topic for radio, and for documentary and feature film. Never, until Chantal Akerman's *Jeanne Dielman* (1979), had so much footage been focused on the banal household chores of preparing and canning food, making and repairing clothing, collecting and recycling materials.

Cinematic fictions were inevitably measured against social changes, even those films whose narratives were set in the remote past. Screen sto-

---

[2] Robert Sklar has described America's domination of British cinema as "one of the most remarkable hegemonies in the history of intercultural communications." Robert Sklar, *Movie-Made America: A Cultural History of American Movies* (New York: Random House, 1975), p. 215.

ries would stand or fall on this ground; even period films invited their audiences to make comparisons with their own present. Laurence Olivier's *Henry V* (1945), prefaced by a word of support for the boys overseas, suggests that Shakespeare's tale of Anglo-French strife should be understood in contemporary terms. And Gainsborough's first successful costume melodrama of the war, *The Man in Grey* (1943), begins at a London auction that is being suspended for contravening the blackout. The flashback to Regency times, for a feature-length story of gypsy fortune-tellers and aristocratic lovers, occurs with the onset of blackness, and ends by returning to the auction again in the light of morning. The two historical protagonists, now redressed in wartime uniform, as they were at the opening of the film, take a modern bus together down the street, prefiguring the wartime spectator's departure from the cinema auditorium. It is as if the conditions of war force even period film narratives into a closer relation with their viewer's lives, while the effort makes the ever-present gap between cinema and experience all the more conspicuous.

The effect of government wartime policy was to mobilize the entire nation of men and women, not only through cinema, but through myriad other media from radio to magazines, from official pamphlets to posters. (The infant medium of television, however, was shut down from 1 September 1939 until 7 June 1946). Through legislation, through the daily experiences of observing the blackout, food rationing, and so on, the individual would come to recognize her role in the crisis. Eric Biddle, writing in 1942 of lessons America might learn from British policy, put the strategy in these terms: ''It was necessary to inculcate in every citizen the maximum feeling of responsibility as part of the actual defense of the community.''[3] Such citizens would then not be terrorized into panic, he wrote, as were the French when they jammed roads in 1940, making the military defense of the frontier impossible. Again making the comparison with the French, Biddle stressed the importance of ''preserving the vital force'' of the nation rather than worrying about saving its buildings and architectural monuments. It was in this more nebulous, mental reshaping of citizens along nationalist lines that the cinema participated.

Wartime films strove to produce in an entire national audience a sense of recognition, a feeling of being that person spoken to by a film. However, achieving such direct and static-free identification was impossible, in part because the wartime audience was literally so dispersed and fragmented. From the outbreak of war until the end of 1945 there were some

[3] Eric H. Biddle, *The Mobilization of the Home Front: The British Experience and Its Significance for the United States* (Chicago: Public Service Administration Press, 1942), p. 26.

34,750,000 changes of address in England and Wales in a civilian population of about 38 million that generally moved very little, and had no history of civilian movement, unlike that of the United States and its West for instance.[4] In wartime England and Wales, almost everyone moved in unprecedented numbers, while contemporaries now described the country as a "nation of migrants," and as having an "atomized" cinema audience.[5] It was partly in response to this fragmentation that members of the nation were individually numbered for the first time ever. A National Register was drawn up by the end of September 1939, and buff identity cards were given out to all on the list. The nation gained an identity, at least as a mathematical sequence.

Under these conditions there was an acute demand for coherent representations of the nation which could show it to be unified despite its real differences of class, nationality, culture, and gender. National differences within the Isle's boundaries were especially visible, and audible, after the influx of European refugees in the late 1930s, the arrival of European forces—Free French and Poles—after the war began, and the G.I. "invasion" of 1942–43. These nationalities supplemented the diversity of Scottish, Welsh, Irish, and English already within the so-called United Kingdom, as well as regional differences between North and South, and the class stratification of virtually all areas. To respond to the conflicting demands of the film industry, government, film critics, and even contemporary audiences, representations needed to pull together these differences in order to emphasize that the most important divide was that between Britain and Germany. Cinema, with its uniquely pleasurable power to shape subjectivity, was peculiarly affected by these pressures. The need to defang the class system led, paradoxically, to an increased representation of, and narrative discussion of, class contrasts on screen, with more central roles for working class characters (and actors), and both upper middle and lower class protagonists sometimes being shown undergoing equivalent hardships. On the other hand, the axis of sexual difference, that foundational structure of visual and narrative categories by which screen men and women are kept distinct yet coupled, became attenuated, less visible, in British wartime cinema: couples were separated or their unions postponed; stories revolved around single-sex, military or civilian groups; the heroine was deglamorized, while the hero was, on occasion, made glamorous.

---

[4] L. Hargreaves and M. M. Gowing, *Civil Industry and Trade: The History of the Second World War* (London: H.M.S.O., 1952), p. 283. Many of these changes of address resulted from temporary moves, to and fro.

[5] Sheila Ferguson and Hilde Fitzgerald, *Studies in the Social Services* (London: H.M.S.O., 1954), p. 100; J. P. Mayer, *British Cinemas and Their Audiences: Sociological Studies* (London: Dennis Dobson, 1948), p. 8.

Sexual difference too had to make way for that temporarily more important difference—of nationality.

The demographic character of wartime cinema audiences was of such urgent concern to government, filmmakers, and producers alike that a plethora of surveys were conducted during the 1940s to establish the character of that audience by class, sex, age, and so on in order to streamline the encounter between individual spectators and screen fictions.[6] But the lack of correlation between these elements is clearly visible with the hindsight of fifty years: the extreme conditions of war produce noticeable failures and discrepancies of address, forced to the surface by mobilization. A couple of examples will illustrate this.

Victory Wedding (1944), a twenty-minute entertainment short starring John Mills and Dulcie Gray, was directed by Jessie Matthews, Britain's top female box office star of the mid-thirties. As the film opens, the male narrator, in voice-over, calls up both men and women, alternately and together, as different pronouns are heard on the sound track. At first the voice describes the feelings of a man, Bill (Mills), who realizes that Mary (Gray) still loves him: Bill loves the simple things that "millions of us like him" also love, says the voice. Here the term "us" refers most unambiguously to men who love women, although the female audience is also being addressed here through the male form. As the film draws to a close, however, the voice-over gradually comes to speak directly to women: "Mary, like all of us in these difficult times, won't give way to self-pity. . . . Mary knows she can help her Bill by working hard and saving hard, and so can you, by putting every penny you can into war savings; you can help your man win that better way of life we're all fighting for." Here "us in these difficult times" includes women alongside men, or may even refer specifically to women, but by the next sentence women have become a distinct and separate group, for "you" is the female who can help her man by saving while "we," men and women, fight for a better life. The pressure of reconciling gender roles to the imperatives of wartime mobilization is registered here in the perceptible strain between meanings of first- and second-person pronouns.

A second example adds the variable of nationality to the search for coherent audience address. *Singing with the Stars* (1943) was a ten-minute short made at the old Paramount studios in Astoria, Long Island, which

---

[6] See, for instance, Kathleen Box, *The Cinema and the Public* (London: Social Survey Report no. 106, Central Office of Information, 1947), based on surveys done with Louis Moss in 1943; John Cross and Arnold Rattenbury, eds., *Screen and Audience* (London: 1947); Mark Abrams, "The British Cinema Audience," *Hollywood Quarterly* 3 (1947–48); Mark Abrams, "The British Cinema Audience, 1949," *Hollywood Quarterly* 4 (1949–50); and Mayer, *British Cinemas and Their Audiences*.

had been taken over by the American Army Filmmaking Unit. Bea Lillie, a British actress well known in the United States for her comedic stage roles, had instigated the project as one of the G.I. Movie Weekly films to be shown both in America and elsewhere, including G.I. camps in Britain. The film is set, as the opening shot announces, in a "British-American Servicemen's Canteen of London," an entirely fictional space (American troops in Britain had their own camps, separate from the local military), existing only on celluloid, and still under construction as the film opens.

A moving camera ushers the viewer through the canteen entrance, past a hostess who is nailing up the canteen's sign, to meet "Miss" Bea Lillie and her other hostesses. The others sport aprons and bows—accoutrements of femininity—while Lillie cuts an androgynous, even mannish figure, with her hair tucked into a fez, and her striped jumpsuit—a cross between pajamas and a clown outfit. She wears army boots underneath the lot, apparently a gift from a midwestern G.I. Halfway through the film, Lillie gives the following instructions, looking toward the camera, preparing the external G.I. audience for a sing-along version of "You Made Me Love You," the popular 1913 tune:

> You fellows on the left—you're the boys.
> And you boys on the right, well, you're the girls.
> Get it? On the left, boys; on the right, girls.

A white "ball" bouncing from word to word in the lower screen encourages the audience to join in, while a chorus of male American voices, laid into the sound track, shifts to a falsetto register when they are "the girls." Lillie periodically reestablishes her rules by holding up alternately first a moustache, and then a rose, to the left and right sides of the screen. The camera pans from left to right, as if synchronized to her gestures, to reinforce the imposed, fictional sexual division on the external audience, the inevitably all-male population of G.I.'s.

This peculiar sexual reorganization humorously feminizes half of the viewers: it asks men to identify either as men or as women, depending on where they sit. The axis of sexual difference is not within the fiction (all on screen are women *pace* Lillie's masculine aspect), nor within the audience (which is all male), but at the interface of the two. This displacement—specifically a product of wartime—becomes the source of the film's humor. At the final chorus "all" are instructed to join in, so that the difference between "boys" and "girls" is merged, a difference that has never existed. Nevertheless, the removal of the fictional difference works as a trope for the production of homogeneity in a band of fighting men. The idea of sexual difference is first introduced, and then made to vanish, to symbolize the new international unity of allies, which is the film's pri-

8

mary job. Further, the maneuver in and out of the gendered divide preserves the idea that the ally is above all male.

The assumption of an all-male audience, which wartime conditions permit, also encourages an unusual sexual joke, a deflation of male pleasure at the spectacle of Lillie. As she adds "rhythm" to one of her songs her breasts start to wobble in time with the music, a movement exaggerated by the stripes of her costume. Lillie acknowledges the involuntary bodily response, first by looking down, and then by looking directly into the camera, and confronting her onlookers with a simple apology: her utterance of the word "sorry" lyses the joke.

Singing with the Stars also produces the identity of the "ally" by articulating and then blending differences of nationality. Included on the canteen menu are food hybrids: "London baked beans," "Hot dogs on crumpets," "Steak and kidney pie à la mode," and "Hot and cold running beer"; cricket *and* baseball are advertised "on the lawn." The film separates and retreads the overlapping categories of foreigner and enemy for its British-based American audience. As Bea Lillie puts it: "I think that underneath the lingo, all of us, Yanks and Tommies, have an awful lot in common. . . . God save Mrs. Miniver and Miss Grable!" She "forgets" that Mrs. Miniver was a fictional, American version of a British mother for the sake of reaching the transplanted American male audience.

These two shorts—*Singing with the Stars* and *Victory Wedding*—invite audiences to shift allegiances during the film, across both gender and national lines: in the case of *Singing with the Stars* one shift (nationality) is expressed through the other (gender). These films do not produce simple, single identities for their spectators, but ask them to reform identity—into the role of the ally, into a state of mobilization, into a state of being a national subject. A multitude of other feature and documentary films were screened in Britain in 1943 besides *Singing with the Stars*. Among the top money-makers at British theaters were *Casablanca*, *In Which We Serve*, *Hello Frisco Hello*, *The Life and Death of Colonel Blimp*, *The Black Swan*, *The Man in Grey*, *The Gentle Sex*, *The Adventures of Tartu*, and *Desert Victory*.[7] In other words, a suspense romance, a naval adventure, an American musical, a Powell and Pressburger political satire, a pirate swashbuckler, a Gainsborough costume melodrama, a women-in-uniform omnibus picture, a spy thriller, and an official documentary could all successfully compete for the substantial wartime box office takings. Such an eclectic group of popular pictures points again to the eccentricities of war-

---

[7] *Hello Frisco Hello*, *Casablanca*, and *The Black Swan* were American; *In Which We Serve*, *The Life and Death of Colonel Blimp*, *The Man in Grey*, *The Gentle Sex*, *The Adventures of Tartu* (U.S. title: *Tartu*), and *Desert Victory* were British. See Appendix II for more information on the 1940s British box office.

time exhibition, production, and audiences: diversity of exhibition locations *and* exhibited films betrays the parallel diversity of audience expressed in the phrase "a nation of migrants." This audience had been reared on a mixed but thoroughly one-sided diet of American and British pictures: Hollywood films, and Miss Grable, were probably far more deeply rooted in British cultural life than was the native product. How then could these native viewers be mobilized for the war effort through their screen experiences? How could cinema be engaged to unify such a diverse population in the interests of national defense?

Establishing gendered genres is one way in which films construct audiences. The "male" combat movie and the "female" "Woman's Film" are two recently investigated Hollywood examples of such gender-specific genres.[8] But in wartime Britain, except for the case of the Gainsborough costume melodramas beloved of women, traditional genre-gender associations were weak; the cinema addressed itself to an audience that, while often dominated by one sex, was no longer characterized by conventional gender distinctions. Under conditions of "total war" women were conscripted to "stand in" for men, and men even stood in for women on some occasions (as at the Forces canteen). Through their arrangement of images and sounds, through their use of point-of-view shots, voice-overs, lighting, music, casting, and so on, wartime British films, as any other films, sought to address this audience. However, such textual elements can never control the sex, class, or nationality of the viewer, or determine every viewer's understanding of a film. It is this gap between the text and its reception that becomes particularly apparent in wartime under the political pressure to acknowledge and address the very complexity of audiences. In the case of *Victory Wedding*, the use of the phrase "your man" requests clearly, if briefly, the attention of a female spectator, whether or not she is actually present in the audience, while *Singing with the Stars* makes a mockery of this kind of invitation by recording fake castrati to accompany Lillie, even though it too invites its viewers to choose between many identities—British or American, male or female, foreign or Allied, or all of these.

Through the formal arrangement of the apparatus, through imagery, characters, and narrative themes, films invite identification by their audiences, but when familiar habits of the cinema, such as its patterning of narrative resolution through gendered reference, is overtaken by vast national changes—as in the case of World War II Britain—then the bonding

[8] See Jeanine Basinger, *The World War Two Combat Film: Anatomy of a Genre* (New York: Columbia University Press, 1986), and Mary Ann Doane, *The Desire to Desire: The Woman's Film of the 1940s* (Bloomington: Indiana University Press, 1987).

of audience to screen becomes all the more fragile. The ready perception by contemporary British women of Hollywood cinema as now having a particular and distinct national style that does not speak to local conditions is a symptom of the new friability of relations between audience and screen. One woman of thirty, interviewed by a mass-observer after the war, considers that most films "are an insult to the public's intelligence."[9] She continues: "Look at the maids in Hollywood films. Do they look as if they've ever done a hard day's work—they're all glamorous girls dolled up to the nines. You can't just sit there pretending." She, along with many other British filmgoers, perceives the rhetoric of Hollywood now as historically specific and national, rather than universal and natural; Hollywood cinema is exposed to be a national cinema unders the increased pressure of national comparison that wartime produces.

It is no accident that the woman quoted above perceives national difference particularly through the imaging of the female body, for in wartime the female screen body performs her own, crucial bout of national service. It becomes a contested site, a place where national allegiances must be fought over, won, or lost in a literalization of "sexual politics." More specifically, the image of glamorized femininity becomes tied to American identity in particular within British cultural productions, and not only screen productions, but also those of critics and of audiences responding to magazines and surveys. The idea of female glamour takes on a heightened national character: femininity too is mobilized for the war effort.

Wartime conditions make conspicuous a further aspect of the way identifications are formed in the cinema auditorium. Wartime spectators are mobilized through a host of media and events besides that of cinema going; the experience of screen narrative and image is not isolated from experience around and beyond the cinema. This is always the case, but the extreme conditions of war now make it visible. The huge and enveloping propaganda apparatus that mass mobilization required meant that any wartime film was entrapped in a vast legislative, discursive web, across which multiple, possibly conflicting images of patriotism and of gender were linked. Women filmgoers had to make sense, for instance, of a range of representations of themselves: from being inessential to national identity, to being central to it, to threatening it. Norms for womanhood circulated through writing, advertising, cartooning, and posters, as well as film; through legislation, rules, etiquette, and upbringing; and through an infinity of other social, psychological, aesthetic, and political forms. Notions of how women should behave and think were shaped and maintained

[9] Income D (March 1950), in Mass Observation Archive, Films Box 15 File H.

11

through these forms, so that however abstract, contradictory, or ethereal they might be, they affected and set limits on male and female behavior.

To convey the texture of the wartime reading of films, to give a sense of the three-dimensional lattice that any wartime film inhabits, this book, while positing films as its central texts, investigates the welter of other materials that adhere to them: cartoons, advertisements, diaries, memoirs, articles, reviews, and so on. In Pierre Macherey's words, it is not just a question of "studying the text but perhaps also . . . everything which has been written about it, everything which has been collected on it, become attached to it—like shells on a rock by the seashore forming a whole incrustation."[10] Any individual film exists within a mesh of other texts that impinge upon it and vary its meaning, particularly as that film text becomes overlain by the deposit of fifty years. For these reasons, the book casts a net wide enough to consider, for example, other traces of wartime femininity, other evidences of its material erosion and reinvention besides that found in films, for it is in relation to these other media that films produced their meanings. It also considers the related phenomena of rationing, illegitimacy, the blackout, and ack-ack fire, and the effect of British cinema's eternally more powerful rival—Hollywood—on the attempt to form an indigenous national cinema. And it looks to cartoons, jokes, and advertisements, for, as Les Cleveland suggests, they can be understood as "uninhibited utterances, reflecting popular cultured attitudes and feelings that are otherwise likely to be censored or concealed in the interests of morale."[11] These are drawn from a variety of magazines which also addressed diverse sectors of the population: the newly founded, popular *Picture Post* (publishing from 1 October 1938), whose format imitated the American *Life* magazine; *Punch*, which spoke to an upper middle-class, predominantly male audience; *Time and Tide*, which historically had a female following; and several others, including *Everybody's Weekly*, whose audience conformed to the magazine's name.

The marshalling of such a wide collection of representations captures the tensions and oscillations underlying the image systems of wartime

[10] Pierre Macherey, interview in *Red Letters* 5 (Summer 1977): 7, quoted in Tony Bennett, "Text and Social Process: The Case of James Bond," *Screen Education* 41 (Winter/Spring 1982): 3.

[11] Les Cleveland, "When They Send the Last Yank Home: Wartime Images of Popular Culture," *Journal of Popular Culture* 18, no. 3 (Winter 1984): 32. The article is concerned with jokes about anxieties over New Zealand women meeting G.I.'s. See also Siegfried Kracauer's argument for "an analysis of the simple surface manifestations of an epoch" in his 1927 essay, "The Mass Ornament," trans. Barbara Correll and Jack Zipes, *New German Critique* 5 (Spring 1975), p. 67. See also Adrian Rifkin, "Well Formed Phrases: Some Limits of Meaning in Political Print at the End of the Second Empire," *Oxford Art Journal* 8:1 (1985): 20–28, for an account of problems studying political cartoons.

films. The films themselves were chosen because they seek to make entertainment from the facts of home front wartime experience. They form an amorphous, loosely tied group that can provisionally be called the genre of the national subject: that is, they are linked through an address to their audience as nationally defined. Focusing on the home front as opposed to the fighting front meant emphasizing the psychological, rather than the physical, aspects of war, and this forced (or allowed) an emphasis on narratives about female experience. Gledhill and Swanson have noted the surprisingly large number of films made during the later war years that elaborate fictions based on women's emotions.[12] It is this group of films that the book examines.

Most of the films discussed were released between 1942 and 1946, dates that not only bracket the transition from war to peace, but also indicate the cultural effects of the government's intensive midwar recruitment drive for women: increasingly difficult war conditions forced the government and the cinema to acknowledge women on the screen after 1941. Before that date, films about the war gave far less space to the female experience. Almost all the films considered are feature films and box office successes, according to the *Kinematograph Weekly* annual surveys, which I have reproduced in distilled form in Appendix II.

Taken as a whole, the study makes reference to most of the major studios, directors, and producers of the period: Ealing and Gainsborough Studios, The Archers, Two Cities, London Films, and the directors and producers Anthony Asquith, Alexander Korda, Frank Launder, Sidney Gilliat, Carol Reed, Michael Powell, Emeric Pressburger, Leslie Howard, Herbert Wilcox, Noel Coward, David Lean, and the great umbrella group owned by Arthur Rank. However, the assembled films are linked through theme and date rather than studio or director. Film is taken to be historically rather than biographically revealing in that wartime conditions worked at a more fundamental level than did individual personality to shape film.

Although costume melodramas are considered in this study, it is the films that explicitly attempt to represent contemporary events that take center stage. These tend to be those films that have been sanctioned and remembered from World War II, but it is my contention that there is more to say, particularly for feminism, because the representation of women in these films is intrinsic to the way they function as mobilizing texts. A consideration of gender must be part of their analysis, not separated off from

---

[12] Christine Gledhill and Gillian Swanson, "Gender and Sexuality in Second World War Films—a Feminist Approach," in Geoff Hurd, ed., *National Fictions: World War Two in British Films and Television* (London: British Film Institute Publishing, 1984), p. 56.

13

it, for if there is one area on which these films consistently wish to stake their identity as British, it is their representation of women.[13] Wartime critics urged a new style of realism on British cinema that would be the basis of a specifically British product, perhaps parallel to the emerging Italian Neorealism. Appropriate subject matter was to be a "native theme," "alive . . . with roots in the contemporary world, in contemporary society."[14] Films were to "reflect the spirit . . . of the terrible national urgency . . . without false emotion or sentimental heroics."[15] One of the main impulses of the style of realism was that it should give a picture of everyday life, but in wartime the "everyday" was startlingly new. A crucial implication of this commitment was that it meant representing women's lives, lives that were radically changed. One critic defined realism precisely in these terms. He insisted that the British audience needed realism because the experience of the war had made it unable to accept any other style, and he cited the maimed, wartime female body as the quintessential sign of recent historical events in Britain: "The earliest thrilling serials—with the heroine snatched away in the nick of time from the circular saw and the oncoming train—instructed us that ladies are never cut up or run over. That was entirely untrue. Ladies are. They are even blown up, these days."[16] He set up the parameters of realism, and the badge of its quality and hence national distinction, through an image and narrative of woman, and thereby implied that matters of femininity and its representation were integral to contemporary understanding of cinematic production during the crisis.

Until recently, feminist writing about the cinema has tended to elide discussions of femininity with Hollywood, producing an ahistorical and apparently international treatment of female representation in film.[17] The

[13] In their study of wartime cinema, *Britain Can Take It*, Anthony Aldgate and Jeffrey Richards write, "We have spent little time on the depiction of . . . women in the wartime cinema" because this subject has been "comprehensively dealt with elsewhere." They refer to Sue Aspinall, "Women, Realism and Reality in British Films, 1943–1953," in James Curran and Vincent Porter, eds., *British Cinema History* (London: Weidenfeld and Nicholson, 1983), and Hurd, *National Fictions*. Anthony Aldgate and Jeffrey Richards, *Britain Can Take It: The British Cinema in the Second World War* (Oxford: Basil Blackwell, 1986), p. 16.

[14] Dilys Powell, *The Film since 1939* (London: British Council Series, 1947), p. 10.

[15] Roger Manvell, "Recent Films," *Britain Today*, July 1945, p. 36.

[16] Elspeth Grant, "From Pearl White to Pearl Harbour," *Sight and Sound* 11, no. 43 (Winter 1942): 62.

[17] Welcome exceptions are: B. Ruby Rich, "From Repressive Tolerance to Erotic Liberation: *Maedchen in Uniform*," pp. 100–130 in Mary Ann Doane et al. eds., *Re-vision: Essays in Feminist Film Criticism* (Frederick, Md.: University Publications of America/American Film Institute, 1984); and Patrice Petro, *Joyless Streets: Women and Melodramatic Representation in Weimar Germany* (Princeton: Princeton University Press, 1989).

case of wartime cinema in Britain asks us to consider how femininity might be constructed differently across different national cinemas, and indeed, how national identity might be imaged through different screen versions of femininity. Women on British screens during World War II were defined, as in peacetime, through their difference to screen men, both British men and, occasionally, American men or men of some other country: thus this was largely a comparison across sex but within nationality. However, British wartime femininity was also defined by comparison to an idea of the American screen woman, an idea more rooted in imagery than in fact, but powerful nevertheless, especially given the increased ''distance'' of America from Britain that austere wartime conditions produced. This comparison was then wholly *within* sex but across nationality. Further comparisons within sex were also made, along class and regional lines for instance, as in the film *The Gentle Sex*. These zones of comparison intersected one another, and can be conceptualized as forming a sort of three-dimensional grid, with male vs. female operating along one plane for instance, and British (national) female vs. American (non-national) female along another. However, the meaning of femininity was not the same along every dimension, and not for every audience member. Femininity defined against masculinity did not coincide with femininity defined against a foreign femininity, or against a different class of femininity. The failure of intersection produced a fracturing and decentering of wartime femininity, and indeed, of the whole gender system, that is particularly visible in British cinema. The zone of sexual difference was invaded and commandeered, in the name of establishing a more urgent difference—that of nationality. Through a subtle, and far from universal repositioning, the war of the sexes was put on hold while a war against a different enemy was being fought.

EACH chapter of this book takes up a different perspective on the relation of gendered to national identity in British wartime cinema. The first chapter examines concrete instances of the projection of national identity on the British screen. The emerging genre of the national subject did not have a clear syntax, as, for example the American Western had, but it did cohere in finding a set of recognizable images and themes—tea-drinking, listening to the radio, family separations, blackouts, and so on—which embodied the idea of a variegated nation pulling together. In the face of massive domestic erosions in male and female roles, this realist cinema developed a new way of delineating male and female spheres, placing them in a strange, yet familiar, vertical orientation—attaching femininity to the land (and even, metaphorically, to underground) and masculinity to the skies.

An account of economic and governmental factors which shaped wartime British cinema is given in Appendix I.

Chapter 2 furthers the investigation of sexual representation in the cinema, linking it to contemporary imagery in other media, particularly in cartoons and advertisements, and describing how the mobilization of femininity for the war effort produced highly contradictory results. The chapter focuses on *The Gentle Sex*, a hybrid documentary/feature production of 1943 which recasts screen femininity in a patriotic direction by making the object of spectacle woman's devotion to duty rather than her individual fetishized body. However, as the analysis also points out, uniforming women ran counter to traditional notions of femininity, and was never easily attained or effortlessly maintained. It required, in the case of *The Gentle Sex*, all the skill that director Leslie Howard could muster.

Chapter 3 proposes that wartime conditions foreground the status of cinema as a "perceptual luxury," to use Paul Virilio's words.[18] The chapter examines a three-way connection between the most universal of home front wartime ordeals—the blackout—the technology of cinema, and the experience of film going. The fictional blackout of wartime texts operated as a multivalent code signifying both realism and fantasy, evoking conditions of wartime loss and deprivation, but also danger, excitement, and daring. The chapter focuses on the film *Perfect Strangers* (1945) to show how the deployment of fictional blackouts is tied to representations of sexual and national difference. If the function of criticism is to expose the divergences between history and ideology, or between one ideology and another, this examination of the figure of the blackout turns out to be a strangely literal way of making the "'absences'" of the text speak.[19]

The specifically wartime tropes of barrage balloons, shelter signs, sandbags, emergency tanks, and military uniforms, present in most home front films, are absent from *Brief Encounter*, the central film discussed in Chapter 4, set in prewar Britain. Encoded in *its* text are such nostalgic items as "prewar" oranges, chocolates, Banburies (a type of bun), Palm Court orchestras, and the peacetime naiveté of Laura Jesson herself, the central female character. Through close analysis of the film and a study of surrounding materials I argue that Laura provided a counterpoint to one Hollywood version of femininity. The broader purpose of Chapter 4 is to investigate the temporal qualities of home front films, as they reinvent femininity. While it is clear that British realist films attempted to deal with contemporary issues, they manifest major difficulties in fixing the actual

[18] Paul Virilio, *War and Cinema: The Logistics of Perception*, translated by Patrick Camiller (New York: Verso Books, 1989), p. 9. Virilio is quoting Henri Bergson here.

[19] Terry Eagleton, "Pierre Macherey and the Theory of Literary Production," *Minnesota Review* 5 (Fall 1975): 138.

times of their diegeses. In most home front films made between 1943 and V-E Day, a large section of the narrative is set in the audience's past, often the Blitz, as in *Perfect Strangers*, or prewar days, as in *This Happy Breed*. The narrative of *Brief Encounter* is set entirely *just before* September 1939. It might therefore not be considered a home front film at all, except that its date of production, the problem of adultery it addresses, and the style in which it does so, demand association with the home front milieu.

The book concludes by comparing the 1944 and 1949 versions of Powell and Pressburger's *A Canterbury Tale*. The 1944 version works as a "limit case": it focuses directly, even excessively, on blackouts, mobile women, and structures of temporal and national difference, ubiquitous elements of wartime cinema. The figure of the G.I. (Sergeant Bob Johnson in *A Canterbury Tale*), an historically "late" development of the war in Britain, displaces other means of representing national difference in that he literally does so: he articulates more easily the relation of rivalry and dependence between British and American cinema exaggerated by World War II.

World War II is still a favorite subject for British film and television, and has been ever since it was fought. It is also a favorite means by which American culture represents Britain. However, films made during the war, as opposed to those made on the same subject but sometime afterward, are distinctive in that they can function far less readily as myth.[20] The contradictions they manifest cannot be so easily naturalized.[21] In these films, clashes between domestic ideals and women's wartime lives remain unresolved, and here lies the interest of this historical moment for feminism. Terry Eagleton writes that under extreme historical conditions, an ideology's "contradictions may be forced from it by its historically determined encounter with another ideology."[22] Wartime ideology, the discourse that explains mobilization, recruitment, fighting, and killing, runs up against the peacetime ideology of separate spheres for men and women and the clear differentiation of men's and women's cultural, economic, and political contributions. In a period as turbulent as World War II the skin of ideology strains and tears; the joins of the pasteup job curl apart, and the evidence of this other battle is strewn in wartime films, for World War II entailed a struggle over the security of gender definitions as much as over national security. We can look to wartime films, therefore, not for progressive images of women, or to see how these images diverge from contemporary experience, but rather to understand how these films negotiate

[20] See Colin McArthur, "National Identities," in Hurd, *National Fictions*, p. 55.

[21] Roland Barthes, *Mythologies* (New York: Hill and Wang, 1972), p. 129.

[22] Terry Eagleton, *Criticism and Ideology* (London: Verso Books, 1978), p. 96.

17

with, and participate in, the war-torn battlefield of representations of womanhood and nationhood.[23]

As we look back with the hindsight of fifty years, the ideological operations of wartime films may have something to reveal about contemporary anxieties over nationality and sexual inequality. Under current immigration laws in Britain, foreign women married to British men may take up British citizenship on entering the country, but foreign men who marry British women may not do likewise. This law suggests, as so much wartime film did, that even today a woman's relation to citizenship and nationality is always more precarious than a man's.[24] Structures of national and sexual difference are as ideologically powerful as ever, but by revealing the operations of those of the past we can produce a more coherent knowledge of those of the present. History becomes a source from which to learn.

[23] See T. J. Clark, *The Painting of Modern Life: The Art of Manet and His Followers* (New York: Knopf, 1985), p. 6.

[24] See my essay "The Female Spy: Gender, Nationality, and War in *I See a Dark Stranger*," pp. 173–99 in Robert Sklar and Charles Musser, eds. *Resisting Images: Essays in Film and History* (Philadelphia: Temple University Press, 1990) for a discussion of woman's tenuous relationship to nationality as presented in Launder and Gilliat's 1946 film.

CHAPTER 1

Projecting National Identity

━━━━━━━━

We lack a unifying belief, a new purpose for a
society devoted to peace. It is easy to have a belief,
if we have an enemy.

J. P. Mayer, 1948

LOOKING BACK in 1939, neither government, filmmakers, nor audiences could remember a time when British cinema had lived beyond the shadow of Hollywood. This cinema was seen as a victim of not only economic but also cultural subjection. Hollywood's tentacles had apparently wrapped themselves around British life itself, bringing with them the contraptions of modern domesticity: "The refrigerator [had] penetrated the fastness of the English home largely as a result of it appearing as a standard fixture in American kitchens as shown in the films."[1] At least since World War I, the American film industry had determined the scale of economic support for most films seen in Britain, and often their content. "So far as films go, we are now a colonial people," Grierson's *World Film News* was able to pronounce in 1937.[2] Repeated counter attempts by British studios to recolonize British screens, or claim a reciprocal slice of the American exhibition pie, had failed. By 1939, eighty percent of films shown in Britain were American, and British producers had secured no more than four to five percent of the United States's domestic market.

The outbreak of World War II put the whole matter of American domination in a new light. The crisis forced the question of nationality into every crevice of public and private life, contaminating everything from leisure to labor, sifting every object into its national category: alien, enemy, neutral, naturalized, Allied. Cinema was caught in this mesh of designations, conscripted for its own bout of National Service. It was the most powerful medium for building national identity in that it reached a wider

[1] Editorial essay, "The Film and the Young Person," *Sight and Sound* 7, no. 25 (Spring 1938): 3.
[2] Editorial essay, *World Film News* 2, no. 8 (November 1937): 5, cited in Margaret Dickinson and Sarah Street, *Cinema and State: The Film Industry and the Government 1927–1984* (London: British Film Institute Publishing, 1985), p. 58.

19

public than any other. Its audience included more women, more younger people, and more of "the lower economic groups and those with elementary education" than those of radio, magazines, or newspapers.[3] As Lord Stragboli reminded the House a month into the war, cinema had a unique "importance for entertainment and in molding the public opinion, and, to speak bluntly, as a means of propaganda, disguised or open."[4] It was a news channel, a source of leisure, and a powerful vehicle for shaping an audience in support of war.

All cinemas address matters of national identity in wartime—we could cite Italian, Soviet, French, and Japanese cinemas as other examples. The question of a *British* national cinema had been on the agenda since its birth in 1896, but the war gave the project new impetus, reviving debates over the reasons for the industry's precarious past, and stimulating proposals for a healthier future. Patriotism mandated that a British screen identity could be produced only in Britain, and by British studios: only a British-made film could represent native culture, and for a film to be British it could not look, nor be, of any other nation born.

The ideology of nationality wears thin when one nation constructs another's screen identity, as would have been the case if America had been the sole provider of filmic images of Britain at war. This threat was well recognized on the eve of war: "Of all people they [Americans] are closest to ourselves in mind and spirit. But to allow these cousins of ours to put a stranglehold on this fundamental power of national expression, which is the British cinema, is carrying blood-relationship a trifle too far."[5] Such an arrangement would have laid bare the absence of any necessary connection between a manufacturer's citizenship and the brand of national identity produced. In addition, handing over the task of representing wartime Britain to a foreign cinema, even one that was soon to be an ally, would immediately have been an admission of the inadequacy of the native film industry and, by extension, of the nation itself. To avoid this erosion of identity, it was imperative that British films be defended, economically and aesthetically, against Hollywood imperialism: there could be no national cinema without a product. Paradoxically, only then could they participate in the battle against Germany.

Government, exhibitors, producers, filmmakers, technicians, critics, and audiences all shaped cinema's wartime fortunes, wielding their pref-

[3] These were the results of a Wartime Social Survey for the Ministry of Information, conducted in June–July 1943 by Louis Moss and Kathleen Box, and republished in Mayer, *British Cinemas and Their Audiences*, p. 273.

[4] Lord Stragboli, *Parliamentary Debates* (Lords), vol. 114, col. 1219, 3 October 1939, quoted in Dickinson and Street, *Cinema and State*, p. 104.

[5] Editorial essay, *World Film News* 2, no. 8 (November 1937): 5.

erences with differentiated power and with little consensus. Film technicians fought first of all to preserve their jobs and sustain at least a skeleton force until the postwar period, a goal that was often in jeopardy. Exhibitors were torn between the patriotism of showing homegrown films and the better returns Hollywood pictures promised. For producer Michael Balcon the dire straits of British cinema were the direct result of cross-cultural— and more specifically, American—contamination. He, along with Ralph Bond, Roger Manvell, and others, welcomed the war's new nationalist pressures because they seemed to provide the economic and artistic foundation for a healthier home-based cinema. He urged producers to remember the domestic audience in the crisis: "For far too long, the American market has been a mirage. . . . The British producer can make no greater mistake than to have the American market in mind when planning and costing a picture. Not in that way will the British film ever become representative of British culture."[6] Other producers, and above all J. Arthur Rank and Alexander Korda, looked to America and the lucrative prospect of a larger American audience when planning and selling their wares. Throughout the war Rank financed Del Guidice's Two Cities production company, whose logo was not a collage of Paris and London, as in Dickens's *Tale of Two Cities*, but of Los Angeles skyscrapers with Tower Bridge opening in front of them, a neat condensation of British cinema's ancestry of impure breeding.

Domestic wartime filmgoers, rapidly swelled by thousands of G.I.'s and European refugees, voted with their feet, bringing British films more success at the box office than ever before, but not necessarily those that critics championed. George Formby's Northern comedies were always among the biggest winners from 1938 to 1943, and an American representation of the British crisis, *Mrs. Miniver*, was the top box office success of 1942. The critically derided Gainsborough costume melodramas also did a roaring trade.[7] Last but by no means least, the government became openly embroiled in the question of wartime cinema. Official guidelines were issued to studios, advocating certain subject matters and forbidding others. Recommended themes were "what Britain is fighting for," "how Britain fights," and "the need for sacrifices if the fight is to be won."[8] Films were

---

[6] Michael Balcon, "Rationalise!" *Sight and Sound* 9, no. 36 (Winter 1940–41): 62.

[7] See Robert Murphy and Sue Aspinall, eds., *Gainsborough Melodramas*, BFI Dossier no. 17 (London: British Film Institute Publishing, 1983) for important discussions of this studio's wartime output plus interviews with its staff.

[8] "Programme for Film Propaganda," Ministry of Information papers, Public Record Office (File INF 1/867), issued by the Ministry of Information in early 1940. Reprinted in Ian Christie, ed., *Powell, Pressburger and Others* (London: British Film Institute Publishing, 1978), pp. 121–24.

to be submitted for security censorship at the Ministry of Information Films Division, and cinemas were warned that they were liable for prosecution if they showed films containing any material that might be useful to the enemy.

However, government decisions over cinema were always inflected by a more pressing desire to maintain the United States's goodwill, especially after Pearl Harbor, resulting in contradictory film policies, which led, overall, to a low but regular output of films from British studios during the war. Wartime filmmakers strove, under the official instruction, to present narratives and images culturally marked as "British," and commentators struggled to isolate and describe these properties in their reviews. Everywhere was the conscious effort to read cinema style as a calibration of national characteristics. For example, when reviewing German cinema in 1938, Vesselo made the connection in the following way: "If it is normally true that the films of a country will in some way reflect that country's national characteristics, it is at least equally true that films produced under an authoritarian regime will in some way reflect that regime's ideology."[9] Further, under conditions in which the definition of nationality was of such pressing importance, the central cultural and political significance of films was understood to be inextricably linked to their economic birth, to the marketplace that permitted their production. Nationalism functioned at two entwined levels—the economic and the aesthetic.[10] In the case of British wartime cinema, the attempt to establish a British national screen identity took place via a battle with the economic and stylistic dominant—Hollywood. The wartime battle with Hollywood had both commercial and cultural dimensions: the content of a film, its ideological presentation, was embrangled with its economic makeup.

The first wartime emergency measure to hit the film industry was the forcible closure of all cinemas and sports stadia for fear of excessive casualties during air raids. This now seems an extraordinary initial misassessment of film's socio-political power in annexing spectators for the national cause, but it also suggests, besides the extreme threat of war to British life, the relative unimportance of the film industry in the constitution of Britain's national identity. Granted, the United States was not under the same physical threat as Britain, but her government ordered baseball games to continue as usual precisely as a sign of normality and fortitude. Further, the enormous success of the American film industry at home, but especially abroad, meant that it too had become intimately tied to ideas of

[9] A. Vesselo, "Babel Cinema," *Sight and Sound* 7, no. 2 (Spring 1938): 128.
[10] I am indebted here to Steve Neale's formulation in his discussion of the German cinema in "Propaganda," *Screen* 18, no. 3 (Autumn 1977): 37.

national strength and domination, and was therefore more immediately obvious as a weapon of war. Given British cinema's rocky past (outlined in Appendix I), the connection between cinema and national identity had never seemed natural in Britain.

The compulsory blackout drew vociferous protests from exhibitors, critics, and producers. Buchanan, a *Sight and Sound* critic, stressed (in an argument reminiscent of Balázs's) the cinema's diplomatic superiority to print and broadcasting. He was convinced that the "celluloid ambassador" was the "surest way of bringing one country before another," making him one of many wartime film personnel who used the adjective "ambassadorial" to cement cinema's relation to national politics.[11] W. R. Fuller, general secretary of the Cinema Exhibitors' Association, claimed that having no cinemas meant "the disappearance of the chief recreation of about thirteen million people a day, the loss to the exchequer of some £200,000 a week, and the danger of unemployment for about 75,000 men and women."[12] He added that industrialists all over the country had been experiencing the bad effects on workers of "no play," and that the cinema's "gigantic contribution to national morale . . . [was] unobtainable through any other medium."[13]

Several (particularly) wartime assets of cinema are being claimed here: that it embodies national identity in the encounter with a foreign cinema; that it makes money for the national coffers; and that it recharges the labor force. Spectators in a mid-1940s poll tended to support the latter point. A thirty-year-old self-described housewife and mother stated, "I definitely go to the cinema to be taken out of myself, and to forget the cares of housework, rationing, and washing babies' nappies. Carry me into the past with Laurence Olivier, Nelson Eddy, Greta Garbo and the others and I'm happy."[14] Another woman concurred: "I've just seen Bette Davis's film *Now Voyager*, and what enjoyment, what relief—*no war*. I have worked in a large office with other women in whose homes the war is ever present by the absence of husbands and sons on service, and who, like myself, snatch their bit of break in a couple of hours each week at the cinema."[15]

[11] Andrew Buchanan, "Let the Screen Help" *Sight and Sound* 8, no. 31 (Autumn 1939): 87–88. For other examples see J. Arthur Rank in Peter Noble, *The British Film Yearbook* (London: British Yearbooks, 1946), p. 7; the Palache Report, 1944; "Newsreel," *Sight and Sound* 10, no. 37 (Spring 1941): 2; "Celluloid Ambassadors," *Sight and Sound* 17, no. 65 (Spring 1948): 39.

[12] W. R. Fuller, "The Exhibitor's Part," *Sight and Sound* 10, no. 37 (Spring 1941): 10–11.

[13] Ibid.

[14] Mayer, *British Cinemas and Their Audiences*, p. 31. Such opinions were collected from 1943 onward.

[15] *Bristol Evening Post*, 28 January 1944, cited in Calder, *The People's War*, p. 427.

We can note in passing that for these two women it is not simply the act of going to the cinema that provides relief, but the viewing of a fictional story removed from war. A seventeen-year-old female filmgoer makes it quite clear that to her even the quality of that escapist plot is unimportant: "I will go and see any musical in Technicolor, even though it has a poor story; any well-acted film, provided it does not concern the war; and any costume films, for which I have a tremendous weakness."[16] One begins to understand the overwhelming success of the Gainsborough costume melodramas during the war.

When no bombs fell on the home front during the first two weeks of war, the Home Office reversed its premature decision and permitted the reopening of auditoria, at first in outlying areas and eventually in cities, provided that blackout regulations were observed and that managers ran Air Raid Patrols and fire-watches during the shows so that spectating citizens could be warned of impending attacks.[17] Neon lights outside cinemas were in fact not turned on again until 1949. Restrictions on transportation and the difficulties of nighttime darkness obviously affected exhibition staff and audiences alike, but audience size gradually increased. Attendances climbed from nineteen million per week in 1940 to an all-time peak of thirty million per week in 1945, an increase roughly proportional to that in the United States.[18]

There were many reasons for cinema's increased popularity, and the increased popularity of British films in particular. For one thing, higher wartime employment freed up spending money, while competing middle-class entertainments such as pleasure motoring and dining out were curtailed by rationing. Secondly, cinema fed the desire for news and information about the war for a wider selection of the population than any other medium. Thirdly, the combination of communal gatherings and spectacular entertainment, promoted through the institution of cinema, mitigated against the fear, exhaustion, and deprivations of war, as the two women quoted above recount. In particular, the cinema's flamboyant light displays

---

[16] Clerk with the Inland Revenue in Mayer, *British Cinemas and their Audiences*, p. 101.

[17] A memorandum was circulated to the managers of the Granada chain of cinemas on 28 August 1939 with the following instructions: "A priority air raid warning will be given to cinema managers when enemy aircraft are sighted over the North Sea. You will not on any account pass on this priority warning to your audience. You will merely give the warning "Red Roses" to your staff so they will be prepared . . ." Quoted in Guy Morgan, *Red Roses Every Night: An Account of London Cinemas Under Fire* (London: Quality Press, 1948), p. 4.

[18] With high wartime employment and limited spending options, the movies became extremely popular in America too. Robert Sklar writes, "In some locations where factories operated around the clock, theaters never closed, and were crowded even in pre-dawn hours by workers getting off late-night shifts." See Sklar, *Movie-Made America*, p. 250.

provided an intensified experience of pleasure, given the surroundings of Stygian darkness, an issue discussed in Chapter Three.

One can also detect a brand of patriotism in the personal policies of some film goers who now claimed to prefer British-made films over American ones. A nineteen-year-old female clerk despised Hollywood's "futile attempts to portray life so showily, gaudily, and synthetically. But in the last few wartime years I have encountered with delight good British films. . . . British films about Britain are now, in my opinion, the best films to see."[19] Another female viewer writes, "I have never liked to see war pictures, especially the American type, which usually are too far from reality, with too many heroics and too much bombast. I don't mind a decent war film of the British *In Which We Serve* type."[20] Another woman, a twenty-year-old civil servant with the Inland Revenue, admits that "although I used to avoid British films, it is now my aim to see every one I can that comes to the local cinemas."[21] This last opinion might include a preference for Gainsborough costume films on the basis that they were British made, as much as because they took one "into the past."

Government vacillations over the home industry, including making distribution concessions to American studios, did little to boost the confidence of domestic producers in the future of British filmmaking, despite the boom in attendance. Proportionally, studios lost far more labor power to the Services than did movie theaters. In all, two thirds of the film technicians were eventually drafted. George Elvin, general secretary of the recently formed Association of Ciné-Technicians, harangued that what remained of the industry survived *only* because film trade unions had three times managed to reverse a government decision to "de-reservation" (or make liable for conscription) all film production labor of military age. To maintain production, studios were forced to "dilute" the remaining nucleus of technicians with women, who now worked as sound camera operators and laboratory printers, two jobs hitherto held exclusively by men. They continued to work as editors, in continuity, and also as projectionists, although it was decided that this form of employment for women "should end immediately at the termination of the war."[22] The role of director re-

[19] Mayer, *British Cinemas and Their Audiences*, p. 70.

[20] Ibid., p. 48.

[21] Ibid., p. 92.

[22] Elvin explained that first preference was given to wives of serving members of the A.C.T. and that "the principle of equal pay for equal work" had been "accepted for dilutees." George Elvin, "British Labour Problems," *Sight and Sound* 10, no. 40 (Spring 1942): 79. In 1939 Elvin had written "This Freedom: An Enquiry into Film Censorship" in *The Ciné-Technician*, journal of the A.C.T., in which he pinpointed censorship as a key inhibitor of film's potential role in national culture: "The elimination from cinematographic subject material of every controversial quotation deprives the cinema of the possibility of

mained a male preserve; Jessie Matthews with *Victory Wedding* and Rosie Newman with *Britain at War* (1945) were rare exceptions. Jill Craigie and Muriel Box were the only women who worked more consistently as film directors in Britain in the 1940s, and neither of them until after the war. As in the United States, women's main contributions to the film industry were as actresses and audience members.

British studios also lost space. Acres were requisitioned for storage, factory use, and official filmmaking. The Crown Film Unit (the G.P.O. Film Unit until August 1940) took over Pinewood, and between 1939 and 1941 thirteen other studios, including Denham, Elstree, Islington, Shepherd's Bush, and Sound City (Shepperton), were converted for non-film purposes. Ultimately only nine studios were left in operation, and home feature production fell from 108 films in 1940 to an average of 60 per year until the end of the war, with a nadir of 46 in 1942.[23] Cinemas did not close for lack of films, however, for exhibitors found ways to overcome shortages by reissuing, having long runs, and renting the ever-available American product: they drew the line only at dropping the double-feature format.[24] Even so, some ten percent of cinemas eventually had to close because of bomb damage, staff shortages, or requisitioning; with horrible irony, the Home Office requisitioned the Tivoli Theatre in the Strand for storing coffins in anticipation of enormous casualties.[25] The Wardour

---

playing any useful part in national life" (pp. 141–46). Quoted in Anthony Aldgate, *The Historical Development of Popular Culture in Britain* (Milton Keynes: Open University Press, 1981), U203, Popular Culture, Unit 7. The reference to C.E.A. strictures on women's employment is taken from Linda Wood, *British Films, 1927–1939* (London: British Film Institute Publishing, 1986), p. 59.

[23] Hollywood maintained production of new features at a level only slightly below that of peacetime. The studios averaged about 440 pictures per annum during the war, as opposed to about 500 in the 1930s. See Steinberg, *Reel Facts*, pp. 42–43.

[24] F. L. Thomas recommended a policy of single-feature showings, extended over longer periods, to bring offerings in line with wartime production capabilities in Britain. Thomas suggested that the "big film," the main feature, be continued while the "small, cheap filler, that second feature . . . be scuttled." He complained that the average theater owner offered too great a bargain anyway, by showing a double feature each week: "There have been cases of programmes as long as four and a half hours, all for the price of a single admission." In peace, let alone war, he argued, the demand for "a change of programme once a week," or even, as is now a very common course, twice a week" could never be met by British producers. His single-feature policy with its attendant extended playing time would be welcomed by the trade and "exhausted" wartime filmgoers alike: the cheaper second features would be eliminated and the demand for first features halved. In fact, in 1940 (and again in 1945) the Board of Trade seriously investigated such a solution, but paradoxically exhibitors opposed it, worried about a falloff in attendance. See F. L. Thomas, "Whither Our Business?" *Sight and Sound* 10, no. 40 (Spring 1942): 64 and 65.

[25] Ernest Betts, *The Film Business: A History of British Cinema, 1896–1972* (London: Allen and Unwin, 1973), p. 209.

Street area was heavily bombed, with United Artists's British headquarters destroyed in 1944 and Paramount badly damaged. The British Film Institute headquarters was also blitzed (Figure 1.1).

Among those who benefited from the crisis were newsreel and documentary teams, needed to provide the war machine with instructional and informational pictures. After two years of fighting, they were busier than ever, showing their wares in touring vans, Service camps, public libraries, and public cinemas, presented free, *pace* the exhibitors.[26] The Films Di-

Figure 1.1. The blitzed British Film Institute makes the cover of *Sight and Sound* in Autumn 1940.

[26] See Dickinson and Street, *Cinema and State*, p. 114. Film societies, which had burgeoned in the 1930s with the growth of the documentary filmmaking movement, were also surviving into the war, proving for Forsyth Hardy "the virility of the movement." In Summer 1941 the societies were actively preparing for their third wartime season, although, as Hardy remarked, "Not many foresaw this possibility, when it seemed almost certain that

vision had rapidly come to heed Lord Stragboli's words, and from 1940 onward was commissioning large numbers of documentaries both from its own Crown Unit and from the private sector. The government's ventures in feature production began with the funding of Powell and Pressburger's *49th Parallel* (1941), but this kind of intervention was so controversial, both in Parliament (which argued that the financial risk was too great) and with producers (who feared the practice would skew the market and even compromise editorial freedom), that it was never repeated. The Ministry of Information's Division continued to shape feature filmmaking, however, by vetting all screenplays, rationing film stock and controlling its allocation, facilitating liaisons between the military and the studios (for the making of *The Way Ahead, In Which We Serve*, and *The Gentle Sex*, for instance), and calling on filmmakers to follow its opinion that "film propaganda will be most effective when it is least recognizable as such."[27] The official view was that feature films were a more subtle and therefore more powerful device than the documentary for molding British public opinion.

J. Arthur Rank was the other chief British wartime beneficiary of the film industry squeeze. By 1943 he had accumulated assets comparable to that of an American major.[28] He used some of his empire profits, which derived chiefly from exhibition in his Odeon and Gaumont cinema chains, for backing independent filmmakers linked to his organization through an umbrella group, Independent Producers Ltd. Here he supported four important director/producer units: The Archers (Michael Powell and Emeric Pressburger); Individual Pictures (Frank Launder and Sidney Gilliat); Cineguild (the Lean/Neame/Havelock-Allan team); and Wessex (Ian Dalrymple). By this arrangement, Rank directly contributed to the diversity of film output during the war and funded and distributed many of the films discussed here, including *A Canterbury Tale, Millions Like Us*, and *Brief Encounter*. He has been enthusiastically thanked for taking these smaller companies under his financial wing while staying out of their editorial operations: Michael Powell remembers him hyperbolically as "huge, monolithic, a

---

film societies, in common with other cultural bodies, would be sucked into the whirlpool of war and destroyed." See Forsyth Hardy, "An Open Letter to the Film Societies," *Sight and Sound* 10, no. 38 (Summer 1941): 29. In fact, film societies were strengthened by the war: new ones sprang up in military camps, and the absence of French films left a gap these societies could fill. They also had access to films (through embassies and independent distributors) that were not theatrically released.

[27] Christie, *Powell, Pressburger and Others*, p. 124.

[28] The story of the consolidation of the Rank Organisation, the foremost vertically integrated film company in England after 1943, is well known and needs only brief mention here. Robert Murphy, "Rank's Attempt on the American Market," in Curran and Porter, *British Cinema History*, pp. 164–78, gives an excellent account. Murphy gives Rank's assets in the mid-1940s as $200 million, while MGM's were $190 million.

fine man, and the sole architect of the British film industry during the war.''[29] From the mid-war onward, Rank worked to build more profitable relations with America. Most of the majors were willing to make U.S. distribution deals for British pictures with Rank, as it seemed a small price to pay in exchange for maintaining what was still their most lucrative over-seas market. Rank was careful to couch these activities in nationalist terms, aware of the contrary interpretation his tactics might encourage un-der war conditions. He stressed the cultural and patriotic importance of his business by describing his main task as the successful presentation of ''British ideas and ideals on the screens of the world. The film is one of the greatest ambassadors.''[30]

During the war, film style had become a moral and patriotic matter: films became ''something more than a commodity.''[31] On this, two people as far apart on the political spectrum as Arthur Rank and Ralph Bond could agree. The war had caused an economic reevaluation of the film industry in terms of ideological need, which had paid off as long as the war had lasted. It had brought into relief the social and political function of cinema, and had directly influenced narrative and stylistic choices—a ''training film'' such as *The Gentle Sex* would be unthinkable in other circumstances. For all its pain and loss, ''total war'' had provided the home industry with the necessary impetus to assert itselfs in the face of foreign competition. The whole apparatus—audience, economics, film going habits, narratives, and visual style—had shifted ground in the crisis, and the mobilized spec-tator had swallowed a new diet of patriotic imagery and bracing narratives. Films such as *The Life and Death of Colonel Blimp*, *A Canterbury Tale*, *In Which We Serve*, and *Millions Like Us* had presented visions of Britain *and* cinema undergoing transformations as a result of the war.

NATIONAL IDENTITY ON THE SCREEN

If there's a war, which God forbid,
then you can say goodbye to England,
home, *and* beauty.

Veteran in *The Way Ahead*

British wartime filmmaking was conceptualized as a renaissance even as the films were being produced. By 1945, statements about the war bringing

---

[29] Michael Powell, with Emeric Pressburger and Martin Scorsese, ''1985 Guardian Lec-ture,'' National Film Theater, London, 28 July 1985.

[30] J. Arthur Rank, ''Introduction,'' in Noble, *The British Film Yearbook*, p. 7.

[31] Ralph Bond, ''What Is the Future of British Films?'' *Picture Post*, 6 January 1945, pp. 11–12 and 24.

out the best in British cinema were commonplace.[32] British films had collected increasing numbers of accolades in American competitions: *In Which We Serve* had earned both the New York Film Critics' Best Picture Award for 1942 and the Special Academy Award, given to Noel Coward "for his outstanding production achievement."[33] Coward's success was followed by others, until 1945 was proclaimed "a banner year for British films."[34] Looking ahead, *Kinematograph Weekly* was especially enthusiastic about Britain's 1946 box office prospects, given the derequisition of studio space and the "speedy release of stars and technicians."[35] The election of the new Labour government in May 1945 on a platform of wideranging social reforms contributed to the British film world's mood of well-being and its optimistic outlook for the postwar years.[36]

A note of anxiety sounded among the celebrations, however. Postwar enthusiasm was dampened by the recognition that war, in all its grimness, had been the catalyst for recent successes, and that, with peace, production might lapse into the shadows again. In Cyril Ray's view, war was not only the occasion of the renaissance but also "the direct cause."[37] Similarly,

[32] See for example, Roger Manvell, *The Art of the Film* (London: The Arts Council, July 1945), p. 10.

[33] Evelyn Russell, "Films of 1942," *Sight and Sound* 11, no. 44 (Spring 1943): 99. Russell ventured of Coward's success that "one swallow doesn't make a summer, but it does usually herald a period of blossoming." He declared that pride in the British School was growing as a result of the awards to *In Which We Serve*: "For the first time in film history an entirely British film has been voted 'The Most Outstanding Film of the Year' by the National Board of Review of Motion Pictures." Earlier British successes, in 1940–42, had been: 1940, *London Can Take It*, Academy Award Nomination for Best Short Subject; 1941, *Target for Tonight*, Special Award to the British Ministry Of Information "for its vivid and dramatic presentation of the heroism of the Royal Air Force in the film" (*The Stars Look Down* and *Target for Tonight* were among the *New York Times* critics' "Ten Best" list for 1941); 1942, *The Invaders* (*49th Parallel*), Academy Award for Best Writing of an Original Story to Michael Powell and Emeric Pressburger, and *One of Our Aircraft Is Missing*, Academy Award Nomination for Best Writing of an Original Screenplay, also to Powell and Pressburger, as well as *Listen to Britain*, Academy Award Nomination for Best Short Subject (documentary) to the Ministry of Information.

[34] Bond, *Monopoly*, p. 9.

[35] R. H. "Josh" Billings, "Good News For Britain," *Kinematograph Weekly*, 20 December 1945, p. 50.

[36] The fiftieth birthday of film in Britain was celebrated the following year, 1946, and in that September the British Film Academy was founded "to promote and improve creative work among persons engaged in filmmaking," with Roger Manvell as its first president. It was to offer prizes equivalent to the American Academy Awards. By 1946 Roger Manvell was research officer for the British Film Institute, editor of *Penguin Film Review,* English correspondent for *Hollywood Quarterly*, and film critic for a number of other journals and broadcasts. See Paul Addison, *The Road to 1945: British Politics and the Second World War* (London: Cape, 1975), for further information on the Labour victory.

[37] Cyril Ray, "These British Movies," *Harper's Magazine*, June 1947, p. 516.

Michael Balcon observed that "the new popularity of British films [had] developed very quickly and under abnormal conditions."[38] Like Ray, he suspected that changes in the form of British cinema and its reception had resulted from extreme circumstances that would not, and could not, be sustained in the postwar period. Both writers recognized that without clear and urgent national opposition, the desire and indeed the possibility of defining British national identity on the screen was ebbing away.

This is exactly how the representation of national identity needs to be conceptualized. National identity is not a natural, timeless essence, but an intermittent, combinatory historical product, arising at moments of contestation of different political and geographical boundaries. In this respect its construction parallels that of the representation of gendered identity. Here, the mutually dependent categories of masculinity and femininity fluctuate according to historical moment, while their ideological power rests with the opposite notion that their meanings are fixed through attachment to biological sex. War produced the need for images of national identity, both on the screen and in the audience's mind, but British national identity was not simply on tap, waiting to be imaged, somehow rooted in British geology. "National characteristics" could not simply be "infused into a national cinema," however much later writers wished that version of the story to be true.[39] Instead, the stuff of national identity had to be winnowed and forged from traditional aesthetic and narrative forms, borrowed from the diverse conventions of melodrama, realism, and fantasy, and transplanted from literature, painting, and history, into cinema. National identity could never be straightforwardly and permanently stated, but instead could emerge only partially, from an insistence on a specifically British nature, definable only through difference from another identity, another place, that was not British.

In the cinema, this other place was above all America. Aesthetic as much as economic distance from America was the crucial yardstick in the patriotic process of differentiation in which all British wartime films were embroiled. The aesthetic dimension of this battle must be read against critical discourse on preferable imagery and stories, and also against the merger of documentary and feature film practices and their specific stylistic and ideological effects. These include the repeated use of visual motifs such as the raid, the poster, the blackout, and the image of urban destruction and its complement, rural rejuvenation, and the use of narrative tropes such as deferred romantic union and romantic partings to perpetuate the

[38] Michael Balcon, "The British Film Today," in Michael Balcon, Ernest Lindgren, Forsyth Hardy, and Roger Manvell, *Twenty Years of British Film, 1925–1945* (New York: Arno Press, 1972, 1st ed. 1947), p. 7.

[39] Dilys Powell, *The Film since 1939* (London: British Council Series, 1947), p. 8.

general condition of imperfect closure in British wartime films—the ideological promotion of "making do" on the part of "ordinary" citizens.[40]

Paul Virilio writes that war is a space "in the geometrical sense," with
its own "reference points" and "landmarks," "its own characteristics."[41]
Virilio's spatial formulation helps us understand the way wartime cinema
staked out its meanings through an emphasis on boundaries, borders,
coastlines, and maps, and through a new stratification, in plot and *mise-
en-scène*, of the realms of air and land. Wartime cinema envisions the
space of the nation in new terms, renovating the severely tested metaphor
of home as an embodiment of nationhood by aligning land and air to domestic and nondomestic spheres, spheres in which traditional gendered
associations are still, intermittently, in force despite the wartime upheaval
in gender roles.

Films representing home front Britain are honed to address an "ordinary" viewer who will recognize himself or herself as a national subject
through the process of filmgoing. The strategies for achieving this cathect-
ing flash are multiple and diverse, and while it will be the job of the next
chapter to detail quite how variable, and ambiguous, the sex of this imagined national subject might be, it is the job of this one to suggest how the
wartime subject could be imaged at all.

ENERGETIC discussions over appropriate styles for wartime films came
from critics, filmmakers, and producers. The "independent" film movement in the 1930s had already denounced the "artificiality" and "psycho-
pathology" of Hollywood spectacle, acting, and narrative form.[42] Ralph
Bond had urged the workers' film movement in 1931 to use its films to
"expose" how capitalist cinema "is used as an ideological force to dope
the workers," and advised them to screen Soviet films at its society's meet-
ings instead.[43] In wartime this anti-Hollywood voice intensified. Balcon
argued that British films were unpopular in America, not "because they
are not comfortably familiar with our idiom," but because these films "are
[a] poor imitation of the American idiom" and consequently a disservice
to the nation.[44] He insisted that Americanized film should be replaced by

[40] These trends are the subject of an excellent article by Andrew Higson, to which the
following discussion is indebted. Higson, "Five Films," in Hurd, *National Fictions*, pp.
22–26.

[41] Paul Virilio and Sylvere Lotringer, *Semiotext(e): Pure War*, trans. Mark Polizotti
(New York: Columbia University Press, 1983), p. 2.

[42] Claire Johnston, " 'Independence' and the Thirties: Ideologies in History," in Don
Macpherson, ed., in collaboration with Paul Willemen, *British Cinema: Traditions of Independence* (London: British Film Institute Publishing, 1980), p. 16.

[43] Quoted in Johnston, " 'Independence' and the Thirties," p. 16.

[44] Balcon, "Rationalise!" p. 62.

British-made films that presented the uniqueness of British culture. Andrew Buchanan agreed that British cinema was not "British—its foundations having been moulded, *by us*, exactly to the American pattern." It was time to "think how to make British films, as distinct from making films in Britain."[45] For Buchanan, the malaise of the British film industry would be solved only by discovering how to "entertain the British public" before entertaining the American one.

Sidney Bernstein used a similar argument in appealing to the government to keep the studios open during the war: "The public has always wanted good British films . . . not the million-pound 'epics' which so often bore them, but the good, honest, unpretentious stories in which we have shown so much promise . . . the records of English every day life."[46] Bernstein's analysis is exemplary of the criteria used by many critics to define what is most "British" about wartime British cinema: it is good, honest, unpretentious, everyday, and restrained in style, budget, and choice of subject matter. It is, in short, "freed from the influence of Hollywood."[47]

Films that conformed to these criteria belonged to what critics termed "the new school of realism."[48] Most of the filmic candidates for this definition had no such pure identity, combining conventions of realism with elements of melodrama and fantasy, but critics used the term liberally and optimistically, bolstering their desire for a transparency in the term by citing ground rules for the new realist style. Realist films had to have simple plots in which plausible events showing plausible characters brought plausible results. Lejeune wanted "situations rather than stories"; Ralph Bond wanted "honest reality and objectiveness . . . real people, real situations, and real instead of synthetic emotions"; Evelyn Russell required "no anachronisms . . . no box office glamour . . . and no loose ends."[49] Good, convincing acting was a plus, while imitation of Hollywood glamour was to be avoided, for glamour and convincing acting were understood to be mutually exclusive. It was mental rather than physical polish and slickness that was required.

The words "truth," "simplicity," and "sincerity" were the corner-

[45] Andrew Buchanan, "Ships and Sealing Wax," *Sight and Sound* 7, no. 26 (Summer 1938): 80–81.

[46] Quoted in Betts, *The Film Business*, p. 309. Bernstein later headed the Granada circuit.

[47] André Bazin, "The Evolution of the Language of Cinema," in *What is Cinema?* vol. 1, trans. Hugh Gray (Los Angeles: University of California Press, 1967), p. 29.

[48] Roger Manvell, "Recent Films," *Britain Today*, May 1945, p. 36. For Manvell the outstanding early example of the "new school of realism" was *Love on the Dole*.

[49] Bond, *Monopoly*, p. 10; Evelyn Russell, "Why Not a School of British Film-making?" *Sight and Sound* 10, no. 37 (Spring 1941): 12.

stones of the critical litany of realism, as indeed they had been for French nineteenth-century realism and naturalism. Only realism could represent British thoughts and ideas, it was argued; this was its "natural and national framework."[50] Critics urged that film should make an account of contemporary events, make some claim on the real—hence their disgust at the costume melodrama and its studio-bound anachronisms. As an antidote, their recipes for national screen flavor recommended heavy seasoning with documentary-style shooting and editing. Pointing the camera at outdoor, living Britain seemed one way in which British films might become distinctive in recording the peculiarities of native wartime life. Location shooting promised a contemporary *mise-en-scène*, to which the opening sequence of Powell and Pressburger's *A Canterbury Tale* was an important and disturbing exception, as discussed in my Conclusion. Here the outdoor footage of Kentish countryside supported both costumed Chaucerian figures and modern military technology, the two worlds narrowly separated by a single shot/reverse-shot cut. This cut challenged the inevitability of a link between locating shooting and contemporary events.

War blurred the distinction between documentary and feature filmmaking in an economic as well as an aesthetic sense. There was now a freer exchange of personnel between the two limbs of the industry because of general staff shortages. The war was also causing film's entertainment and informational roles to merge. Many feature films as well as documentaries contained instructions on how to "carry on," and emphasized the need for increased effort and sacrifices. This intermarriage of style and address was credited with producing a new, specifically British quality in filmmaking: "*The Way Ahead* represents at its best Britain's distinctive contribution to film art—the successful wedding of the documentary technique with that of the fiction story."[51] In Harry Watt's documentary short *London Can Take It* (1940), intended chiefly for American viewers, the male voice-over narrator is especially eager to certify the genuineness of his representation vis-à-vis American conventions, and cries out over footage of a blitz, "These are not Hollywood sound effects. This is the music they play every night in London: the symphony of war."

Target for Tonight (1941) and *Diary for Timothy* (1945) exemplify the kind of hybrid films, often of unconventional length, that grew from this documentary/feature merger. The former deployed R.A.F. members rather than actors, while the title sequence informed viewers that the R.A.F. men would "reenact" their daily routine for the filming of the fictional story of their real plane "F for Freddie." *Diary for Timothy* incorporated a real

[50] Noble, *The British Film Yearbook*, p. 18.
[51] Bond, "What is the Future of British Films?" pp. 11–12 and 24.

miner, Goronwy, and an injured pilot (whose undeniable leg battle-scar we are shown), but wove their lives through the fictional power of film into the life of "Timothy," a generic middle-class baby born on the fifth anniversary of war. This baby symbolizes the whole of the coming postwar generation. In the film's closing scene, documentary and fictional elements are thoroughly intermeshed through a cutaway shot that makes Goronwy's portrait seem to hang above Tim's cot in his nursery.

Many feature films incorporated documentary footage of fleets, flypasts, parades, and explosions, pulling narratives away from the stagey interiors and theatricality of which British cinema had so often been accused. Shots of Cathy Wilson (Deborah Kerr) steering a motorboat in *Perfect Strangers* are intercut with high-contrast imagery of actual bombing raids over the Thames. Documentary elements such as the use of location shooting, non-professional actors, military footage, voice-over narration, montage passages, and less goal-oriented closure served to place the experience of film characters in a larger world picture, encouraging audiences to do the same with their own lives as they switched between watching different levels of fiction, some documented, some acted (played and unplayed, to use the Soviet distinction)—in short, encouraging them to be mobilized.

The war caused every fiction, no matter how apparently remote from the crisis, to be understood in its terms. The presence of documentary style within feature filmmaking gave aesthetic form to this connection, above all through the kind of audience address it promoted. Basil Wright explained the appropriateness of the "documentary approach" to the crisis in precisely these terms. He stressed its closeness to real social experience in that it was based on "the observance of reality and on many years' experience of the handling of ordinary people." This approach could therefore "make the public feel that the subject dealt with is really a part of their own lives and responsibilities, and not a fictional episode divorced from their own experience."[52] Wright understood the way the inclusion of elements of documentary style served the war effort by speaking to, and of, in his terms, "ordinary people." Documentary filmmaking in Britain since the 1930s had been directly associated with "ordinariness" as a euphemism for working-class subject matter, so that the merging of documentary and fictional strategies offered a way to imagine that sector of the population that needed, above all, to be incorporated into the idea of nationhood and hence into the fight—those who formed not only the majority of workers but also the majority of cinema-goers.

[52] Basil Wright, "Realist Review," *Sight and Sound* 10, no. 38 (Summer 1941): 21. See also Thorold Dickinson, "Why Not a National Film Society?" *Sight and Sound* 7, no. 26 (Summer 1938): 75. He writes, "Everyone nowadays admits that the best British films are the documentaries."

The government decreed in its "Programme for Film Propaganda" that films about "How Britain fights" needed to include the sacrifices and contributions of "all classes of workers." It recommended, on a related point, that "the documentary element is made part of a dramatic story" in fashioning feature films.[53] These twin aspects of subject matter and style buttressed the imaging of ordinary people, and hence the address to a similarly ordinary spectator. The genre of the national subject enhanced empathy with filmic characters by imagining a patriotic, intelligent, but above all ordinary spectator who is in the process of surviving extraordinary events.

References to this combination of the ordinary confronting the extraordinary abound in wartime films: "We're living in strange times, darling," says Captain Kinross in *In Which We Serve*; "These are not ordinary times," chimes a London civil servant in *Tawny Pipit*. The male voice-over of *London Can Take It* describes "the greatest civilian army ever to be assembled . . . ordinary by day, heroes by night," while a similar voice-over in *Victory Wedding* notes that "the simple things that make life worth living . . . mean everything to Bill, and millions of us like him." The titles of *Millions Like Us*, as Andrew Higson points out, include a credit to "millions like you," while *Brief Encounter*'s Laura Jesson describes herself as "just an ordinary woman," and Fred Blake of *Millions Like Us* mutters shyly that he's nothing more than "an average, ordinary sort of chap," to which his future wife replies, "I'm ordinary myself, come to that."[54] Such films drum home the idea of a continuity between screen character and audience member in their shared ordinariness.

Characters are shown performing the ordinary tasks of washing up and cleaning house (*Waterloo Road, Millions Like Us*) and responding to the media that addressed ordinary people. They go to the cinema and watch newsreels (Walter and Kath in *In Which We Serve*, and Laura and Alec in *Brief Encounter*), read *Picture Post* (in *Next of Kin* and *The Way Ahead*), and listen to music and government announcements on the radio (in *I See a Dark Stranger* and *Millions Like Us*). This is one of the many ways in which films perpetuate the effects of government propaganda. In *Millions Like Us* the radio advises housewives, absent as characters in the film but presumed present in the audience, to make better use of the potato. At such a moment the cinema redoubles government efforts to engender thrifty wartime habits. (See Figure 1.4.)

The most direct implantation of official propaganda through film takes place via the filmic image of the poster, whose very presence is a sign of

[53] Christie, *Powell, Pressburger and Others*, pp. 122 and 123.
[54] Higson, "Five Films," p. 26.

film's documentary power. Posters, familiar to wartime audiences from official campaigns, decorate the war film's *mise-en-scène*, and are sometimes mobilized to support elements of the plot. In *Next of Kin* several posters referring to the dangers of gossip paper the fictional environs. "Keep It under Your Hat," "Careless Talk" (by Fougasse), and "Telling a Friend May Mean Telling THE ENEMY," are all shown but disobeyed in the film, with the result that Allied lives are lost. *Waterloo Road* is strewn with air raid shelter signs and a poster for precautions during an air raid, which is also ignored as the two rival men, Ted and Jim, fight over Tilly. Here the poster generates tension through its juxtaposition to contrary narrative events, while proposing to the audience a responsible, moral reading of the scene consonant with national concern. *This Happy Breed* (1944) contains the poster "Get Your Gas Mask Now," old by the year of the film's release, and one of the film's visual elements that holds the ending of its story distinctly in the past, in the early war. *Tawny Pipit*, with its rural setting, boasts a "Dig for Victory" poster, while *Millions Like Us* includes "Serve with the Men Who Fly," "Firebomb Fritz," "Russia's Fight Is Ours," "Tighten Your Grip" (an image of pliers crunching a swastika), and "Is Your Journey Really Necessary?" cruelly appearing as Celia and Fred set off for their honeymoon.

The poster as a representational form has no original. A film character has, as original, the body of the actor, but the poster is from the start a reproduction, which the film merely duplicates, thereby seeming to fictionalize it less. The poster conveys a wartime message and enhances the "reality" of the film's setting through its status as a peculiarly wartime document. It seems to carry the power to address the viewer in the same manner both on-screen and off. It cuts into the fantasy state so readily promoted in the cinema auditorium, purveying another, more sanguine level of discourse within its walls. Audiences familiar with the "Is Your Journey Really Necessary?" slogan, posted at every "real" railway station, are asked to weigh its message against the peacetime conventions of the honeymoon, a personal journey of no immediate strategic, public value, when they see the poster incorporated into the *mise-en-scène* of *Millions Like Us*. The juxtaposition makes romance appear an uncertain indulgence in wartime, and subtly prepares the audience for Celia's later loss of her husband over Germany.

Documentary strategies were adapted for many feature films from *The Gentle Sex* to *The Way Ahead*, both of which required cooperation from the Forces and hence the government during production. The plots of these two films, and many others, are composed of multiple narrative strands following several characters with equal interest instead of singling out a central romantic couple or hero.[55] These films thus appear to have a rather haphazard structure, lurching from one round of duties and crises to the next in the conversion of citizens to soldiers. The films do not build toward a particular event but are nevertheless ordered, merely through belonging to the unique space of war. That space brings them narrative organization, although it also brings these films to their most abstract moments in terms of visual style.

During the German raid on the refugee train in *The Foreman Went to France* all rules of classical cinema are momentarily broken. A shot of a small girl's face is intercut several times, in quick succession and from different angles, with explosions and shots of airplanes flying in multiple directions, producing in the spectator a chaotic, spinning effect. A similar disorientation occurs while viewing the air raid sequence over Freihausen in *Target for Tonight*. Here the alternating dark and light flashes of attack and defense, which have the character of documentary footage, cannot be assigned to either Allied or enemy action. We see silhouettes of Germans—literally the faceless enemy—and shots of British pilots, but our psychical orientation toward the abstract light patterning is left unanchored, since we cannot locate who attacks and who is being attacked. The inclusion of the motif of the raid in both films entails a temporary collapse of visual convention and is one of the ways through which these films signal their historical specificity.

Because of their imbrication in contemporary events, British films about the war cannot sustain conventional narrative chains of cause and effect, those which would usually result in the classical ending of lovers fading out in a "happily ever after" embrace. Instead, marriages occur precipitously, on twenty-four-hours' leave, and they rarely conclude British films.[56] Many more romantic unions are deferred or lost rather than secured. Wartime acts as an historical constraint on this cinema, exposing the inadequacy of romantic liaison for narrative resolution, and thus tending, retrospectively, to unmask the ideological function of such endings in "normal," peacetime cinema. This exposure of cultural convention may explain the high number of wartime viewers who voiced the following type of opinion, particularly of American film: "I think I have always realized, quite clearly, that films *are* just films, and that the exotic glamorous kind of life some of them depict is not to be found anywhere in reality"; and similarly, "I never sighed with envy at the synthetic beauty of the stars or for their magnificent houses and trains of servants—simply, I think, be-

[55] Ibid., p. 25.
[56] Precipitously formed romances are also to be found within Hollywood cinema of the war years, for instance in *The Clock* (1945).

cause I did not connect them with reality.''[57] And in the same vein, ''Seeing films has made me want to go to America and see for myself how the Americans live—probably half the population live in penthouses, and the rest wallow in dirt in filthy tenements.''[58]

For another viewer, an eighteen-year-old shorthand typist, it was precisely when the representation of war was attempted that the conventions of American cinema became most irksome: ''Maria Montez and Jon Hall in their fairy-tale films filled me with a wild desire to travel, to see for myself, even though my inner self told me that the Baghdad I was seeing was constructed by carpenters under the direction of a director, who saw everything through rose-tinted glasses. This fact was brought home to me in *Four Jills in a Jeep*. How distorted is the American idea of Britain. We don't all hunt the fox and talk county.''[59] She objects to the foreign cinema because it fails to respond to changed wartime conditions that to her, the mobilized spectator, are all too visible. *Four Jills in a Jeep* generalizes about the British population, remaining insensitive enough to impute to all citizens the same privileged class status, which she does not share. The film thus fails to address her as part of the nation pulling for the war effort: it is not tuned to specific, national conditions.

The shortcomings of romantic union for wartime closure are most openly and self-consciously acknowledged in *Love Story* (1944). Toward the end of the film Lissa (Margaret Lockwood) cries, ''We're all living dangerously. There isn't any certainty anymore. . . . How long have any of us got?'' to which her lover Kit (Stewart Granger) answers, ''Let's take all the happiness we can, while we can.'' However, the film does not end with their embrace; it finishes in further parting, as Kit flies over the Cornish cliff with his squadron while Lissa, now his wife, watches from the headland below. Such an ending is typical of the way this entire genre of films asks its audience to accept emotional loss, separation, and uncertainty about the future while still demanding its commitment to ''living through.''

Wartime closure's lack of definition takes literal form in *The Way Ahead* as, at the end of the film, the few remaining men of the Duke of Glendons (the DOGS) walk with fixed bayonets toward the Germans, and, in several shots, away from the camera, disappearing into rousing music and smoke. The final shot shows a World War I DOGS veteran back home reading of his regiment's exploits in the newspaper; his facial expression suggests he

---

[57] Forty-seven-year-old housewife and fiction writer, in Mayer, *British Cinemas and Their Audiences*, p. 121; nineteen-year-old female clerk, Mayer, *British Cinemas and Their Audiences*, p. 68.

[58] Nineteen-year-old female typist, Mayer, *British Cinemas and Their Audiences*, p. 66.

[59] Ibid., p. 38.

is impressed by their record, but the audience remains unsure, since no text is given them to read, and there is no dialogue, only music. This film's ending is as vague as the fog, though in the context of the rest of the film, the veteran's expression is probably one of pride in his troop's bravery before death. At the beginning of the film he had expressed skepticism about the ''young chaps' '' ability to fight a modern war with the words: ''It's all this education and machinery and going to the pictures. . . . Where are the *men*?'' But now ''the way ahead,'' if unclear, is at least shown to be forward. The words, ''the beginning,'' appearing last on the screen, suggest the necessary price of an initial loss of life for the greater, patriotic good and the eventual victory against Rommel in North Africa.

These films cannot be described as vigorously ''war-affirmative.'' Their endings are too contaminated by the moral anxieties of a nation entirely engaged in war, for the first time in its history. The collaboration of so many citizens, of so many nations, in the bombing and destruction of others brings an unprecedented burden of fear and guilt to a whole generation. As Ann asks David in *The Gentle Sex* as she contemplates their futures: ''Are we different to any other generation?'' *In Which We Serve*, *The Way to the Stars*, *Diary for Timothy*, and *Waterloo Road* all manage the anxiety of this aspect of ''total war'' by producing a fictional son in the course of their narratives who will inherit the unknown consequences of his parents' wartime mobilization; *Tawny Pipit* also promotes a pronatalist stance through its production of a family of pipits by the closing shot. *Waterloo Road* ends as Dr. Montgomery turns away from the Colter boy's pram and looks toward the rubble and railroad of a blitzed street: ''I wonder what they'll think of their Mums and Dads? Probably never understand why they allowed all this. And yet maybe they'll have to admit that, take it all in all, they didn't come through so badly. Well, Jimmy, me boy, look at you, it's all yours.'' The last shot frames the unhappy coalition of a child grinning and gurgling in the grim surroundings of bombed-out London.

Similar questions about the next generation's stake in the war are addressed to Timothy via Michael Redgrave's voice-over in *Diary for Timothy*. The film closes with intercut shots of Tim screaming for his bottle and bombs falling over the Rhine. The penultimate image of explosion dissolves to Tim in his cot, flames lashing around him as the war footage fades away. Redgrave asks Tim of the war, ''What are you going to say about it, and what are you going to do? . . . Are you going to make the world a different place? You and the other babies?'' This film, like so many others, finds that the nation's narrative cannot simply be exhausted, resolved because the celluloid runs out. Whether Beethoven, as a German composer, should not now be listened to in Britain, as Redgrave also asks, is the least of the postwar world's unanswerable questions. All these

40

films—from *Love Story* and *Waterloo Road* to *Diary for Timothy* and *The Way Ahead*—demonstrate that despite the urgings of government memoranda, pronatalist discourse, and the plethora of critical guidelines, the extreme conditions of war mitigate against the possibility of a conventional closed ending.

THOSE FILMS repeatedly praised by critics during the war have a recognizable iconography comprising determinedly banal, quotidian locations shot with a restrained acting and camera style, save for those moments during a raid. Corner shops, bomb sites, front-door steps, and station platforms provide these films' typical settings, while parlors, pubs, and spartan dance halls, lit by lonely, revolving mirrored globes, add a modicum of luster to the austere wartime environment. The illicit, indulgent nature of Ted's tea trip with Tilly to the Palais de Danse in *Waterloo Road* is suggested through the glittering presence of just such an orb. More usually, the surfaces in the *mise-en-scène* of these films are dull and nonreflective, with camera techniques similarly subdued. Blimps, blackouts, and banded curbs, teapots, draining racks, and patterned upholstery frame the omnibus narratives. Hot tea is the pervasive social lubricant, and the whistling kettle is one of the most common home front sounds—except for those specific to war. The wailing siren, the all-clear, the B.B.C. announcement, and the droning aircraft engine overhead are heard across the genre. These films abound with imagery of maps, beaches, cliffs, and lighthouses, efforts to demarcate and resecure the nation's threatened border. Dancing in aircraft hangars, pub drinking, listening to the radio, fighting together, and other scenes of group activity collectively symbolize community strength and the surmounting of class difference in the face of possible defeat.

The ideology of national unity could not permit differences within the nation to jeopardize the war campaign. Distinctions between England, Scotland, Ireland, and Wales, between classes, accents, races, and generations, and between men and women, are noted in the films, but then lessened, often through the suggestion that a set of internal differences is precisely what makes Britain distinctive, and hence unified. Skepticism over such egalitarianism provoked a welter of wartime jokes on the subject of its impermanence (Figure 1.2). In this late war *Everybody's Weekly* cartoon, Miss Pamela and the new maid have already refound their old class niches, only a short time after their war work together. *The Gentle Sex* and *The Way Ahead* are paradigmatic in attempting to blend regions and classes of Britain through the selection of polyglot bands of recruits, a strategy that also characterizes the Hollywood World War II combat film. The choice of a large, single sex group of protagonists for both these films

41

"It seems Miss Pamela and the new maid were in the same ATS outfit in the Normandy campaign, Mrs. Van Giltgold."

Figure 1.2. Class collision as spectacle in *Everybody's Weekly*, 3 February 1945, p. 13.

produces a unity of identity on at least one level—sex—which mitigates against disunities of class.

In *The Way Ahead*, Parsons and Davenport are simultaneously called to the same army unit, but the problem is that Davenport is Parsons's peacetime boss. On the train down to camp, itself a trope for the mixing of classes, Davenport ventures, with difficulty, that Parsons might "disregard any difference in status that pertained in peace" between them. Emerging from the class-blending capsule the train represents, the narrative then more-or-less plays out this instruction, showing war to be a force that makes employee and boss equals. The train was significant in class terms because, to increase wartime efficiency, the peacetime stratification by class had been suspended on trains to and from London: there was only third class, so classes mingled on the train as well as on the platform.[60] In

[60] See Bernard Darwin, *War on the Line* (London: Southern Railway Company, 1946), and Robert R. Bell, *History of the British Railways during the War, 1939–1945* (London: The Railway Gazette, 1946).

Millions Like Us, Forbes, the aircraft factory foreman, is more skeptical of war's egalitarianism, explaining in a marital discussion with his more middle-class employee—a conscript—that there are two sorts of people: "You're one sort and I'm the other. Now there's a war on we've got to be together. What's going to happen when it's over? Are we going to go on like this, or shall we slide back? That's what I want to know." The conversation occurs right at the end of the film, which thus fails to provide an answer.

Scenes of communal leisure activities abound in home front films, included for their value as images of national cohesion among citizens whose loves and lives run close to those of the audience. The dance hall is a favored location—found in *Listen to Britain*, *Millions Like Us*, *The Gentle Sex*, and others—since it can present an image of a large group reassuringly subdivided into heterosexual couples (*pace* Jennings's pairs of dancing women in *Listen to Britain*), moving in unison, coordinated, and yet registering the conventional peacetime pairing of the sexes, all too rare with wartime separations. Dancing in these films takes a social form, is a participatory event, rather than an opportunity for female spectacle. For Peter Roper, *Diary for Timothy*'s injured pilot, relearning to dance is a sign of his recovery and inclusion back into the working nation: his last shot in the film shows him heading for the cockpit again. When dancing takes its more usual cinematic form, as an occasion for female display, as in *Next of Kin* or *Piccadilly Incident*, that female, on the stage and separated from the internal diegetic audience, may well not survive the film: in *Next of Kin* she is a drug addict and threat to national security, while in *Piccadilly Incident* she is killed in one of the last air raids of the war. (Vera Lynn, however, tended to survive, as in *We'll Meet Again* [1942].)

Communal singsongs, another recurring vehicle of national unity, are shown to arise spontaneously in these films, to tunes old and new. An international band of allies—French children, British soldiers and civilians, and an American woman—join forces for "Glory, Glory, Hallelujah" in *The Foreman Went to France*. *Two Thousand Women* ends with all the prison camp interns bellowing "There'll Always Be an England" in the faces of their German captors. *Tawny Pipit* includes a vigorous rendition of "Land of Hope and Glory" in honor of the visiting Russian "Lady Sniper," and ends with a choral version of "All Things Bright and Beautiful" sung by the villagers of Lipsbury Lea. The company of *The Way Ahead* does "She's My Lady Love" to the sounds of Strainer's ukulele while waiting for Saharan battle. Jennings shoots carol-singing in the Anderson in *Diary for Timothy*, while Lissa drops her classical, high-culture repertoire in *Love Story* to play the more popular "Take Me Off to Dear Old Blighty" for the troops to join in with on the North African front.

43

At the end of *Millions Like Us*, group singing helps Celia overcome the loss of her husband, overwhelming her personal misfortune in an image that Higson aptly describes as "both of melodrama and of national identity."[61] With cruel irony, the cheerful song's lyrics include the line "he left me in the lurch."

The genre of the national subject adapted some of the conventions of family melodrama for wartime needs. The genre treats the experience of sons, fathers, mothers, and daughters, the archetypal figures of melodrama, but these characters are no longer in conventional relations to one another, let alone in their conventional space—the home. The idea of home, so valuable to the ideology of national unity, was under siege; films trying to make sense of wartime had to manage the relation of this ideal of home to its patent wartime disintegration. They had to install the notion of "home," while mobilizing the spectator to defend it, and reconstruct it, because it was in danger of being lost. Such conditions explain the proposition made by a disembodied male voice-over in *This Happy Breed* who explains that home has been changed because of the absence of *men* (rather than because of adjustments to female experience). Describing the end of World War I he comments: "After four long years of war, the men are coming home. Hundreds and hundreds of houses are becoming homes once more." Speaking over an image of clouds followed by camera panning and tilting down onto London and row upon row of terraced Victorian houses, with male choral singing in the background, he implies that a house is only a home when the whole family is there. More troubling to wartime Britain, and an issue that *This Happy Breed* avoids by being set between the wars and by referring to World War I, is the effect that the absence of *women* from the house has on the concept of "home," an absence that World War II enforced by law.

The idea of a "home front," borrowed from World War I, was a powerful component of the rhetoric of national unity. Although in peacetime "home" could mean everything from not-foreign, not-abroad, not-a-colony, to a house, family, fireside, or England and the nation itself, the 1939 crisis required that the category be legislated by the government to ensure its continued existence. A new ministry was created, the "Ministry of Home Security," responsible for planning and supervising A.R.P. services, with the Home Secretary at its head. The "Home Guard," "Home Intelligence Unit," and "B.B.C. Home Service" were all instituted in the first few months of war. In all instances the word "home" is virtually interchangeable with the word "national." The Home Guard was Churchill's inspired new name for Local Defence Volunteers, while the Home

[61] Higson, "Five Films," p. 26.

Service was national radio's own gesture toward mobilization.[62] It was first aired on the evening of 1 September 1939, two days before war was declared. It opened with the now famous announcement, "This is the B.B.C. Home Service," repeated on the sound tracks of so many home front films. One single program across Britain had never before been heard.[63] In addition, by using a low frequency, the B.B.C. could continue to broadcast during bombing raids without giving away geographical locations; German radio had to shut down under similar circumstances. Radio thus seemed to bring the nation together through a mechanism unavailable to the enemy. The government certainly preferred radio over cinema as its main communication channel to the nation in wartime, and as the *Everyman's Guide* advised at the outbreak of war, "The Government gives information and instruction to the public by means of broadcast announcements. These . . . are of vital importance to everyone, and . . . listeners should have pencil and paper ready to make notes of important matters concerning themselves."[64]

This power of radio to link up the nation must account in part for the large number of communal radio-listening scenes in home front films. Domestic images of families clustering around radio sets perfectly encapsulate the notion of the home front: small units of patriotism at home, resourceful, bound by familiarity and linked by the radio, ready to act when required. *In Which We Serve* is one of several films that replay the announcement of the start of war by the Prime Minister. *I Live in Grosvenor Square* opens with a scene of Alvar Lidell delivering his evening program for the B.B.C. *I See a Dark Stranger* shows characters listening to the announcement of D-Day in a Northern Irish pub, and *Diary for Timothy* begins with a broadcast of the "B.B.C. Home Service" on the fifth anniversary of war. The cinematic space of war is given aural character through repeated reference to the power of the radio's sound waves.

Of course, despite government legislation and rhetoric, the European home and combat fronts overlapped in reality. British radio was received in Germany and vice versa; bombing raids killed and injured civilians and troops alike. British films such as *In Which We Serve*, *The Foreman Went to France* (1942), and even *The Gentle Sex*, with its ack-ack fire and

---

[62] Churchill instituted the change to "Home Guard" on 24 August 1940, soon after his appointment as Prime Minister.

[63] See Asa Briggs, *The History of Broadcasting in the UK*, vol. 3, *The War of Words* (London: Oxford University Press, 1970); Anonymous, *Ourselves in Wartime: An Illustrated Survey of the Home Front in the Second World War* (London: Odhams Press Ltd., 1944), pp. 45 and 201.

[64] S. Evelyn Thomas, *Everyman's Guide to the War Regulations* (St. Alban's: Donnington Press, 1939), p. 9.

convoy driving, articulate the contiguity of the two fronts, and indeed in terms of screen time, *In Which We Serve* is almost evenly divided between the two. This is less true of films made after the immediate Nazi threat had passed, and of films that represent the American home front.[65] While *The Fighting Sullivans* (1944) and *The Eve of St. Mark* (1944) represent both fronts, in *Since You Went Away* or *Tender Comrade* the fighting front is simply unimaged. The absent men are present in the form of bedside photographs and as prewar memories of their womenfolk, but never present as characters on the distant location of the battlefield. (For this we must wait until the war is over, as in Walsh's *The Revolt of Mamie Stover* [1956].) The patriotic contributions of these men are never intercut with the domestic narrative, and the American home thereby remains the "Unconquerable Fortress" that Selznick's *Since You Went Away* announces in its opening credits, separate from the space of war.

British home front films are forced to confront the urban destruction and conscription of women that distinguish their subject from its American equivalent, but, interestingly, this confrontation is embraced in that it promises to engender national difference on the screen. While they might be expected to have been read as highly demoralizing images, British films did not shy away from bomb site scenes; rather, they are an almost compulsory element of their iconography. *Waterloo Road* begins with establishing shots of the railway station, focusing next on Dr. Montgomery walking down the Colters' street in 1944. As he stares at the destruction, passing piles of rubble and blown-up terraced houses, his voice-over is heard, as if expressing his thoughts: "Gosh! I feel that here I'm walking in a battlefield." As he remembers "the Winter of 1940–41," the shot dissolves to one in which the row of houses is complete, in its earlier, pre-Blitz form, and two women walk down the street, Ruby and Mum Colter, central characters for the film to come. The time span of the film thus stakes out the journey from the past up until the physical destruction of the home in the present.

Despite such destruction there is very little spectacular, bodily violence in home front films, at least nothing equivalent to armed combat. Bombing raids in *Piccadilly Incident* and *In Which We Serve* result in women's deaths, but the unseen attacker is vaguely "above," signaled by a screaming siren or humming engine. Deaths result from collapsed ceilings in these two films, but the enemy's aerial viewpoint is absolutely never shown. In later home front films combat footage is more rarely intercut

---

[65] Jeanine Basinger makes this point indirectly when she writes of the American combat film: "It's very hard to be in war and not be in combat (although the effect of war on civilians has become a familiar genre-type in foreign films, since when civilians sat at home they were still in a war zone)." Basinger, *The World War Two Combat Film*, p. 10.

with domestic scenes, so that in *The Way to the Stars* (1945) Johnny Hollis loses his life on the local airfield, after his return from the Frankfurt raid. Roger Manvell praised this film (and *Waterloo Road*) precisely because "war scenes were excluded . . . the emphasis was wholly on the experiences of the individuals, and the impact of the war on their emotional lives."[66]

The physical destruction of homes is frequently figured metaphorically through the incomplete or irregular family whose absent components are left unexplained: absence is simply a condition of war. In *Millions Like Us* Celia has no mother; she must leave her father alone at home after recruitment. In *Waterloo Road* Tilly lives with her in-laws; she seems to have lost her family. In *The Way to the Stars* Johnny, the father, survives only a third of the film; in *The Gentle Sex* farewells to the seven recruits are never made by two parents; and none of the three pilgrims in *A Canterbury Tale* have any identifiable relatives, at least not in the 1944 version, although Sergeant Johnson's father is mentioned during the discussion of lumbering. The nuclear family exists more or less intact in narratives set in the prewar period, as in the two Coward/Lean films *This Happy Breed* and *Brief Encounter*, though the Gibbon family in the former film certainly experiences its share of deaths and departures. This temporal displacement of the narrative is crucial in enabling the representation of a cinematic world in which more conventional families endure, even if their mothers, as in Laura Jesson's case, are not conventionally nurturing.

The key narrative location for films of the home front genre is as often a training camp, a factory, a village, or a city, as a home. These new sites permit and encourage the representation of different social structures, more communal than those of the traditional home, structures that serve the national interest better. Instead of conventional families, home front films produce makeshift, pseudofamilies, diverse groups of characters united through the Navy, R.A.F. or A.T.S., through their journeying on a train together, through beer-drinking in the local saloon, or through pulling together as a "working village," as in *Great Day* (1945). Unrelated characters take up the family melodrama's archetypal roles. In *Tawny Pipit*, nurse Hazel Broome and convalescing pilot Jimmy Bancroft guard the pipit's nest with two evacuated boys from London, thus forming a uniquely war-based family. A similar configuration arises in *The Foreman Went to France*, in which unmarried—but eventually engaged—Fred and Ann travel with orphaned French children. Even *Since You Went Away* and *Tender Comrade* present new kinds of extended families, in which char-

---

[66] Roger Manvell, "The British Film, 1940–1945," in Balcon et al., *Twenty Years of British Film*, p. 88.

acters play out family roles of father, son, mother, and daughter, irrespective of their biological sex.

The concepts of family and home are under such pressure in wartime that they can function only intermittently, or partially, as metaphors for national unity in cultural representation. Precisely because of the inability of the literal image of home and family to constitute a stable notion of nation, a number of other linguistic and representational tropes come to their aid, such as "home front" and "Home Guard," and those affectionate nicknames for the country—"old blighty" in *The Way Ahead*, or "the old lady" in *This Happy Breed*—which proclaim her identity with such disarming force and familiarity that the need for further definition is obviated.

Overt pronouncements on national character are everywhere in wartime films, although these now seem but lame shorings up of clichés of Britishness, so easily are they refuted, or even inverted. In *This Happy Breed* the British are "a nation of gardeners"; in *Brief Encounter* they are "kind to mad people"; in *Tawny Pipit* a "love of nature and of animals has always been part of the British way of life" (rather than the German), and "the English aren't very good at saying what they feel"; in *In Which We Serve*, "we are an island race"; and in *The Foremen Went to France* the French are exasperated at "les anglais avec leur thé." National identity is also built up through repeated references to idiosyncrasies of local culture, as found both in canonized texts and in daily traditions that war could at any moment disrupt or forget. Elgar and Shakespeare, Cromwell and Victoria, the Domesday Book and 1066, teatime and cricket, remind and educate the spectator, middle and working class, male and female, in his or her national past. Knowing you are British, for a film spectator, stems from sharing this knowledge with other Britons. Films invite this recognition, spreading culture to the edges of the national boundary and if possible beyond it, to leave no place for ideological difference, no place for Fascism.

Britishness is also constructed through more explicit comparison with other nations, as in *The Lion Has Wings*, in which Nazi and British mores are lined up cheek by jowl. *This Happy Breed* shows Sam and Vi watching *Broadway Melody* in 1929, "the all-singing, all-talking, all-dancing marvel," and their first sound film. Sam comments, "You know, I don't understand a word they say," to which Vi rapturously responds, "No, but it's marvellous, isn't it?" The female spectator, Vi, is shown here to be too absorbed by the form of cinema to observe the national boundary, a lapse explored in the next chapter in a discussion of woman's relation to national security. In the opening moments of *Waterloo Road*, set in 1944, Dr. Montgomery overhears some passing G.I.'s as the film flashes back to

1940: "Americans, eh? Funny how we take them for granted now, just as if they were our own boys." In both films it is the sound rather than image that bears the weight of national specificity: Britishness is coded through verbal language, in that the sounds of the two Englishes are different.

A more unusual example of the comparative establishment of nationhood occurs in *The Way Ahead* as the troop enters a small Tunisian town and encounters a foreign culture. The audience hears the following exchange: "What a dump. Where the hell are we? Not even a flick 'ouse with an army picture. I'd hate to be an Arab in peacetime." "How about them hareems?" "I haven't seen any yet. Nothing but them flies. Talk about the mysterious East. I reckon Lyons Corner House, Coventry Street's got more mystery than what this has." Here, the value of the Middle Eastern location for defining national difference shifts from its usual status of being more exotic, as in *Morocco* and *Casablanca*, and even *Desert Victory*, to the obverse position of being more banal—and deprived of women and movies. Tunisia can remain otherwordly only while it is still distant; under scrutiny of troops it seems ordinary, indeed *more* ordinary than London. The point above all is that it still remains different.

The iconography of urban destruction—demolished shops in *Perfect Strangers*, the truncated church in the later *It Always Rains on Sunday* (1947), the forlorn shop signs of "moved" in the Canterbury rubble in *A Canterbury Tale*—are counterbalanced in home front films by an emphasis on the rural, and on the few miraculous wartime architectural survivals, St. Paul's being the most famous, briefly sighted in the opening moments of *Perfect Strangers*. Landscape imagery provides the best visual antidote to war, for the continuity it evokes. The physical existence of the land, and especially its distinctive geological features, confirms the continued political existence of the nation despite the demolition of human constructions. In *Tawny Pipit*, for instance, successful incubation of a new generation of pipits means their "field will go down in history": the *land* will become a national monument through war, a repository for history, a safer storehouse than the architectural, human record. The same theme is developed in *A Canterbury Tale*, as discussed in the Conclusion.

In several film and advertising representations the regenerative power of the land is of psychic benefit in its ability to overcome war's disruptions. In *The Foreman Went to France* Jimmy suggests to the foreman, Fred, "Come down to the old allotment tonight. Nothing like a bit o' gardening to make you forget your troubles." A Hartley's jam advertisement claims that in spite of war its product "has not altered in quality by one single berry." The countryside in which this jam survives and flourishes is imaged through a black and white scraperboard drawing of a thatched cottage, hayrick, drystone wall, and orchard, an idyll with no sign of war and nothing to give it period, not even a hay wain. The advertisement is captioned: "In such a countryside grew the fruits for this real jam."[67] A wartime advertisement for Vita-Weat suggests a similar power of earth: "This is the land that grows the wheat for Vita-Weat," runs the caption, beneath a trouble-free picture of fields, horse-drawn cart, and windmill, set in a mandorla of wheat ears.[68]

Home front characters are well able to "dig for victory," as government posters urged them. They have a special sensitivity to the soil and the elements, liking "planting things, and watching them grow, looking out for changes in the weather" (in *This Happy Breed*). When Bob Mitchell, the Gibbons' neighbor in *This Happy Breed*, evacuates his London home, his compensation is that he'll have a garden, "a sight better than the one I've got here." But this optimism for British earth is accompanied by an anxiety about the environment's ability to defend itself in the crisis. The rare nesting pipits of *Tawny Pipit*, allegories both for refugees and for the precious, threatened nuclear family, are menaced by egg thieves (described as the "fifth columnists" of the Association of British Ornithologists), by the curiosity of young boys, and even by the war machine itself: the Ministry of Agriculture and Fisheries orders compulsory tractor plowing of the nesting site, while the Army conducts tank training maneuvers on the same piece of land. By cutting swiftly between shots of ripe crops, apple harvesters, and shimmering poplars, with spitfires, pill boxes, and A.R.P. wardens surveying the moonlit shore, Humphrey Jennings produces an equivalent sense of menaced nature in the opening sequence of *Listen to Britain*.

In many feature films imagery of the land is politicized, legally bound to the concept of nationhood through the films' inclusions of maps and their natural corollary, the coastline. Borders and boundaries proliferate in these films, responding especially to the occupation of the Channel Islands at the end of June 1940, the first step in the German invasion plan for England, though the only portion of British native territory to be taken. *Millions Like Us*, *Listen to Britain*, *Diary for Timothy*, and *A Matter of Life and Death* all exhibit the embattled shore: shots of slowly unbarbed beaches and detonated mines ensure that babies like Tim will not get "blown to bits" when they vacation after the war. In *Next of Kin* and *Target for Tonight* maps crowd military headquarters in a backdrop of national wallpaper. In the former film a map of Norville in Brittany, the film's enemy target, is shown upside down on the screen as if from the British point of view, Britain being "above" (that is, north of) France.

---

[67] Advertisement for Hartley's Jam, *Picture Post*, 27 January 1940.

[68] Advertisement for Vita-Weat, *Picture Post*, 3 February 1940, p. 56.

Powell and Pressburger's wartime films frequently begin with a screen map, which becomes a parodic map of the universe by the time they make *A Matter of Life and Death*: it foregrounds the problem of naming the owner of the aerial master shot, for this film marks it as God's.

Maps substitute for a particular kind of land imagery absent from home front films: the bird's-eye view. This component of the image track can be understood to have equivalent power to the disembodied voice-over of the sound track. That this shot is largely missing in home front pictures points to the strategic importance of the position that gives rise to the aerial view. Under conditions of war, a country, in this case Britain, proclaims ownership of the skies above her territory—"air rights," as it were—but there is no physical barrier that marks off the boundary between one nation and another in the sky, between Ally and enemy. The aerial point of view can be taken and owned by the enemy, unknown, and especially at night, by bombers, spy planes, parachutists. This is the supreme voyeuristic position, and the one through which the nation becomes most vulnerable in a war so governed by air power. It is "the vision of God," in the words of Raoul Ruiz, describing wartime filming in *Of Great Events and Ordinary People* (1979).

When the aerial shot appears in home front films, it is always explicitly installed as the point of view an an Allied subject, the male pilot, and never included as part of a montage, documentary-style sequence, which would not imbricate the shot in an individual, Allied look. In *Target for Tonight*, aerial photographs of Freihausen are the vital documents that enable the R.A.F. to destroy a German fuel depot. The viewer sees overhead shots of Germany both in the form of these photographic prints, and as soon as the British plane "F for Freddie" crosses to Europe and the captain announces "Freihausen, here we come." These second types of shots are not strictly tied to the crew's lines of sight: a collage of cuts suggests a general aerial access to the image of Germany. Any aerial shots of England are withheld, however, until the mission over Germany has been accomplished and the plane is returning home. At this juncture a shot of the Channel and British coast is deftly marked as the point of view of the British pilot in a shot/reverse shot edit typical of fiction film's conventions. The preceding montage arrangement, relating the British plane to its cloudy environment and to the German land, is here forsaken for continuity editing to secure an Allied gaze for the precious aerial shot of Britain.

With its unique ability to entertain and to organize looking, the medium of cinema arrogates differential social power and pleasure to different fictional looks through the way it disposes shots, images, and words. British wartime cinema performs a special ideological task in rationing that rare and powerful view from the air, by giving it both a nationality and a gender. The aerial gaze promises to encompass the entire nation, to embrace its physical structure, its people, and all its material and cultural wealth: it might therefore be called the "national look," when held by the right pair of eyes. Home front films always fictionalize this look as male, in contrast to the land-bound female look, which in so many ways supports the skies as a male preserve.

The filmic home front is above all the territory of women: the presence of any menfolk there is always carefully explained, usually by reference to injury, age, infirmity, or illegality. Thus most men of home front fictions, save the notoriously sexy G.I. waiting to go abroad and the uniformed soldier on furlough, diverge conspicuously from ideal constructions of masculinity. They are either permanently medically disqualified, wounded, A.W.O.L., draft dodgers, or beyond serving age. Ted Purvis, the spiv of *Waterloo Road*, claims two of these: he evades conscription, and then finds he has a dicky heart. Several films include an overt address to older home front men, acknowledging that sector of their audience through the old codgers in *The Way Ahead*, through *Waterloo Road*'s Dr. Montgomery and Tom the lodger, and through Captain Ellis, the disgruntled veteran of *Great Day*. The hobbies of older home front men on film are quintessentially noncombative: bird-watching, gardening, and pigeon-fancying. Older men play Air Raid Precaution wardens, foremen, fire guards, postmen, doctors, stationmasters, and publicans, characters who regulate and stabilize the new home front communities. In that these kinds of jobs were indeed largely held by the older generation of men—a fact satirized in the television series and film *Dad's Army* (1971)—these peculiarly wartime characterizations represent another way in which wartime cinema strives more earnestly to approximate its viewers' domestic lives.

It is the young, temporarily injured men of home front fictions, those with the potential to regain an unproblematic masculinity, at least in the films' terms, who long for the powerful aerial gaze and who sometimes earn it, in recovery, thereby also clarifying their gendered identity. John Ellis, the World War I veteran of *Great Day*, is depressed, and his heart is not fit enough for the Home Guard. He steals money for drinking and gets arrested, but through it all his solace is to wander out to the long barrow and admire a soaring kestrel through his old military Zeiss binoculars for its "lovely lines, like a spitfire." He never gains the bird/plane's realm, but yearns for the release from earthbound cares he imagines it would provide.[69] The recovery of the younger Bancroft in *Tawny Pipit*, suffering

---

[69] The bird/plane comparison of *Great Day* is paralleled by that in *A Canterbury Tale* in its opening sequence, and also by that in *Tawny Pipit* when a plane flies over the pinfold and the young boys train their binoculars on it. Bancroft scolds them, saying they are supposed

from Battle of Britain wounds, is accomplished at the film's end as he takes to the air again, in the final shots, in a plane named *Anthus Campestris* (Latin for the Tawny Pipit), seeing with his now magnificent aerial vision not only the English countryside, but the pipit's nest in close-up! Squadron Leader Peter Carter in *A Matter of Life and Death* suffers from a distortion of vision in his left eye (caused by ''retinoid adhesions of the olfactory nerve''), and ''highly organized hallucinations''; he recovers his visual power during an operation that enables him literally to view from on high, for he wins the girl at a heavenly trial. Kit in *Love Story* is also an ex-pilot with an ocular disorder deriving from pressure on the optic nerve. He is threatened with blindness but also mends in the operating theater. The film concludes with his squadron's flypast, shown from the point of view of Lissa, his wife, while she forms the last image, seen below on the cliff through the pilot's godlike aerial gaze.

In all these films the sky becomes a masculine sphere, signaled through the strategically powerful aerial gaze it supports. This gendered stratification is reinforced by another, complementary iconography, this time of home front women looking toward the sky from land. Lissa's respect for the flypast recurs for Celia in *Millions Like Us*, for Toddy in *The Way to the Stars*, and for the whole home front community at the end of the American *Mrs. Miniver*. It is in this context that we must understand the extreme generosity of Colonel Barton Barrington in *Tawny Pipit*, who gives the visiting female Russian sniper, as a gift, his ''telescopic rifle'' to empower her vision.

Another related cycle of images, in both films and surrounding cartoons and advertisements, shows women contributing to national defense by filling the sky with barrage balloons. (These balloons were floated above cities, ships, and other likely targets. They were tethered to the ground and dangled hausers intended to snag low-flying enemy dive-bombers.) The blimps' phallic symbolism lies undeniably close to the surface in these images, especially in the advertisement for Maclean's toothpaste, with its slogan, ''Yes, I keep it up,'' and in the Ministry of Food's plea for the potato, which begins, ''*He* leads a double life—our old friend the potato.'' In this advertisement the potato doubles as vegetable and as protective balloon via an illustrative arrangement of three potatoes in the disposition of male genitals (Figures 1.3 and 1.4).

The image of barrage balloons became part of the filmic shorthand for war, but the image is always shown from land-eye level, as in their hoisting in *Millions Like Us* and in their appearance in the opening frames of

---

to be ''watching birds'' (i.e., guarding the pipits), to which they answer that the plane *is* a bird.

Figure 1.3. Women support the aerial war effort
from the land beneath in Maclean's toothpaste
advertisement, *Picture Post*, 20 June 1942.

Love Story and *Perfect Strangers*. The absence of this image presented as
an aerial point-of-view shot results from similar ideological pressures to
those which regulated the aerial image of the British landscape: the aerial
shot of the barrage balloon connoted either danger for the airborn Ally, or
superior vision for the enemy. Either option threatened fictions of national
cohesion.

The trope of the barrage balloon, and of men recovering vision in the
form of the aerial viewpoint, and of women living below the space of flypasts and dirigibles, can be understood collectively as restratifying vision
into two gendered registers of asymmetrical cultural value: the air becomes
a masculinized sphere, while women remain close to the land, on the territory vacated by men, actively supporting the reign of the upper domain
by their work and the direction of their look. Women are now ''on a man's

Figure 1.4. The Ministry of Food harnesses
vegetable power. Government information bulletin,
Time and Tide, 20 November 1943, p. 957.

job—and equal to it,'' in the words of a Weetabix advertisement, but the
job's masculine nature is secured through the placement of the balloon
image *above* the woman—in the same spatial arrangement as in the films.
(Figure 1.5). This intricate layered division is a consequence of the wartime toll on conventional distinctions between male and female roles. The
opposition of masculinity to femininity, which helped to guarantee social
stability in peacetime, had been thrown into torsion as women donned uniforms, entered factories en masse, and left their children in day-care cen-
ters, and as men's bodies failed medicals and proved all too vulnerable to
military technology in battle. The representational division is one of the
ways in which British film refashions a semiotics of sexual difference in
the face of wartime change. In the absence of traditional schema of separate, gendered spheres—of domestic and public spaces—on the ground,
the cinema images a gendered cleft in new, vertically stratified terms, ex-
panding its ideological volume, as it were.

Virilio's concept of a ''space of war'' is thus literalized in miniature in
the case of wartime cinema. Film viewing takes place under new conditions, often in new spaces, and the fictional spaces of narratives take on
new meanings with revised gendered allegiances. Lastly, axes of vision—
vertical and horizontal—assume national and sexual significance, a topic

Figure 1.5. Trespassing on masculinity: hoisting the
dirigible. Advertisement for Weetabix in
Picture Post, 6 June 1942.

that will be discussed further in Chapter 3 in the context of the wartime
space of the blackout.

ONE of cinema's primary cultural roles has been to invent and reproduce
a set of images and tales that sustain the rift of sexual difference. The
image of the fetishized woman has been central to this endeavor, as Laura
Mulvey first argued.[70] However, wartime demands—of rationing, conscription, and patriotism—required a new version of femininity, with
which the glamorized Hollywood image of woman was incompatible. The
veteran in *The Way Ahead* was right to include "beauty" when he proclaimed that "'if there's a war, . . . you can say good-bye to England,

[70] Mulvey, "Visual Pleasure and Narrative Cinema," *Screen* 16, no. 3 (Autumn 1975):
6–18.

home, *and* beauty.'' Woman's pivotal place on the screen as a specular object had to be modified for war, for female beauty became at once a political liability and a symbol of peace. Both were linked to the imaging of national identity.

Over and over again, critics single out female acting and appearance as the litmus test of Britishness within British film. In an account that, in its disparagement, typifies much British opinion of the women who populated American wartime films, Helen Fletcher describes how Toddy, hotel keeper in *The Way to the Stars*, takes the news of her husband's death: ''Thousands of women, and no Hollywood heroines, have heard the news she heard and taken it just like that, going back afterwards to finish up filling up the mustard pots.''[71] A woman's restraint and levelheadedness are held to be the screen's signs of nationality here, by measurement against American production. In a similar vein, recommending the censorship of glamor, Fletcher sketched Lana Turner's gradual molding for soldiership in the W.A.C.S. in *Keep Your Powder Dry*, but noted, ''If only she were to cut off that blond hair one feels the conversion would be complete.''[72] With the hindsight of a few years, Wilder's *A Foreign Affair* (Paramount, 1948) is able to be still more explicit about the function of American screen femininity as a marker of that cinema's national character. Marlene Dietrich, playing Erika von Schlütow, remarks to her visiting female counterpart in Berlin, Congresswoman Frost (Jean Arthur), whose name connotes Erika's opinion of her sexuality, ''You are an American woman? I see you do not believe in lipstick. And what a curious way to do your hair, or rather, not to do it. . . . I'm a little bit disappointed, to tell you the truth. We apparently have a false idea about the chic American woman. Oh, I suppose that's publicity from Hollywood. . . . Perhaps if you would change the line of your eyebrows a little . . .''

All these examples charge Hollywood with distorting, or synthesizing the female form in a way that suggests the imbrication of images of woman with the establishment of national identity (Figure 1.6). In the words of a *Colliers* cartoon, ''The Swedish film star was beautiful, but the moment she arrived in Hollywood her studio imposed a new face and form.'' Further, as the Dietrich character suggests, Hollywoodian femininity was an ''idea,'' an overall impression from ''publicity'' rather than a truth about every female screen representation emanating from the States. However,

---

[71] Helen Fletcher, ''Films in Review,'' *Time and Tide*, 16 June 1945, p. 499. This was a period in which several influential female film critics were working in Britain: Catherine de la Roche, Penelope Houston, Catherine Lejeune, Dilys Powell, and E. Arnot Robertson. See Marsha McCreadie, *Women on Film: The Critical Eye* (New York: Praeger, 1983), for biographical details of some of them.

[72] Helen Fletcher, ''Films in Review,'' *Time and Tide*, 7 April 1945, p. 290.

The Swedish film star was beautiful, but the moment she arrived in Hollywood her studio superimposed a new face and form

Figure 1.6. Hollywood imposes a new femininity on the foreign film star.
Colliers, 5 March 1949, p. 18.

as Dietrich also indicates, this idea was very powerful, amounting to a sign of national identity which the congresswoman lacked, making her citizenship unrecognizable. It was against this monolithic and, for them, stigmatized femininity that British filmmakers and critics searched for some essential, undoctored, non-American strain that would secure a different British, national identity on the screen, but, as the following chapter will argue, there was no such stable femininity to be found.

The Mobile Woman: Femininity in Wartime Cinema

Millions of girls and women have to be registered,
interviewed, reserved, deferred, called up, directed,
transferred, and . . . frequently reshuffled.

J. B. Priestley, *British Women Go to War*

LESLIE HOWARD, J. B. Priestley, Frank Launder, and Sidney Gilliat all
chose to represent wartime's mobile woman in their work. They stated in
explanation that the phenomenon of the mobile woman was *the* paradigm
of war: her story crystallized for them the unique character of the crisis.[1]
If we look to other British films of the 1942–46 period, we find this
emphasis on female experience in wartime narratives reinforced, leading
to the paradoxical situation of a wartime cinema apparently revolving
around female experience. Many factors contributed to this state of affairs.
Certainly the discourse on national film style with its emerging realist aesthetic demanded a focus on home front life, causing an expansion of the
war genre to include women. Another component, this time economic,
was the recognition, through survey data, of the increased size of the female audience, whose past viewing habits suggested that further patronage
might be encouraged by an emphasis on stories about women. The most
important factor, however, was the sudden strategic significance of women
for national defense, and the consequent need to present her contribution
as part of the greater national effort. Women now had to be figured as part
of the nation's political body.

The production of a coherent national identity depended on a basis in
stable and reassuring gender roles, and in particular on the maintenance of
that traditional femininity that the war was rapidly undoing. The categori-
zation of a new femininity proved a particular challenge for the cinema,

---

[1] Geoff Brown, *Launder and Gilliat* (London: British Film Institute Publishing, 1977),
p. 108; Ronald Howard, *In Search of My Father: A Portrait of Leslie Howard* (London:
Kimber, 1981), p. 125; J. B. Priestley, *British Women Go to War* (London: Collins, n.d.
[1944?]).

59

because of its foundations in images of glamorized womanhood, inherited from the dominant, American form. The British experience of women being bombed out, conscripted, subject to rationing, and joining, nay replacing, the male workforce led to a deglamorization of the national heroine in which cinema had to participate. Films worked to redefine femininity, but they had, by their very focus, to dramatize its concurrent disintegration.

Ideas about femininity and war have rarely reinforced one another: the story of Boadicea had to undergo convoluted transformations in order to deploy her as a warring figurehead, and Delacroix could paint a semi-naked female to lead a revolutionary movement in *Liberty Guiding the People* (1830) only at the price of an uneasy alliance between eroticism and politics.[2] Even when Queen Elizabeth I (Flora Robson) bellowed "I am England!" to her Spanish visitors in *Fire over England* (1936) it smacked of the awkwardness of equating woman with a belligerent nation, even in an historically remote setting. (Surely one of the appeals of the figure of Cleopatra for cinema, from the silent period onward, including one film in the period of this book—Gabriel Pascal's expensive 1945 British version, *Caesar and Cleopatra*—was her promise of combining female sexuality with the politics of war.) The oxymoronic title *Tender Comrade* or the archaic *The Gentle Sex* suggests a survival of the tension into World War II, since notions of women as tender or gentle had been deformed by their wartime jobs as convoy drivers, riveters, and muckrakers.

Wartime cinema occasionally gives overt expression to male anxiety over these new configurations. In *Great Day*, Ellis constantly makes disparaging remarks of the type, "No wonder the country's going to the dogs, with a pack of women running it." Ted, a farmer character in the same film, remarks of his new female farm hands that "it's not like old times with all these flibbertigibbets about," while Culpepper refuses outright to hire a Land Army girl in *A Canterbury Tale* on account of her sex. "In my day we used to call them 'the gentle sex,' " says veteran Colonel Barrington in *Tawny Pipit*, conceding the fact of historical change while keeping the Victorian past in view. *The Way Ahead* cites the incompatibility of women and wartime needs in specifically visual terms: Luke (John Laurie) has worked on a farm until joining the Army but now he has been replaced by a "lassie." As he says, "She's better looking than me, but not for that

[2] See Sharon Macdonald, "Boadicea: Warrior, Mother and Myth," in Sharon Macdonald, Pat Holden, and Shirley Ardener, eds., *Images of Women in Peace and War: Cross-Cultural and Historical Perspectives* (London: Macmillan Education Ltd., 1987), pp. 40–61. See also Marica Pointon, "Liberty on the Barricades: Women, Politics and Sexuality in Delacroix," in Sian Reynolds, ed., *Women, State and Revolution: Essays in Power and Gender in Europe Since 1789* (Amherst: The University of Massachusetts Press, 1987), pp. 25–43.

kind of work." His words make unusually clear the way the ideal of glamorized womanhood was threatened by labor, or indeed by any movement at all.

As these examples suggest, changes in female experience challenged men's understanding of themselves, and their country. But elsewhere in films, advertisements and magazine columns are traces of women's anxieties, resentments, and desires in the face of the same changes. For instance, an advertisement for Jeyes Fluid must address itself primarily to the female consumer, but does so by acknowledging the contradictory demands war makes upon her: "Are you leading a double life? Are you doing national service as well as looking after your home? . . . Jeyes Fluid will protect you . . . A supply of Jeyes Fluid should be an essential part of both your domestic and your A.R.P. arrangements" in the event of the "interruption of Public Health and Sanitary Services through enemy action."[3] The image accompanying the text is of a woman's body split in half vertically, dressed as a nurse on the left, holding Jeyes, and dressed with an apron on the right, wiping a dish, but also using Jeyes. The syndrome of the "double life" was not specific to war, but war changed its meaning, so that women were now encouraged to identify with this split identity and to understand it as a symptom of patriotism.

An advertisement for Rinso juggles the same issues. The copy claims: "Holder of riveting record is also Model Housewife." We learn that this woman manages to excel at the two roles by washing the "Rinso no-boil way" because it saves her an hour and a half and because it also saves fuel. Thus patriotism is infused into the purchase of Rinso, while the appeal is again made through a glimpse of the conflicts experienced by wartime women.[4] The myth is that Rinso will bridge the gap.

More explicit references to the contradictions of war experienced by women are available on the letters page of *Time and Tide*, which printed many female readers' complaints about official policy toward women. In a letter of 8 November 1941 a "woman doctor," as she signs herself, describes being turned down for a job on the basis that she was a "lady" doctor. She continues: "We are constantly hearing of the need for women to help in the war effort, yet this is the sort of rebuff that many of us, married or single alike, are meeting when we offer our services." Another woman of thirty-eight describes how "women like me, no longer young,

---

[3] Advertisement for Jeyes Fluid, *Picture Post*, 6 July 1940.

[4] Advertisement for Rinso detergent, *Picture Post*, 24 January 1942. Sue Harper describes the discontent and anxiety of conscripted British women during the Second World War in "The Representation of Women in British Feature Films, 1939–1945," in Phillip M. Taylor, ed., *Britain and the Cinema in the Second World War* (London: Macmillan, 1988), pp. 168–202.

dependent on their own efforts for their means of livelihood, dare not throw up such jobs as they possess, knowing full well as they do that not for them will employers two, three, four years hence be waiting with open arms.'' She adds that although ''we have heard a good deal about the reluctance of women to take their fair part in work of national importance,'' this is surely understandable given the experience of unfair hiring practices in peace.[5] The government needed to assure women such as herself of an adequate livelihood after the war in order for her to be able to volunteer.

Even in film, a medium thoroughly permeated by masculine fantasies of female subjectivity, we catch glimpses of women's wartime predicaments. In *The Way Ahead* Parsons tells his army boss that his wife back home is being bullied by finance companies for loan payments ''just because she's a woman.'' While on the one hand his comments imply that it takes a man to handle the family's fiscal matters, they also acknowledge that discrimination might occur solely on the basis of sex. In *Great Day* Meg Ellis (Sheila Sim) announces to her father, ''It's all very well for you. You usen't to have to think. You always had Mummy to do your thinking for you. We women have to accept responsibility and make the best of things. . . . I'm bitter about the kind of life that Mother's had.'' In another scene in *Great Day*, a young woman expresses her response to new government legislation in these bald terms: ''I've got to have a baby or go into a factory. What am I to do?'' Even in the more conservative *This Happy Breed*, Ethel Gibbon is able to retort to Frank after he returns from World War I: ''There'll always be wars as long as men are such fools as to want to go to them.''

The general point is that while wartime cinema might attempt to figure the nation through an image of stable femininity—through, for example, the image of the mother based at home, as in Mrs. Colter of *Waterloo Road*, or, more problematically, Mrs. Ellis of *Great Day*—it also had to mobilize discourses that could speak to real women as historical subjects, subjects who were being moved out of the home. The interest of this material lies both in its failure to achieve a coherent replacement feminine for ideal wartime, and in the space opened up that makes visible the contradictions of wartime female subjecthood. This forked pattern leaves its mark in the textual structures of films, especially in the way they solicit their audience's attention. Many films strive to speak to women, acknowledging and encouraging their labor and sacrifice, while also reassuring men of these women's continued femininity. I shall analyze just such a dichotomy at the end of this chapter, in *The Gentle Sex*.

[5] *Time and Tide*, 8 November 1941, p. 967.

62

WARTIME'S erosion of the feminine ideal was not immediate. Material inroads such as clothes rationing and home front bombing came on by degrees. The military need for womanpower was not at first apparent, permitting for instance an advertisement of 1940 for Clarks Shoes in which the female consumer is reassured that "it would be a dreadful bore if *every* woman went to war" (Figure 2.1). The ideological construct of the "waiting women" became unthinkable, even traitorous, after Mr. Bevan's mid-war female recruitment drive. The screen's most serious attempts to come to grips with women's war experience coincided with this drive, when the Ministry of Information Films Division commissioned titles specifically dealing with female experience; *The Gentle Sex* (1943) and *Millions Like Us* (1943) were two of the results. By then the war machine required images and narratives of total mobilization, in which the word "total" was a euphemism for, above all, the inclusion of women.

Despite their content, films like *The Gentle Sex* and *Millions Like Us* were not marketed specifically as "Woman's Films."[6] Such a nomenclature would have run counter to the ideology of national unity, whose rhetoric finessed the peacetime ethos of the sexes' separate spheres. The king's statement, issued on cards on 8 June 1946 to all children, exemplifies this principle of the equal importance of every citizen's contribution: "Today, as we celebrate victory, I send this personal message to you and all other boys and girls at school. For you have shared in the hardships and dangers of a total war and you have shared no less in the triumph of the Allied Nations." Though knowing its audience to be composed mainly of women, the film industry could not be certain of that audience's rapidly changing self-identity, nor did it wish to draw attention to gendered or classed rifts through the construction of sex-specific or class-specific fictional worlds: the machine of patriotism forbade it. Instead, under wartime, woman-centered narratives were understood to be of wider, national significance and not the exclusive concern of women. Similarly, the number of stories of working class, "ordinary" people increased on the screen, in both documentary and feature films, sometimes entwined, as in *The Way Ahead* and *In Which We Serve*, with upper middle-class stories of that more priviledged Briton who had dominated the prewar cinema. In such a way the lives of the ordinary are advertised as the concern of everybody.

American home front pictures form a more obviously gynocentric genre, positing an opposite, "man's" genre, the combat film. *Tender*

---

[6] William Everson remembers that the trailer for *The Gentle Sex* showed Lilli Palmer firing a machine gun, an activity excluded not only from the film itself, but also off-limits for actual British women in wartime. It seems that this trailer footage was intended to attract men as much as women to the cinema to see the film. (I have not been able to find a viewing copy of the trailer.)

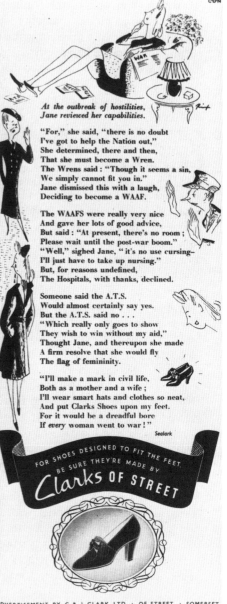

At the outbreak of hostilities,
Jane reviewed her capabilities.

"For," she said, "there is no doubt
I've got to help the Nation out,"
She determined, there and then,
That she must become a Wren.
The Wrens said : "Though it seems a sin,
We simply cannot fit you in."
Jane dismissed this with a laugh,
Deciding to become a WAAF.

The WAAFS were really very nice
And gave her lots of good advice,
But said : "At present, there's no room ;
Please wait until the post-war boom."
"Well," sighed Jane, " it's no use cursing—
I'll just have to take up nursing."
But, for reasons undefined,
The Hospitals, with thanks, declined.

Someone said the A.T.S.
Would almost certainly say yes.
But the A.T.S. said no . . .
"Which really only goes to show
They wish to win without my aid,"
Thought Jane, and thereupon she made
A firm resolve that she would fly
The flag of femininity.

"I'll make a mark in civil life,
Both as a mother and a wife ;
I'll wear smart hats and clothes so neat,
And put Clarks Shoes upon my feet.
For it would be a dreadful bore
If *every* woman went to war ! "

Sealark

FOR SHOES DESIGNED TO FIT THE FEET.
BE SURE THEY'RE MADE BY
Clarks OF STREET

ADVERTISEMENT BY C & J CLARK LTD · OF STREET · SOMERSET
MAKERS OF LADIES' AND CHILDREN'S FINE SHOES SINCE 1825

Figure 2.1. Six months into the war
this Clarks advertisement encourages
women to "fly the flag of
femininity" by buying their shoes.
Picture Post, 17 February 1940, p. 3.

Comrade and *Since You Went Away* represent a world more materially intact if emotionally incomplete, and women remain largely within the domestic sphere; their factory jobs get scant representation. Grouping of films by gendered address was always weaker in Britain because of different, less genre-oriented traditions of production, but domestic conditions of greater national upheaval in wartime compounded this trend. The home front's contamination by combat activity was a crucial factor in orienting realist British film output along the lines of a national rather than gendered address.

After 1941 and the beginning of the female recruitment drive, several British films, from musical comedies to romances, imaged life in the female forces: in the A.T.S. in *Old Mother Riley Joins Up* (1941), *King Arthur Was a Gentleman* (1942), *Next of Kin* (1942), *Women Aren't Angels* (1942), *Somewhere on Leave* (1942), *Miss London Ltd.* (1943), *The Gentle Sex* (1943), *English without Tears* (1944), and, much later, *The Small Back Room* (1949); in the Air Transport Auxiliary in *They Flew Alone* (1941) (U.S. title: *Wings and the Woman*), and *The Hundred Pound Widow* (1943); in the W.A.A.F in *The Balloon Goes Up* (1942), *I Live in Grosvenor Square* (1945), and *A Matter of Life and Death* (1946); and in the Wrens in *Fiddlers Three* (1944), *Perfect Strangers* (1945), *Piccadilly Incident* (1946), and *The Weaker Sex* (1948). The most frequently represented branch of the Forces, as this list suggests, was the A.T.S. Such films were cheaper to make, since no rentals of planes or boats were required, and they also perpetuated the association of women's work with the land, with ground level, supporting the spatial model proposed in Chapter 1.

Other jobs held by women on-screen included factory worker in *Millions Like Us* (1943) and *Sally Gets a New Job* (1943) (an M.O.I. short); Army nurse in *The Lamp Still Burns* (1943); barge hand in *Painted Boats* (1945); Women's Land Army recruits in *A Canterbury Tale* (1944), *Great Day* (1945), *Went the Day Well?* (1942), *Up with the Lark* (1943), and *Tawny Pipit* (1944); and troop entertainers of various sorts in *Piccadilly Incident* (1946), *I Live in Grosvenor Square* (1945) and *Love Story* (1944). In other films peripheral parts are taken by women specifically to enhance the wartime atmosphere so that, for example, a female bus conductor and station porter can be spotted in *Tawny Pipit* and *Love Story*, British equivalents of the female cab driver in the American *The Big Sleep*. Even films focusing on male experience began to include scenes of the female encounter with war: *In Which We Serve* incorporates a home front raid on women; *Desert Victory* includes the labor of female factory workers whistling while they work; and *The Way Ahead* takes note of shifting sexual roles by including an all-female musical band (albeit a disappointing one) and the news from

Stainer's local, the Knave of Hearts, that the hearts have gone. "Betty's in munitions and Joyce is in the A.T.S.," the barmaid informs him.

By 1945 the question of whether the war had had a permanent effect on women was *the* topic on film's and others' lips. An immediately postwar *Punch* cartoon diagnoses the legacy of war for women in positive yet trivial terms by showing a daughter in a Wrens uniform visiting a department store with her mother. As the mother tries on hats in front of a mirror, the daughter tilts away, exclaiming of the hat's angle. "Oh, *no*, mother! At *least* ten more degrees to starboard."[7] The cartoon proposes that female concern with fashion has survived the war merely polluted by military lingo.

The cover of the first *Picture Post* of 1945, subtitled "Problems of 1945," prods the possibility of female transformation more warily (Figure 2.2). Anxieties and desires of both men and women are condensed in the cover's clashing arrangement of a bounteous, tutti-frutti hat atop the regime of female military dress. The problem of 1945, the cover suggests, is the juxtaposition of women's recent experience with her future place in peace, presented here as a matter of "looks," of dislocation in sartorial style. The woman in uniform reaches upward to a fantastic cornucopia, a hat that works as a synecdoche both for prewar norms of femininity—notions of frivolity and attention to decoration—and for the woman's desire for an end to austerity conditions. Both aspects recall the traditional stereotype of woman as Eve, as susceptible to temptation. But this cover is in no sense a simple image of returning woman to an imaginary prewar place by restoring her to the position of visually entertaining object, and to the pleasures of female decoration. It is rather a picture of speculation and uncertainty, appropriate to the sliding character of wartime femininity, here still unresolved at the war's end.

Femininity's unstable wartime nature is most perfectly expressed in the government's lingo for the deployable female, "the mobile woman," the central topos for this chapter. These pages explore the effects on representation—and on women—of a shift away from her exclusion from the concept of nationhood (not least in the omission of her suffrage until 1919) toward the acute need for her incorporation into the nation, in the midwar period, and then the relaxation of that pressure again after Germany's defeat. We will see that the war produced a weird laminate of multiple femininities in conflict, to which remnants of the pleasure, anger, and distress of those women this imagery addressed still adhere. Wartime women faced irresolvable contradictions in the versions of femininity that surrounded them, and by which they built their images of themselves.

[7] *Punch*, 18 July 1945, p. 59.

Figure 2.2. Peace symbolized as a Carmen Miranda hat. *Picture Post*,
6 January 1945.

MATERIAL RESTRICTIONS ON GLAMOUR

Any investigation of wartime femininity must reckon with the practical constraints war placed upon its continued existence. Clothes were put on points rationing from June 1941 to reduce demand and thereby free garment workers for more urgent tasks. In 1942 the Civilian Clothing Order introduced ''utility'' garments (alongside utility furniture and other economy measures) to ensure access to basic clothing and to conserve resources. This resulted in a subtle uniforming of the entire nation, with its own powerful ideological effect of producing national unity. Prices were rigorously controlled, and many citizens welcomed the Order's egalitarian outcome despite its strictures, for it would no longer be solely the wealthy who could afford clothes.

The Order limited the variety of clothing styles that could be made by any one company, to promote long and economical runs. This restriction affected women's clothing above all. The numbers of pleats, seams, and buttonholes permissible in female clothing were all reduced. The manufacture of jewelry—both costume and real—was simultaneously prohibited. Substitutes appeared for banned forms of decoration: stencils were used instead of embroidery, metal studs took the place of sequins, and the more infamous pencil lines on flesh simulated stocking seams. Utility clothing eventually accounted for four-fifths of all clothes produced in Britain.[8] Even the couturiers Norman Hartnell and Hardy Amies designed suits that echoed women's forces uniforms in their cut, their thrifty use of fabric, and their standardized look. The mutilating effects of these measures on contemporary notions of womanhood seep down to us through a wartime joke as it slashes the female body: ''Heard about the utility woman? She's single-breasted.''

The changing fate of toiletries during the war provides a clear indication of the importance of a stable femininity in the signification of national health and strength. Since the late eighteenth century's ''Great Masculine Renunciation'' in which ''man abandoned his claim to be beautiful,'' lipsticks and other cosmetics have been key to defining sexual difference—at least when applied to women.[9] (They have usually signaled sexual deviance when applied to men.) Shortages of lipstick, rouges, and vanishing cream were reported early on in the 1939–45 conflict, but the government

[8] Calder, *The People's War*, p. 323.
[9] The phrase was coined by J. C. Flugel, *The Psychology of Clothes* (Hogarth Press: London, 1930), p. 119. It refers to the radical simplification and increased uniformity of male dress with the onset of industrialization. Flugel is quoted in Kaja Silverman, *The Acoustic Mirror: The Female Voice in Psychoanalysis and Cinema* (Bloomington: Indiana University Press, 1988), pp. 24–25.

made special efforts to maintain a supply, since it deemed cosmetics "essential to female morale."[10] The implications of this policy are intriguing. Firstly, it understands self-decoration as a positive female pleasure. However, it is perhaps also the case that women's use of these products was essential to *male* morale, in that their use secured, through difference, masculine identity. Such cosmetic traces of womanhood were especially desirable given the concurrent compulsory renunciation by women of spectacular clothing. This contributed to the erosion of masculine identity, by proposing its dissociation from the male biological sex, in that women were understood to be looking increasingly like men, especially when in uniform. A wartime cartoon of 1942 reassures the middle-class, predominantly male readers of *Punch* that women and men really are the same as their old prewar selves under the uniform (Figure 2.3).

In 1942 the Board of Trade considered prohibiting the most inessential cosmetics but decided against it.[11] Instead, a stricter order was introduced, which included licenses for manufacturers. In December 1942 the use of certain vital, scarce materials in toilet preparations was prohibited, such as the solvent in nail varnish and nail varnish remover. When a new product for stopping ladders in stockings appeared, the Board passed another order prohibiting the packaging of the substance in less that half-pint containers. Even so, evasion was rife throughout the makeup industry. Creams were accredited with medicinal properties to avoid the order (see the Lacto-Calamine advertisement discussed below), while advertisements and labels made clear to women that the products were really "cosmetics in disguise."[12]

Black market activites could never be fully stamped out in an industry that "required little or no machinery, . . . used small quantities of raw materials with large profit and . . . produced goods that were easy to transport."[13] In addition, a nation of women reared to equate the attainment of female beauty with the application of makeup, and raised on the pleasures of painting the body, must clearly have fueled the black market trade. Norman Longmate even records an increased use of cosmetics by women during the war years, and several homemade recipes to get around the short-

[10] Calder, *The People's War*, p. 321.

[11] "Toilet preparations were considered too important a part of morale to be the subject of prohibition." E. L. Hargreaves and M. M. Gowing, *The History of the Second World War: Civil Industry and Trade* (London: H.M.S.O., 1952), p. 533 (hereafter cited as *Civil Industry and Trade*).

[12] Hargreaves and Gowing, *Civil Industry and Trade*, p. 533. The notion of "cosmetics in disguise" is another rather curious instance of wartime's redoubling habits, discussed more fully in Chapter Three.

[13] Hargreaves and Gowing, *Civil Industry and Trade*, p. 536.

When John Smith gets away on leave—   *a subtle change takes place :*

the same is true of his sister Joan—   *only rather different.*

Figure 2.3. On leave, femininity resurfaces.
Fougasse cartoon, ''Joan and John,'' *Punch*,
2 September 1942, p. 183.

ages.[14] In any event, the baroque structure of wartime cosmetics legislation is testament to the powerful cultural place the tiny products held. By the end of 1943 regulation of the production and sale of toilet preparations was described as ''one of the most complicated of the controls over manufacture and supply that had been evolved within the Board of Trade.''[15] Cosmetics had acquired a strategic importance, worthy of legal protection, even as the (directly contradictory) stereotype of the painted lady as lethal for fighting men persisted in official posters and films (Figure 2.4).

The use of makeup in wartime had a distinct political valence with interesting ramifications for the institution of cinema, whose imagistic mainstay, the glamorized female body, bedecked in cloth, jewels, and creams,

[14] Norman Longmate, *How We Lived Then* (London: Hutchinson, 1971), pp. 276, 278–79.

[15] Hargreaves and Gowing, *Civil Industry and Trade*, p. 531.

70

Figure 2.4. Female sexuality disguises female
intelligence, and so jeopardizes the war effort
in "Keep Mum, She's Not So Dumb!" a poster
from the Careless Talk campaign.

was now stigmatized, since all these products had become subject to restriction. Conventional screen femininity survived the war more or less
unscathed in narratives set outside its domain—in period films or films set
in exotic locations—or in home front films that diegeticized display
(through scenes of troop entertainment, for example), but elsewhere in
home front films the presence of female glamor could no longer be an
"invisible" given. It always had to be narratively explained.

Like the government, and like women, the cinema was unwilling and
unable to banish the pleasures and profits of female glamor in the name of
civic-minded austerity. However, under pressure of the ethos of wartime
unity, film narratives and imagery embarked on a conspicuous strategy of
ranking and reclassifying femininities, endowing each scene of a woman's
attention to her image with patriotic—or, equally, anti-patriotic—signifi-

cance. The verdict on the meaning of female attention to appearance could go either way, just as the government's convoluted policies did, so that scenes of female maquillage become narratively controversial, and betray the more general search for a "normal" wartime femininity, made urgent by its absence.

In *Millions Like Us* (1943) Celia's elder sister Phyllis is first seen, near the opening of the film, polishing her toes. In the narrative, it is the summer of 1939, but nail varnish in 1943, at the time of the film's release, was one of those precious rarities of peacetime Britain. Through the audience's retrospective wartime glance, from 1943, the lacquer taints Phyllis with an irresponsible care for the trivial vis-à-vis her younger sister. Their father, Mr. Crowson, alerts us to this when he dubs his elder daughter "Lady Muck" and warns Celia against learning her way with boys. Phyllis has a diminutive part in *Millions Like Us*, though she too is eventually shown to have joined the war effort. Her chief function, however, is to serve as foil to Celia, whose shyness, unworldliness, and unpaintedness can now be understood as appropriate wartime virtues. The crisis has here provided the conditions by which a film can validate a degree of despecularity in its central female protagonist, who is of course not ugly, but merely gleams less with the sheen of the fetish.

This ranking of femininities parallels that which Mary Ann Doane has described as occurring in the American "Woman's Film" of the 1940s, particularly in that subgroup of films on women's illnesses and treatments. Referring to *Now Voyager* (1942), among others, Doane observes that the woman's disease is frequently imaged through a despecularization of her body, and a displacement of spectacle "in other directions," especially onto the doctor/patient relationship, which becomes eroticized instead.[16] By the end of the film, the restoration of the woman's health is made legible through the opposite maneuver, so that the woman pays attention to her image again, and becomes a specular object. In British wartime films the woman's body is often similarly despecularized, but the reasons are the opposite of ill health: the cause is the patriotism that informs the rearticulation of gender divisions defining conscripted or volunteer women like Celia.

In *Millions Like Us*, Celia is not cured of her ordinariness, unlike Charlotte Vale (Bette Davis) in *Now Voyager*, because the parameters of the home front genre preclude such fantastic transformations of characters' bodies, or at least they do until the need to address the ordinariness of the British wartime audience becomes less pressing, that is, as an Allied victory becomes certain. More openly sexual femininity may be present in the

[16] Doane, *The Desire to Desire*, pp. 39–42.

wartime films, as in the character of Phyllis in *Millions Like Us*, or Good-time Dot in *The Gentle Sex*, but only in peripheral characters.

It is partly because it was released two years later, in 1945, on the cusp between war and peace, that *Perfect Strangers* can present its female protagonist, Cathy, going through a similar metamorphosis to Charlotte Vale. In *Perfect Strangers* war parallels medicine as the "cure" for impaired female narcissism. In this film Dizzy is completely *au fait* with the arcane techniques of make-up application and sexy dressing, even in a uniform. She teaches the habit to lackluster Cathy, who has hitherto lacked the necessary knowledge or tools on account of her sheltered married life. As the film ends, Dizzy is revealed to have been pining for a fiancé all along, causing Cathy, and the audience along with her, to reinterpret retrospectively Dizzy's pleasure in her appearance as preparation for the future. While earlier it had seemed to connote self-confidence and strength, it is now (partially) recuperated as preservation for a man. Both Cathy's transformation, and our new knowledge of Dizzy reestablish the cultural peacetime importance of narcissism in women. Further, Cathy's beauty lessons will now make her a more compatible postwar wife for Robert, who has also been specularized as a result of his patriotism, a point of divergence from the American "Woman's Film" and a matter I will discuss in Chapter 3.

In Gainsborough's *Love Story* (1944) two brands of femininity are again compared; the star image of Margaret Lockwood, by now fixed in the firmament by the success of *The Man in Grey* (1943), bears directly on the outcome of the contest between two women for a single man, Kit Firth. Lissa Cambell (Lockwood) and Judy Martin (Patricia Roc) typify two facets of wartime womanhood constructed as mutually exclusive: frail, sexual beauty (Lissa) and vigorous robustness (Judy). Lissa's femininity is presented as excessive in the context of reigning austerity conditions, even though the manager at her hotel has asked her to "dress for dinner" as it is "good for morale." Lissa shocks two young female dinner guests with her slinky, low-cut black attire: "Fancy dressing like that, and in wartime," exclaims one of them at Lissa's entrance. "Oh! Stop beating," retorts the other, "There are plenty of men to go round."

However, Lissa's appearance is relatively restrained compared with that of Lockwood in her Gainsborough costume film of the previous year, *The Man in Grey*, one of the biggest winners of 1943. This was an intertextual relation readily perceived by one contemporary viewer, a young chemist's assistant who found the level of fashion in *Love Story* quite attainable but was angered by comments overheard from neighboring members of the audience: "I think I can honestly admit that no dresses have ever attracted me as much as those worn in *Love Story* by Margaret Lockwood.

They were very simple but were of the type that most young girls could wear and afford.''[17] The viewer then recalls the irritating prejudices of fellow Lockwood fans at the screening, preconditioned by her recent period role: ''When I saw *Love Story* I heard a loud voice say, 'That isn't Margaret Lockwood playing so and so?' I was so annoyed I got up and found another seat but heard this remark again.'' While the fictional female diner was alarmed at Lissa's high ration of femininity and the competition she represented for men, these historical spectators seem to have trouble recognizing their star disguised as a contemporary woman. The transformation of Lockwood's image, however moderate, registers Gainsborough's own austerity measures.

Lissa's femininity in *Love Story* comes to occupy a middle ground between Lockwood's role in the incipient Gainsborough costume cycle and Judy's appearance and behavior. Judy is always dressed in overalls, smokes a cigarette, and keeps a knotted scarf in her hair in a guise reminiscent of the sturdy Land Army look. She digs her hand into her pockets and asks for a light on almost every entrance she makes. She is first seen organizing an open-air, amateur production of *The Tempest* in a cliffside amphitheater. Lissa scrutinizes her from afar, a perplexed look crossing her face, and then descends, following Kit, to meet her. Judy comments that Lissa is different from Kit's other ''bits of nonsense'' who are ''two hundred percent female: alive from the neck down''; Lissa likewise remarks that Judy is not what she had expected (her earlier puzzled look can now be read as one of trying to discern Judy's sex from a distance). Kit is systematically excluded from this female to female assessment, both through editing, and through his inability to answer Judy's request for a light, a task Lissa then readily accomplishes with Kit's equipment. Kit's failure to produce a flame, on this and several other occasions, becomes the film's symbol of his impaired masculinity—a lack based on his disqualification from military service on medical grounds.

If comparison with *The Man in Grey* made Lockwood's appearance in *Love Story* seem relatively restrained, remaining doubts about Lissa's patriotism were alleviated for the audience through her diegetic profession as entertainer, and through the knowledge that she has wanted to join the W.A.A. F.'s but has been disqualified early in the film by the diagnosis of a weak heart, the result of childhood scarlet fever. The film's internal concert audiences naturalize Lissa's function as an object for the external audience's visual consumption, and if she too tends to look two hundred percent female, it is sanctioned by her being less then one hundred percent healthy underneath, in an inversion of the scopic relations of *Now Voyager*:

[17] Mayer, *British Cinemas and Their Audiences*, p. 81.

here illness authorizes moderate specular display. In sum, the wartime female spectator is able to overlook the unpatriotic potential of Lissa's glamor: she can retain a patriotic stance while watching *Love Story*, enjoying the visual escape from wartime austerity, though in this case the film offers no narrative escape.

FEMININITY AS COLLABORATION

The advent of rationing politicized female glamor, as I have explained, but its contentious status also stemmed from long-held fantasies about the liability of female sexuality at times of war. Its association with war's destructiveness is still familiar to us through expressions such as "blond bombshell" to describe Jean Harlow; through the fact that the B29 bomber dropping the first uranium bomb was named after its pilot's mother, Enola Gay; and in the fact that the name Gilda, after Rita Hayworth's screen role, was written on the bomb itself.[18] Even the term "dilutee," used to describe women wartime workers, connoted the weakening effect of women's presence in war. The problem now was to incorporate woman into the idea of nationhood despite her precarious past relation to it—hence, presumably, the efficacy of "Mae Wests" as a nickname for R.A.F. pilots' life preservers, which swelled up into two inflated "breasts" upon their chests. The winning of the right to vote was still a recent victory, only twenty years old at the outbreak of war, with equalized rights in Britain only since 1928; Allied women in Belgium and France were still without suffrage. It is not surprising, given this legal, social, and cultural history, that so many wartime images of women, on film and elsewhere, cast doubt on her national allegiance, despite their best efforts to ensure it.

As a founding model of feminist theory proposes, the power of gendered division rests on the fact that social, economic, and political inequalities between real men and women are made to seem natural in being aligned with, though not actually determined by, biological sex. The biological division legitimates other culturally constructed ones: culture vs. nature, intellect vs. intuition, activity vs. passivity, and so on. Woman then becomes a kind of cultural dumping ground, as Judith Williamson puts it— the main vehicle for the representation of difference and otherness within mass culture.[19] This system buckles under the weight of World War II, when the primary meaning of the opposition "them" and "us" shifts from

[18] Marsha McCreadie, ed., *The American Movie Goddess* (New York: John Wiley and Sons, 1973), p. 32.

[19] Judith Williamson, "Woman Is an Island: Femininity and Colonization," in Tania Modleski, ed., *Studies in Entertainment: Critical Approaches to Mass Culture* (Bloomington and Indianapolis: Indiana University Press, 1986), p. 101.

referring to the two sides of gender—the battle between the sexes—to the two sides of war, the battle of nations. "Woman versus man" is all too readily transposed onto "enemy versus Allied." In this way women are always potentially marked as collaborators in wartime, despite the representational upheavals that work to circumvent the inference. For while British wartime propaganda demands patriotism in women, the message that women, especially young single women, are a national risk is never far below the surface.

In the early war, before it was apparent how dire the *man*power shortage would become, images of incipient female collaboration were fairly common, and overt. In a Fougasse poster proclaiming "Careless Talk Costs Lives," women jeopardize security by gossiping too loudly on a bus, since they are within earshot of men whose national allegiances are invisible, and therefore in doubt.[20] In "Keep Mum, She's Not So Dumb" the dangers of female gossip are allied with female sexuality, in that a highly sexualized woman in a transparent, breast-revealing dress takes a parallel place to the male passengers on the bus: she is eavesdropping on the military men who surround her (Figure 2.4). The same message is repeated in "Don't Tell Aunty and Uncle," another poster that warns against telling military secrets to anyone, even your relatives, but especially not to a young, apparently naked woman, another painted lady (Figure 2.5). In a VD poster it is again female sexuality that threatens national security: a feminized skull sports a pink hat decorated with vaginal flowers while the slogan reads, "The 'easy' girlfriend spreads Syphilis and Gonorrhea, which unless properly treated may result in blindness, insanity, paralysis, premature death" (Figure 2.6).

This configuration is alive and well in films from the early war as well. Thorold Dickinson's *Next of Kin* (1942) was first made as a training film, before the Dieppe raid, but was then developed for public release under the encouragement of Churchill. At one point in the film, information is passed to a network of German spies by an English music-hall actress who leaves messages in lipstick on her dressing-room mirror. German agents pay her backstage visits and depart with military secrets extracted by her from her enlisted "boyfriend," while he himself is distracted by her sexual charms. She files her nails nonchalantly while withdrawing information, and trades it for money to support her cocaine habit (a detail cut from the American release version of the film). Thora Hird, playing an A.T.S. woman, also jeopardizes security through her relationship with a soldier. In another scene, British male officers discuss security and one tells the

---

[20] Fougasse, poster, "Careless Talk Costs Lives," illustrated in Joseph Darracott and Belinda Loftus, *Second World War Posters* (London: Imperial War Museum, 1972), p. 30.

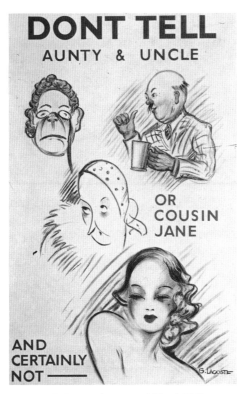

Figure 2.5. Lacoste's poster, "Don't Tell
Aunty and Uncle," depicts a young, glamorized,
sexualized woman as the greatest risk to
national security.

other, "Let me know where you think we're weakest." The shot immediately dissolves to an image of a woman in a halter-neck dress with almost bare midriff, dancing onstage before an audience. The juxtaposition through editing implies that the answer to the officer's question is nightclub women, which in the film's terms is true. The poster artwork for the film corroborates the idea: in it giant, explosive female lips devastate the landscape of soldiers (Figure 2.7).

In Powell and Pressburger's *The Life and Death of Colonel Blimp* (1943), young officer Spud Wilson discovers that "War begins at Midnight," and is thus able to make the preemptive (albeit mock) strike at the bath-house, precisely because his girlfriend Angela "Johnny" Cannon (Deborah Kerr) has "carelessly" leaked the news to him in the course of their intimacy. In *I See a Dark Stranger*, Bridie Quilty (also played by

Figure 2.6. In Mount's anti-VD poster the lurid
hat decoration symbolizes the dangers of
female sexuality for male health and hence national
strength.

Deborah Kerr), a neutral Irish spy (an impossible category) intends to assist in the escape of a Nazi agent from the British police by seducing David
Baynes, whom she believes to be a British agent; she is incensed when it
transpires that he is no such thing.

In all these representations women are, to put it in the most benign
terms, a risk to the nation; at worst, they constitute an internal enemy.
Female sexuality, coupled with female inadvertence, amounts to collaboration. The particular interest of *I See a Dark Stranger* lies in the fact that
it links female collaboration explicitly to the question of nationhood, making visible the barely concealed ambivalence of woman's role in wartime,
and that it does this in the context of Ireland, for Ireland too was feared to
be an internal enemy for Britain on account of her decision to remain po-

Figure 2.7. A woman's lethal pillow talk provokes another Dunkirk in this poster artwork for *Next of Kin* (1942).

litically neutral throughout World War II. It is the shared fate of women and Ireland, in a neutral yet suspect place, entitled to autonomy yet not to be politically embraced, that Launder and Gilliat recognize when they personify Ireland as a female spy in their film. They treat Ireland and woman unevenly, however, foreclosing on female independence but necessarily leaving the vexed question of Irish nationhood raw and unhealed at the end of the film. By its conclusion, their film demobilizes the rhetoric of nationalism and reconstructs gender for the postwar world.[21]

BEAUTY IS AT THE CROSSROADS

The precarious status of feminine glamor in wartime was a particular challenge to manufacturers of beauty products. The intimation that female sexuality was threatening to wartime security, as well as the climate of austerity both came into direct conflict with the promotion and sale of cosmetics. One solution, used by advertisers throughout the war years, was to suggest that the maintenance of a legible femininity was an integral part of national service: slogans such as "Hair Beauty—is a duty, too!"; "Beauty answers the call . . ."; and "Instant Beauty for women in wartime"—Potter and Moore's Powder-Cream make her "ready for action" convey the sense that buying such products is patriotic, because the survival of femininity is a sign of strength and perseverance (Figures 2.8, 2.9, and 2.10). In publicity campaigns for shampoo and cream from 1939–

[21] See my essay in Sklar and Musser, eds., *Resisting Images: Essays in Film and History*, for further discussion of *I See a Dark Stranger*.

79

Hair Beauty—
is a duty, too!

Sparkling Loveliness

EVAN WILLIAMS BRILLANTINE imparts a natural lustre to the hair and keeps it in perfect condition. It may be used regularly without fear of producing that lank, matted appearance which is so objectionable. In several shades.

1/3 PER BOTTLE

YOU really must make your hair exceptionally nice for the Christmas re-unions . . . the men of the Services on leave will expect and deserve it. "Evan Williams" is famed the world over . . . the ideal cleansing medium for the hair. A weekly shampoo with this perfectly balanced product is all that is needed to restore tone, colour, health and beauty to even the most delicate hair.

A Necessary Precaution: Look for the name " Evan Williams " on the packet

"ORDINARY" FOR DARK HAIR   "CAMOMILE" FOR FAIR

EVAN WILLIAMS
SHAMPOO

Figure 2.8. Maintaining hair beauty with Evan Williams is a wartime duty; according to the caption, the men of the Services expect and deserve it. *Picture Post*, 16 December 1939.

42, military terminology papers over the contradictions of profit-seeking in war: Kemt hairspray is said to induce "Regimental Curl," for instance, as well as a "crisp, new war-time hair-style" (Figure 2.11).

In the first two of these advertisements vignettes of women in uniform are placed alongside an image of a naked women to mitigate against the promotion of an excessive or public eroticization of the female body in time of war. Such advertisements walk the tightrope between being unpatriotic by suggesting that women should be thinking about their looks rather than war, and being war-affirmative at the risk of undermining both the demand for their product and the category of traditional womanhood altogether. A symptom of this tension lies in such advertisements' repeated

Figure 2.9. Military discourse, as in "answer the call," is deployed to sell soap for a "natural beauty treatment." *Picture Post*, 18 April 1942.

references to a so-called "natural beauty," femininity built on a critique of an imaginary type of prewar womanhood allied to the American female cinematic image. According to this discourse, natural beauty certainly required effort and maintenance, but both had to be invisible vis-à-vis American glamor.

An advertisement for Crookes' Lacto-Calamine powder-based "skin food" stakes out the parameters of "natural beauty" quite clearly, and is fascinating in the precise ways it articulates the challenge to glamorized beauty war presents.[22] In the advertisement's copy a doctor lends the

22 Advertisement for Crookes' Lacto-Calamine, *Picture Post*, 10 February 1940, p. 3.

Figure 2.10. Wartime women need instant beauty: lingering over visual effects is deemed unpatriotic by comparison. *Picture Post*, 19 October 1940.

Figure 2.11. Kemt hair spray stimulates regimental curls supportive of war. *Picture Post*, 2 March 1940.

weight of his profession to the skin product while pronouncing on the wartime erosion of women's looks: "Most women have recently been undergoing an unusual amount of nervous strain. . . . The therapeutic action of Lacto-Calamine would be beneficial to every woman's complexion just now." The advertisement shows a bust-length photograph of a woman apparently without clothes, bare-shouldered, and with loose, long hair adorned with poppies. The caption implies that this is her natural state, even though the image is obviously artificially lit and carefully composed. The text begins: "Whither beauty? Beauty's at the crossroads. Many young women now have less time for make-up, and more occasions when they would rather not look made up at all. Everyone wants to know a new way to look lovely, and very few really know what to do about it. Why don't *you* set the fashion and be one of the first to learn the new approach to beauty—via loveliness of the skin?" The reasons that women might rather "not look made up at all" are not listed, but we could speculate that they are linked to those same cultural associations of female glamor with national liability, and, further, with the idea that single women, or women separated from their husbands, should avoid looking made up in order to avoid appearing to solicit other sexual encounters, since these also endanger the nation's health. The phrase closes off the possibility of *female* pleasure being taken in using makeup, or in viewing a made-up woman. The overall message is that not looking made-up is the appropriate wartime appearance.

A nineteen-year-old female student nurse from Mayer's survey of cinema-goers was certainly caught in the web of these new definitions of femininity. She wrote: "I always used to imagine that Hollywood hairstyles, clothes and make-up were well out of my reach, but since the advent of natural beauty has arrived, it has become apparent to me that the rest are only appendages to produce the desired effect."[23] American film standards of femininity—a remoter possibility than ever in wartime—now seemed excessive, and irrelevant to her on account of the crisis. A seventeen-year-old shorthand typist expressed a similar subduing of habit and taste: "I have certainly envied Rosalind Russell's and other film stars' clothes, but under present day conditions I have never yet managed to get new material, or felt justified in ordering something else in order to copy."[24] These comments suggest, as I argued at the end of Chapter 1, that the Hollywood female star made American cinema seem distant and parochial, rather then apposite and universal, to British wartime audiences.

An August 1945 Home Office survey of probation officers blamed the imagery of women in American cinema, combined with the arrival of G.I.'s in Britain, for the rise in the illegitimate birth rate during the war: "To girls brought up on the cinema, who copied the dress, hairstyles and manners of Hollywood stars, the sudden influx of Americans, speaking like the films, who actually lived in the magic country, and who had plenty of money, at once went to the girls' heads. The American attitude toward women, their proneness to spoil a girl, to build up, exaggerate, talk big, and to act with generosity and flamboyance, helped to make them the most

[23] Mayer, *British Cinemas and Their Audiences*, p. 58.
[24] Ibid., p. 64.

attractive boyfriends. In addition, they 'picked up' easily, and even a comparatively plain and unattractive girl stood a chance."[25] According to this social worker, mimicking American screen femininity clouded a "girl" 's judgment, deluding her into a corresponding belief in Hollywood's version of reality at the sight of any American male, and the consequences were again detrimental to national health.

What emerges from these varied sources—from films, advertisements, and social workers' and audience members' statements—is an elision between Hollywood screen femininity and the negativity of female sexuality in war. The suspect political valence of glamor became a particular liability in government poster design. It was the specific problem of recruitment posters to represent women in a way that made war jobs attractive but that also encouraged women to identify with the poster image and hence enlist. The fate of an A.T.S. poster by Games is instructive, for it had to be withdrawn on the grounds that its female image was too glamorous. Loftus and Darracott describe how it was replaced with an image based on a photograph rather than a painting, and contemporary Eric Newton used the phrase "a slightly Russianised young lady" to express the new character of non-fetishized womanhood thus produced.[26]

The withdrawal of the poster suggests the War Office's (understandable) lack of faith in glamorized images of women for speaking to real women of national need. The risk that a female audience would not recognize itself in this imagery—that it would remain a fantastic, unattainable femininity—was indeed too great. Of further interest is the invocation of the Soviet Union as the source of an alternative, more politically compatible femininity. Comparisons of different national populations of women was, as I have been arguing for female screen populations, pivotal in the construction of British wartime womanhood: "Are you equal to two German women?" asked an article in *Woman and Beauty* magazine.[27] In a parallel maneuver, Soviet women were held up as appropriate models for emulation by working British women in a poster that read, "Cover Your Hair for Safety: Your Russian Sister Does!" The poster showed a simple headscarf knotted at the nape of the woman's neck, and a hammer and sickle decorating the larger scarf on which the whole image was presented.[28]

[25] The survey was conducted in ten areas, including London and Liverpool. Quoted in "Illegitimacy and War," in Ferguson, Sheila, and Hilde Fitzgerald, *Studies in the Social Services* (London: H.M.S.O. 1954), pp. 97–98.

[26] Darracott and Loftus, *Second World War Posters*, p. 65.

[27] *Woman and Beauty*, 1942, Douie Collection, Fawcett Library, London. Cited in Jennifer Uglow, "The Fawcett Library," *Times Literary Supplement*, 7 September 1984.

[28] This poster is also illustrated in Darracott and Loftus, *Second World War Posters*, p. 65.

There are several other indications that the idea of the Soviet woman as unglamorous counterbalanced American screen goddesses in the British wartime discourse on femininity. Such notions of Soviet femininity came at least in part from the showing of Soviet films in Britain, and it is in this light that we can understand the *Herald Tribune*'s comment on *Brief Encounter*, that it was "between Hollywood and Moscow in style and quality."[29] Further, knowledge of Soviet women's wartime experience boosted their association with a despecularized femininity. The Soviet Union was the only combatant nation to make more extensive use of female labor during World War II than Britain. Soviet women saw combat; they were trained as snipers and fighter pilots (dubbed the Night Witches by the Germans). One of the most successful snipers made a tour of Allied territory, the model for the visiting Russian aviatrix in *Stage Door Canteen* and the "Lady Sniper" in *Tawny Pipit*. Lieutenant Bocolova, as she is called in the latter film, is the most successfully gynandromorphic character of the entire home front genre. She is the "brave and beautiful representative of our gallant Russian ally," according to Colonel Barrington, has killed over a hundred "Hitlerites," and can sling the Colonel's telescopic rifle effortlessly over her shoulder. Her combination of strength and attractiveness, sustained for just a few minutes on the screen, tantalizes the local Land Army girl, who ponders: "I want to see what she's got that I haven't." It is a comparison female audience members are also asked to make.

The Mobile Woman

The mobilization of labour eventually became
a swing over from man-power to woman-power. . . .
It was as though with the passing of the
National Service Act No. 2, the country
at last realized we were in for total war.

Ourselves in Wartime

With the passing of the British National Services Act on 2 September 1939, men between the ages of 19 and 41 had become liable for conscription, but women's contribution was still made on a voluntary basis. However, from November 1940 Labour M.P. Aneurin Bevan began to describe the country's urgent need for "the employment and training of women," and a year later, on 10 December 1941, the controversial National Service Act (No. 2) became law. This was the first time in British history that women had been called up. By 5 March 1942, all British single women between the ages of 20 and 31 could be conscripted, a form of legislation

---

[29] *Herald Tribune*, 15 September 1946.

never introduced in the United States and implemented in Germany only as a last-ditch effort in 1945. The conscription of women therefore established national difference, as the male voice-over in *Desert Victory* proclaimed: "In no country are women so thoroughly organized for war."

"Mobile" and "immobile" were Ministry of Labour classifications designating women who could either be moved to work anywhere in the country (mobile) or who had to work locally because they had dependents or were married (immobile). In a letter to *Time and Tide* one married woman described the limbo she experienced in this reclassification of women, for she was married and could therefore not be mobile: "The present call-up of women is not exactly conscription and not exactly voluntary service, so the poor unfortunate married woman is torn in half between her public and her private duties and made thoroughly unhappy as a result. Hers is not to do or die but to decide, which in most cases is far more difficult."[30]

The term "mobile" clearly had both a literal and a metaphorical meaning, the metaphorical resting on the literal. The category of woman was on the move: it was impossible to pin down with certainty, constantly having to be resighted through wartime imagery and tales. J. B. Priestley described this commodification as an "intricate" task: a question of finding as many immobile women as possible to release mobile ones, since, by 1943, the latter were in "rapidly dwindling supply." He explained that it was far more difficult to "mobilize" women than men, because women were not "free" and could not "be moved about in the casual fashion that will do for the male."[31] Training and mobilizing them was a "highly complicated and difficult task."[32] He added that it was *so* difficult that most countries, in this and other wars, had refused the challenge even if they were "desperately in need of manpower." He was referring to the German wartime emphasis on women's roles as mothers rather than fighters. Germany was so ideologically overinvested in the image of woman as mother of the Aryan race that it could not resort to the military conscription of women, even when its survival was at stake. Further study would presumably show that Germany was unable to tolerate the kind of contradictory and fluid definitions of femininity in circulation in Britain.

[30] Anonymous, "Women's War Service," *Time and Tide*, 24 October 1941.
[31] J. B. Priestley, *British Women Go to War*, pp. 14 and 19.
[32] Ibid., p. 20. His full text is interesting: "Finally, the mobilization and direction and wholesale transfer of women workers is a highly complicated and difficult task just because it is so new, because most women are not used to being regarded as units in an industrial system, because their idea of themselves as workers and wage-earners is often sketchy, because the whole business of machine production often seems unreal to them, and finally because there is always the danger of arousing sex prejudices."

Priestley's vocabulary in describing the mobile woman registers the fragility of this new category of femininity. Its friable status is more overtly revealed in a contemporary political cartoon, "La Donna è Mobile," directed toward a middle-class female audience, the readership of *Time and Tide* (Figure 2.12). The cartoon's joke stems from the perceived incompatibility between "innate femininity" and the waging of war. A single woman sits passively on a park bench with her arms folded, while a couple cuddle in the distance. She wears a long, constricting Victorian dress with the slogan "Victory" written across her lower skirt. Three Allied leaders court her: Churchill with chocolates, and Stalin and F.D.R. with bouquets of flowers. Seduction is their method, not businesslike bargaining or official recruitment. Churchill has abandoned his attributes of hat, cane, and briefcase to concentrate on the task, but the woman seems as yet unmoved, perhaps because she is an allegorical figure—a personification of victory—being bribed with all too material means.

In the foreground Hitler clutches a large handkerchief and cries out in a bold operatic gesture as if delivering "La Donna è Mobile," Verdi's famous 1851 aria from *Rigoletto*. In *Rigoletto*, the melody is first sung by the Duke of Mantua as he laments the fickleness of women. In the cartoon

La donna e mobile

Figure 2.12. The mobile woman becomes "La Donna è Mobile," in this *Time and Tide* cartoon, 16 October 1943, p. 841.

Hitler does the same. He bemoans the fact that things are not going his way, for he now knows, as Priestley promised, that those nations that woo and organize their women for war will gain victory. In this way the cartoon foregrounds the importance of women's wartime contribution. But in turning the expression "mobile woman" into "la donna è mobile," and in reducing her actions to allegory, Hitler (and the cartoon) cast doubt on the status of that very contribution. The new Italian phrase invokes the stereotypical idea of women as flighty and undependable and permits an image of woman *not* as vital contributor, but instead as a stationary sign of Victory, potentially swayed by seduction, by flowers and confectionary. The suggestion yet again is that women are always susceptible; it would only have taken Hitlerian chocolates for history to have followed quite a different path.

It may seem farfetched to invoke Verdi in this wartime context, but the expression "La donna mobile" [*sic*] crops up elsewhere in wartime representation, suggesting that the government terminology "the mobile woman" was both risible and discomforting. When asked by the Ministry of Information to work on a home front film, Launder and Gilliat came up with a narrative based on the mobile woman's story, which we know as *Millions Like Us*.[33] Gilliat recalled that they were "very impressed with the fate . . . of the conscripted woman, the mobile woman," and that they had wanted to call their film that "if it hadn't been such a silly title." Their embarrassment at the term is a symptom not only of the difficulty of representing female wartime experience filmically in a realist mode, but also of the government's difficulty in finding a name for it at all. Further evidence of the nomenclature's awkwardness is to be found in *Waterloo Road*. In this film, as two older men, beyond conscription years, chat with an American G.I. in the local pub, Tom Mason, pigeon fancier and family lodger, looks across the bar towards a furtive couple, Ted and Tilly. He nurses his pint, sighing, "If you ask me, the youngsters are having the toughest time in this war." The G.I. casually replies, "What war? I ain't found it yet." Just then a uniformed woman walks past. "La donna mobile," enunciates Mason carefully, following her with his eyes. "What's that?" asks the G.I. "Italian!" "What's it mean?" his neighbor repeats. "What's it mean? It means women is [*sic*] mobile." "Who said that? Mr. Bevan?" In desperation Mason ends the exchange exploding: "Females are a problem all round. Blooming crossword puzzle. Give me pigeons everytime. Not so blinking whimsical." His pigeons are homing pigeons, which fly home to East London even after Tom has evacuated them as train

33 Geoff Brown, *Launder and Gilliat*, p. 108.

freight for safety. By contrast, the homing instincts of mobile women are, as their name suggests, in suspension.

The coexistence of these two contradictory reputations of the mobile woman—the reliable, invaluable war-worker on whom victory depends, and the capricious, whimsical, flighty companion and potential collaborator who distracts male attention—resulted in part from the anxiety attached to shifting women's primary place of work from the home to the barracks or factory, an anxiety compounded by the relative absence of the male population. This absence underlined the actual independence and self-sufficiency of women, but was also feared to encourage alternative sexual activity among women outside marriage, both hetero- and homosexual. One way of coping with this anxiety was precisely to generate a new stereotype of femininity—the mobile woman—which would encompass the contradictions. Homi K. Bhabha theorizes that the stereotype has precisely this capacity, for it "is a form of knowledge and identification that vacillates between what is always 'in place,' already known, and something that must be anxiously repeated."[34] The vacillation in this case is between a traditional notion of femininity and one that accommodates women's war work.

Because of such ambivalence, stereotypes do not offer secure points of identification for their viewers, but rather they can be misread, or read in a contradictory way. They can, to quote Christine Gledhill, "potentially open up a challenge to patriarchal assumptions, making visible a whole regime of practices, modes of feeling and thought which generally go unrecognized even by women themselves."[35] It is in this ambivalence that we can recognize the conflicting demands on women of this particular historical moment, and the instability of the models of femininity it produced.

ADDRESSING WOMEN: THE CASE OF
THE GENTLE SEX

The Gentle Sex is an excellent film through which to study the ways women might be addressed through a filmic text embedded within the contradictory sets of meanings described above. Directed by Leslie Howard and the uncredited Maurice Elvey, it is a feature-length film about recruiting women to the Auxiliary Territorial Service (A.T.S.), the women's branch of the Army. It clearly manifests the double problem of trying to produce a new cinematic image of woman appropriate to the British realist film

[34] Homi K. Bhahba, "The Other Question . . . the Stereotype and Colonial Discourse," *Screen* 24, no. 6 (November/December 1983): 18.

[35] Christine Gledhill, "Recent Developments in Feminist Film Criticism," in Doane et al., eds., *Re-vision*, p. 43.

style and of finding a workable audience address that would not only constitute the nation as unified, but also promote the recruitment of women. In the end the film cannot generate a coherent mode of address, but instead combines a number of contradictory ones to women, to men, to all classes, and to that impossibly ungendered group, the nation. It is a film that speaks both to the women whom it wishes to mobilize, and to a national audience in which gender and class difference must be played down or elided. Above all, however, it seems to want to speak to men.

The Gentle Sex confronts the question of female wartime migration head on, but from the start it has trouble defining its target. The first shot following the credits gives a high-angle view of a morning jam at Victoria Station. Indistinct passengers and porters mill far beneath a heavy, four-faced station clock which tells 10:05 precisely. Here are the people, the stuff of busy Britain, from which director Howard will shortly select seven women to play the parts in his film. He will, as his voice soon says, "swoop down for a couple of armfuls," cull from the crowd a cross section from the national spectrum. In the foreground right of this frame a hatted, Mackintoshed, silhouetted man leans over a high parapet, his face largely hidden (Figure 2.13). The preceding credits have hinted at his identity: "Observations of a mere man written by Moie Charles and spoken by Leslie Howard." However, it is the familiar, avuncular radio voice of Howard delivering the following speech that secures who he is: "Women! Women all over the place. This station seething with women! They think they're helping, I suppose, rushing about. But what good can it do them? Or us? . . ." That it is Howard on the screen is now clear, but who is down below him? and more to the point, who is presumed to be watching this film?—who is the audience imagined by this text? The first title credit, "The Gentle Sex," and subsequent embroidered credits have already solicited a female, middle class spectator, but is the ultimate address of Howard's discourse to her? He opposes "them" to "us" in his speech, so is "us" the British women in the audience yet to join up, or the diverse potential audience of British wartime men—those too old and too young to fight, those A.W.O.L., or on leave, those G.I.'s waiting to go abroad?

The pronoun "them" is a placeholder more readily filled. "Them" are without doubt the seething women down below, already laboring for the nation. But they are tarnished with the term's recent use, "them" and "us" in wartime referring to the polarity of Allied/enemy, suggesting again women's suspect political place, separate from men. It will become clear that it is the film's question that revolves around "them," around the masses of British wartime women already participating in the defense of the nation, and the ones that are still to do so, and it is a question that must be urgently asked by men.

Figure 2.13. Howard looks down from the parapet. Frame enlargement from
The Gentle Sex.

Howard's speech evidences the difficulty of addressing and reaching
women directly in a medium and culture that conventionally speaks to
women through men, that builds her self-image inside a masculine frame.
The Gentle Sex was sponsored by the government's Ministry of Information explicitly to boost female recruitment, but both the masculine author-
ity of Howard's voice—*the* patriotic voice par excellence—and his impos-
ing silhouette "between" the spectator and the diegetic space of the film,
in the foreground of the shot, tend to exclude a female viewer. Indeed,
Howard's view from the balcony (and his plan to "swoop down" on the
female crowd) recalls that of the male pilot looking down from the air,
described at the end of Chapter 1; the opening of *The Gentle Sex* repeats
that same spatial arrangement of gendered spheres.

After Howard has handpicked the seven women, restaging, reflexively,
the director's part in the filmmaking process, the story moves on to cover
their training and dispersal from the A.T.S. barracks. The seven women
are from diverse class and cultural backgrounds, as are the eight men in
The Way Ahead; indeed, the latter film was recognized at the time as a
pendant to *The Gentle Sex*. Both films mobilized gender for war: the im-

pression of uniformity produced from using seven female characters, or, equally, eight male characters, served to counterbalance, and even over-shadow, the class and regional divisions among members of the same sex. In *The Gentle Sex*, Dot is a beautician, Joan a dance teacher, Anne an officer's daughter, Gwen a cockney waitress, Erna a Czech refugee, Betty a sheltered only child, and Maggie a daughter of Scottish fisherfolk. As in other films, the act of contributing to the war effort is shown to bring together a varied bunch, and the motif of the train, with its powerful new connotations of class dissolution, initiates the process. The seven climb aboard at Victoria Station and travel down together to camp.

On completing training, four of the characters—Anne, Joan, Erna, and Maggie—become convoy drivers, while Betty and Dot join an ack-ack unit, and Gwen, the peacetime waitress, remains at camp as a Mess orderly. As is typical of the genre of the national subject, there is no single star character or couple to follow here, but instead a range of possible audience identifications is offered, dispersed across the seven characters, whose narrative strands interweave and displace one another. However, at an All Ranks dance (another staple of wartime iconography), a romance develops when Anne meets Flying Officer Sheridan and Maggie falls for a fellow Scot. Anne is now singled out for the audience as the more important character who will eventually lose her man, like Toddy in *The Way to the Stars* and Celia in *Millions Like Us*.

After an all-night convoy and some transfers, the seven are brought together again. During a blitz there have been casualties at the ack-ack unit, and Anne hears that David Sheridan has been killed, but the film ends with all seven women queuing up the following morning in a field for steaming tea and sandwiches dispensed from a mobile canteen. The parting image of queuing, in which all seven recruits participate, is needed to reaffirm class solidarity, given the diverging experiences of occupation and rank that the group has by now encountered. The camera tilts up and pulls back as the now disembodied voice of Howard closes the film with a thank you to its women, and a reclamation of a position of mastery for men: "Well, there they are, the women. Our sweethearts, sisters, mothers, daughters. Let's give in at last and admit that we're really proud of you. You strange, wonderful, incalculable creatures. The world you're helping to shape is going to be a better one because you're helping to shape it. Pray silence, gentlemen. I give you a toast. The gentle sex!" Men are reassured that women really are illogical, strange, "incalculable," just as prewar femininity would have it. But like so many other British wartime films, this one can offer no resounding closure: the problems posed outrun the usefulness of peacetime convention. All Howard can do is "give in," and postulate the subject as male once more, through the high-angle mode and disembodied voice. The arrangement of camera and point of view reassert that vertical stratification of vision and space in wartime cinema, hinted at in the first, Victoria Station scene, that consigns the feminine to the land, the masculine to the skies.

The Gentle Sex PREMIERED on 18 April 1943, coinciding with the peak of female wartime employment and forming part of the first wave of wartime films to focus on women.[36] It is extraordinary among them in including almost no male characters, inviting comparison with a predecessor such as *Maedchen in Uniform*, with its representation of lesbian love, which was in regular theatrical distribution at art houses in the early nineteen-thirties in Britain, later being taken up by film societies, and still being much praised and shown during the war. Although *The Man in Grey* took the box office crown for 1943, *The Gentle Sex* was among the top money-making films, indicating that it must have had a certain appeal for women, given their predominance in the cinema audience. Part of that appeal lay in the scope the film gave to female experience, and especially the representation of female-to-female relations.

The Gentle Sex had been ''rescued'' from production difficulties by Leslie Howard, who on a *Britain Speaks* radio broadcast justified his acceptance of the directorship on the grounds that this ''was obviously one of the most remarkable aspects of the war.''[37] His ostensible project, in line with his backers at the Ministry of Information, was to make a promotional film of the A.T.S. that would have a broad audience appeal and generate recruits for the war effort. He asserted that the part played by women ''these days'' was ''so far-reaching and important that the least a mere maker of films'' could do was ''express on the screen the significance of their work.''[38] But this expression took a complicated form, from the title frames onward.

The film's first image is of an empty floral border, containing just a date, ''1838.'' The pattern is laboriously hand-drawn on paper to simulate embroidery. Into it fades a stitched Victorian proverb: ''THE GENTLE SEX. In whatever station in life a woman is placed, a spirit of modesty, humility, obedience and submission will always be required of her'' (Figure 2.14). As the text dissolves to leave an empty center frame again, the romantic

---

[36] *Millions Like Us* was released in the same year for similar reasons. It has a simpler narrative structure with fewer characters, but also deals with class and gender issues, in wartime factories as opposed to in the Forces. It has been written about more extensively than *The Gentle Sex*. See several essays in Hurd, *National Fictions*, and Harper, ''The Representation of Women.''

[37] Ronald Howard, *In Search of My Father*, p. 125.

[38] Ibid.

music lurches into a strident, regimented rhythm in preparation for the subsequent embroidered title, "1938 ONWARDS—THE GENTLE SEX" (Figure 2.15). Although the style and content of these two titles is broadly the same—that is, the sex is still the gentle sex—the change in score signifies a massive upheaval in meaning. The use of embroidery now seems to be ironic, and to suggest that, in wartime, existing stereotypes of femininity, which to Howard in 1943 seem to have been largely Victorian, have become outmoded.

Nine more fades, in and out of the embroidered frame, allow the rest of the title credits to appear, and the music shifts several more times, from a Stuart lilt to regal pomp and circumstance, to a fulsome melody enhancing the acknowledgment of the cooperation of the A.T.S. The domestic icons decorating the credits (embroidered trees, baskets, dolls, passionflowers, hearts, a horse and carriage, and a symmetrical Georgian-style house) all invoke a pre-1939 (or, rather, pre-twentieth century) idyllic rural past, forever sealed off by two World Wars. These icons often work in bizarre contradiction to the title they decorate, not to mention the subsequent events of the film. The A.T.S. acknowledgment is embellished with a prim doll-like woman in a long dress, who stands hands clasped together near a flowering passion tree, hardly garbed for ack-ack duty (Figure 2.16).[39] She is more reminiscent of the cartoon version of "La Donna è Mobile," while the passionflower, a favorite motif of sexual desire for the Victorian Pre-Raphaelite painters, could only connote lesbian love in the training camp context.

Carriages and crinolines plainly contradict the imagery of the machinery of war—of trucks, tanks, and uniforms—which will occupy the film to follow. Indeed, as the credits roll by, their forms foretell the arabesques generated in the attempt to make a contemporary representation of women's wartime role: the difficulties of reconciling, or even promoting, femininity and national productivity. In fact, the credits themselves have a synecdochichal relation to the whole film: they dramatize the awkward transition that has to be effected from domesticated woman to professional, dependable war-worker. Embroidered close-work and soldiering could not be more opposed.

In her study *The Subversive Stitch*, Rozsika Parker unravels the varied significations of embroidery, and its role in constructing notions of femi-

---

[39] Caroline Lejeune appreciated the "pleasantly ironic touch . . . provided by a Victorian sampler, bidding women cultivate 'a spirit of obedience and submission.' " But, she added, "the film's most subtle irony may be an unintended one—a cross-stitch credit to the War Office and the A.T.S." Caroline Lejeune, "The Gentle Sex," *The Observer*, 11 April 1943.

Figure 2.14. A woman's Victorian station in life will be measured against the wartime scenes at Victoria Station to follow. Frame enlargement from *The Gentle Sex*.

Figure 2.15. The Victorian sampler is brought up to date by adding "1938 onwards" to the shot. Frame enlargement from *The Gentle Sex*.

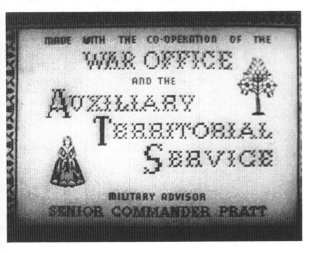

Figure 2.16. *The Gentle Sex* makes a cross-stitch credit to the War Office. Frame enlargement.

ninity over the last five hundred years.[40] She identifies a consistent, intractable bond between embroidery and a certain Victorian notion of femininity as innately passive, submissive, and non-threatening: "Women embroidered because they were naturally feminine, and were feminine because they naturally embroidered."[41] A nineteenth-century embroidering woman was coded as upper class, genteel, leisured, and in the process of being educated into the feminine ideal. The Victorian sampler, which the opening credits of *The Gentle Sex* imitate, was associated with this preparation for domesticity and a life of good manners among a refined female society. The activity of embroidering also connoted innocence, sincerity, and purity: it was the archetypal occupation of a virtuous, betrothed woman who kept her hands busy while awaiting her wedding.[42] Indeed, samplers were often characterized as works made by women simply "for love."

Collapsing the categories "woman" and "embroidery" reinforced the sexual division of labor by suggesting that women's embroidered work was inessential, amateur, and symptomatic of feminine weakness. According to this logic, embroidery required patience and perseverance, but little else. It was (and is) largely perceived as contentless, mindless, delicate, and decorative—not an art, but entirely the expression of femininity as "service and selflessness"; "women work for others, [but] not for themselves."[43]

Embroidery accrued a new, additional significance in wartime Britain: that of luxury. Sixteen-year-old Norah Kirk worked as an embroiderer in a Singer dress factory, and she recalled that in 1942–43 "all of a sudden, silks went off the market—couldn't get them at all—so there was no embroidery done on dresses, the war had put a clamp down on it."[44] The Austerity Regulations of summer 1942 had forbidden such trimmings. When peace came *Embroidery Magazine* editorialized thankfully: "What a feeling of prosperity it gives to realize once again that silks, wools, fabrics, and all embroidery equipment are available in all abundance. These things can never be taken for granted again after the lean war years, when

---

[40] Rozsika Parker, *The Subversive Stitch: Embroidery and the Making of the Feminine* (London: The Women's Press, 1984).

[41] Ibid., p. 11.

[42] See Wayne Anderson's anthropological discussion of this practice in *Gauguin's Paradise Lost* (New York: Viking Press, 1971), p. 31.

[43] Parker, *The Subversive Stitch*, p. 6.

[44] Norah Kirk (b. 1926, Nottingham), quoted in Sheila Rowbottom and Jean McCrindle, eds., *Dutiful Daughters: Women Talk about Their Lives* (London: Allen Lane, 1977), p. 196.

one felt guilty plying the needle for any purpose but 'make do and mend,' and wools and silks were impossible to get.''[45]

The point here is to emphasize how powerfully suggestive the titles of *The Gentle Sex* would have been to the wartime audience, even though the aesthetic choice of cross-stitching seems so deliberately at odds with the film's ostensible recruiting aims. Recourse to Victorian stereotypes may seem an extreme maneuver for a 1943 training film about modern warfare, albeit the training of women, but it would not have been sufficient merely to invoke a prewar past, because women had seen service before, in World War I, even if they had not been conscripted. Mrs. Sheridan, Anne's potential mother-in-law, functions as a reminder of this in *The Gentle Sex*. When Anne remarks to her that ''for the first time in British history women are fighting side by side with the men,'' Mrs. Sheridan corrects her and says that in 1917 she was driving an ambulance for the W.A.A.C.'s at Etaples, and that was how she met her husband. Victorian femininity, signaled through the style of embroidery, through a Keats poem that Howard recites at the end of the credits, and through the Victorian proverb about a woman's station in life, takes us to a period prior to suffrage days, to a period when in popular memory sexual difference was more clearly defined—in effect, a period of relief to conservative male spectators of war.

A Victorian notion of privileged and protected femininity was totally out of kilter with the wartime necessity of training women for ack-ack duty and truck-driving, except for its connotation that women were submissive and could be trained for any purpose. Skills in handmade, nonmechanized embroidery were as relevant to the needs of a uniformed military unit as domestic cookery was relevant to factory work, even though many jokes were founded on the idea of their compatibility (see Figures 2.17 and 2.18). However, these jokes are part of the process of mobilizing femininity for war, asserting women's real capacity for learning new skills, while also absorbing anxieties stemming from female migration into traditionally male jobs—in these cartoons, of foundry and munitions. In *The Gentle Sex*, the conjunction of domestic craft with national defense was surely meant to be ironic, as was the bare fact of the title, the use of a Keats sonnet, and the reference to a ''station in life'' that precedes the first postcredit shot, the shot of Victoria station. These women are physically at Victoria Station, the film says, but not psychically.

Such ironic choices work in a similar way to the sampler style of lettering. They wait to be undercut by the activities of the A.T.S. women, func-

---

[45] Cited by Penelope Dalton, ''Issues in the Role and Status of Needlecraft in Secondary Schools,'' unpublished M.A. thesis, University of Sussex and Brighton Polytechnic, 1980, and quoted in Parker, *The Subversive Stitch*, p. 202.

"It's practically the same as making a fruit jelly—without adding fruit, of course."

Figure 2.17. The factory as kitchen. *Everybody's Weekly*,
20 March 1943, p. 13.

tioning like the lawyer's technique of setting up a false line of reasoning only to knock it down dramatically. But how successful could addressing women as upper and middle class Victorians be, even in irony? Embroidering for pleasure was a very upper middle-class habit, not the experience of working class women whose encounter with stitchery occurred in the mills. In *The Gentle Sex*, the irony sets up a problem, both for the spectator and the director—that of closing the gap between conventions of femininity and the realities of class and war. This problem gives the narrative momentum, sets it on its way, but also draws attention to its insoluble nature. The very difference between the cross-stitch embroidery of the titles and the manufactured khaki uniforms that follow plays out the ideological divergence that exists between fighting and femininity. The titles' elaborate structure and laboriously constructed appearance work in opposition to the aesthetic of "realism," promised through the idea of charting history (1838 to 1938), the disciplinarian music, the promise of documentary footage, and the credit acknowledgment of the War Office and A.T.S. But because of embroidery's history as a powerful trope of femininity, it can still insist, in framing the film, that femininity exists whether women are soldiers or not, and from whatever class they come.

"Now add a quart of molten lead, and T.N.T. to taste."

Figure 2.18. Women's domestic knowledge is mobilized for destructive ends in *Everybody's Weekly*, 24 July 1943, p. 13.

UNIFORMING WOMEN

Broadly speaking, mobile women worked either in factories in overalls or in the Forces in uniforms, but in terms of filmic representation, the potential for glamor and self-confidence associated with a uniform lent itself more readily to screen spectacle. To some extent, therefore, *The Gentle Sex* "skirts" the worst of the difficulties by focusing on the uniformed A.T.S. and avoiding the image of women-in-overalls present in a film such as *Millions Like Us*. In this film Celia is adamant that she'd "hate it in a factory," adding "besides . . . I'm mobile." Here she hints at the additional prestige that she, and most of the audience, would have associated with mobility, taking the word to be synonymous with wearing a uniform. One of the propaganda purposes of *Millions Like Us* was to counteract the impression that only Forces women were truly mobile.

The film poignantly dramatizes the process of interviewing that determines Celia's mobility status. While waiting in line at the Ministry of Labour National Service Office, Celia fantasizes about her life in the Forces. She gazes up at a recruitment poster emblazoned with the words ''Serve in the WAAF with the Men who Fly,'' yet another reminder of the gendered classification of air and land in war (Figure 2.19). On the poster, a young woman looks upward and outward like Celia, with a flier behind her right shoulder and a British R.A.F. flag and strong white clouds illustrated beyond. The shot cuts to a slow track in on Celia's face. As the focus softens, romantic music swells up and a sequence of dissolves shows Celia sporting different Forces uniforms as she helps a pilot into his cockpit, drives war officials in an open saloon car, smiles to light their cigars, and

Figure 2.19. Women serve the men who fly. Poster by Jonathan Fosse for the Air Ministry, 1941-43, appearing in *Millions Like Us*.

coyly acknowledges a gentleman on horseback who doffs his cap to this pastoral version of Celia as a Land Army girl. She then fondles an imaginary engagement ring. Her fantasies traverse all four branches of the women's Forces, providing a veritable military fashion parade. In each fragment she serves and defers to men, while the camera movements, focus, framings, and systems of exchanged glances suggest that her job is as much to entertain these men as a sexualized accoutrement as to work with them.

The poster enables Celia's daydreams of sartorial transformation, but they end abruptly as her interview starts. When she turns down the traditionally "female" jobs of cook and typist, the Ministry of Labour official suggests factory work, but Celia is still disappointed. The interviewer finally convinces her (perhaps along with "millions" of disgruntled women like her in the audience) that "Mr. Bevan needs another million women, and I don't think we can disappoint him at a time like this. You can help your country just as much in an overall as you can in a uniform these days." Celia is never again seen in the glamorizing uniforms or under the fetching lighting effects of her fantasy.

In American feature films of the war period, the relative ease or difficulty with which different women's jobs could be incorporated into contemporary narratives depended to a large extent on the ease of conversion of the role to spectacle. *Stage Door Canteen*, *Four Jills in a Jeep*, and *Tonight and Every Night* all dramatize the work of female troop entertainers and their special dilemma of having to be seductive to be patriotic, while still being faithful to one man, in preparation for peace. In *Tender Comrade* and *Since You Went Away*, though both narratives contain characters who are factory hands, their work is barely represented and most scenes take place within the home, even if it is a new kind of home. There is a patriarchal point to Doris's heinous crime in *Tender Comrade*: she hoards one hundred and twenty-seven different shades of lipstick because, as her roommate Barbara says, "with all those you can hold out for seventy-five years." Even at the Douglas Aircraft factory, Jo Jones (Ginger Rogers) does not wear overalls but instead a slim-fitting, waisted dress with padded shoulders and dramatically widening straps, a fashionable outfit in sum. While driving a small vehicle across the shop floor (present as a back-projected image behind her) she nonchalantly turns the wheel with her right hand while smiling to her co-workers as she passes by. The use of back-projection, plus the composition of the shot—throughout it she stands facing the camera, the steering wheel conveniently just to the side of her svelte body—save her from over-contamination from war labor. Her glamorous aspect is further preserved in that her work hat, a dark pill box perched on the back of her head, is only slightly larger than the one she has worn in the previous scene at the troop train, seeing her husband off before she has signed up for war duty. Jo retires from factory work, pregnant, shortly after her ride in the factory.

There were certainly pressures on American wartime femininity, but they were different from those in Britain: American women were never conscripted, for example. By comparison, the deglamorization of the national heroine in Britain was overdetermined, setting in train a series of nervous male symptoms, expressed in cartoon and film imagery. Several British cartoons, especially those about the Women's Land Army, evidence a pervasive male fear that the adoption of uniforms or overalls by women will actually diminish sexual difference, that women will lose their femininity (Figures 2.20 and 2.21). If women and men *looked* similar, were they not indeed similar? One of the problems of combining femininity with uniformity stemmed from the powerful notion of femininity as incompatible with cohesion, rationality, and public dependability (Figure 2.22). Several cartoons support the idea that femininity is irrepressible and seeps out into war work in unexpected and detrimental ways. A *Punch* cartoon from December 1942 is captioned, "I understand you've been riveting in your name and address," and shows a tank factory manager reprimanding an overalled woman who limply holds her riveting gun.[46] She

"And then we'll have that little dream cottage with a tiny white gate, roses round the door and a hundred acres of arable at the back."

Figure 2.20. Life in the Land Army changes women's fantasies. J. W. Taylor cartoon, *Punch*, 23 June 1943, p. 524.

[46] *Punch*, 16 December 1942.

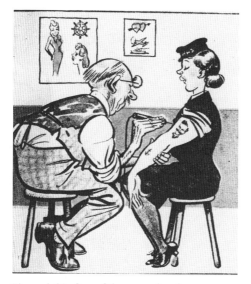

Figure 2.21. One of the cross-dressing
implications of uniforming women. *Everybody's
Weekly*, 9 January 1943, p. 13.

has apparently used war work to engineer romantic encounters with tank
men. In "Aircraftwoman Smith," a woman has the urge to dry her laundry
while on duty (Figure 2.23). She improvises by hanging clothes on a balloon hauser, to the dismay of the officer in charge. But the joke inadvertently gives away the condition of the overburdened woman who must lead
that "double life" the Jeyes Fluid advertisement imaged. As a corollary,
the price paid for an image of public responsibility in women, for a male
audience, seemed indeed to be one in which women were more interested
in their jobs and less interested in appearances. As another *Punch* cartoon
of 1942 suggests, patriotism expected, permitted, and even required a degree of despecularization in women (Figure 2.24).

In British realist cinema, so interested in representing unglamorized
womanhood, yet so anxious about the longterm price of changed sexual
roles, obsessive attention is paid to those private moments in films such as
Perfect Strangers, *Millions Like Us*, and *The Gentle Sex* when women
educate each other about lipstick, hat angles, and hairdos in preparation
for the postwar world. Most of the first reel of *The Gentle Sex* concerns the
reorganization and training of the seven female recruits into a disciplined
and controlled unit, able to drive trucks and ambulances and spot enemy
aircraft. The process of removing their civilian clothes, and replacing them
with standard issue, is documented through several scenes, so that camp

Figure 2.22. Uniformity and women are at odds in the
A.T.S. supply room. *Everybody's Weekly*,
24 July 1943, p. 13.

training is presented almost entirely in terms of undressing and dressing
for action. It is as if Howard needs to assert over and over again the presence of a female body beneath the uniform.

In one shot a notice-board lists the intimate attire that will safeguard
women's femininity for the duration: "3 prs. panties, 3 vests, 4 shirts, 8
collars, 2 studs, 3 brassieres, 3 prs. knickers, 2 corset belts" (Figure
2.25). Other shots show women squeezing in and out of skirts, practicing
hat angles, and checking the effects in mirrors. The last scene of the wom-
en's first day in the A.T.S. shows Good-time Dot, former beautician, being assisted in her nighttime grooming ritual (Figure 2.26). She has
brought all the accoutrements of femininity to camp and declares, "It'll
take more than a war to stop me combing my hair," thus assuaging male
fears that femininity will be lost in the course of duty, while also entertaining her co-recruits gathered around her, one of whom willingly lies on
Dot's bed and holds up her mirror.

It is no accident that it is Dot's *hair* that is singled out in this scene as a
sign of continued femininity in the military environment. Nancy Huston
argues that the diversion of men's sexual energy into murderous energy

" Aircraftwoman Smith, there's a time and place for everything !."

Figure 2.23. Aircraftwoman Smith leads a "double life." *Everybody's Weekly*, 16 January 1943, p. 13.

for war is signaled through the ritual of head shaving on the first day of military service.[47] In this ritual, hair is understood as an outward sign of active sexuality that is removed in order for the ability to fight to emerge. We can use this proposition to understand how the equivalent motif of hair might operate for women across wartime films, posters, and cartoons, even though the U.K. custom was for the male individual to take care of trimming his hair, as opposed to having it forcibly removed on day one (Figure 2.27). Women are urged to tie back their hair for war work, and squash it under their cap, and are warned of the dangers of Veronica Lake's languorous locks. However, at night, as in this scene, long hair tumbles out, for it is one of those key elements of femininity, part of a culturally

[47] Nancy Huston, "The Matrix of War: Mothers and Heroes," *Poetics Today* 6 (1985): 154–55.

" This photograph's rather flattering, isn't it ? "

Figure 2.24. War requires women to be uniformed, and
uniformly unattractive. Fortunately for the middle-class
readers of *Punch*, not all women can conform.
David Langdon cartoon, *Punch*, 9 September 1942,
p. 216.

constructed dimorphism, that at least during the nineteenth century distin-
guished male from female.

In wartime cinematic representation there was a tension between representing uniformed or overalled women in order to meet the demands of the
British realist aesthetic and contemporary political needs, and the pressure
to foreground difference through spectacle in order to produce the more
stable peacetime.

In this light, we can consider *The Gentle Sex* a variant of the cross-
dressing genre, that is, of films that probe the rigidity or flexibility of gender identity by detaching gender signifiers from the expected biological
sex. While most films explore cross-dressing by disguising the male as a
female, as in Hawks's comedy *I Was a Male War Bride*, which puts Cary
Grant in a W.A.C. uniform, ''women-in-uniform'' or ''women-in-over-

Figure 2.25. The list of female undergarments assures viewers that women
really are the same under the uniform. Frame enlargement from
The Gentle Sex.

all'' dramas work in the opposite direction. While in male-to-female films
''sexually disguised characters are subject to being constructed as spectacle'' through the use of soft focus, lingering close-ups, and point-of-view
shots, as in *Some Like It Hot*, in *The Gentle Sex* (among other wartime
films) the sexually ''disguised'' characters—the women—must not, for
patriotic reasons, be too obviously glamorized.[48]

A further cross-dressing implication of uniforming women is traceable
at the edges of film texts and cartoons. It was feared that legislating wom-
en's dress, by equipping them with practical uniforms in order to unify
them, might have the power to disguise, alter, or even reconstruct their
real selves. The connotations of male strength attached to a military uniform might permanently empower a female wearer. The question was,
''What would be the effect of the uniform on the 'real' woman underneath?'' Would it promote lesbian relations among women? Jean Mor-

[48] Annette Kuhn, *The Power of the Image: Essays on Representation and Sexuality* (London: Routledge and Kegan Paul, 1985), p. 66.

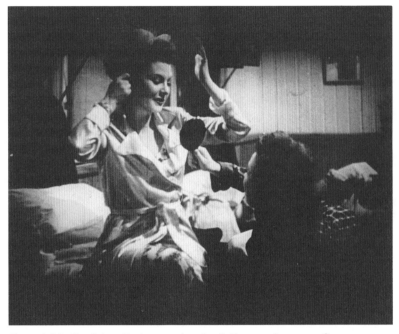

Figure 2.26. Good-time Dot's grooming ritual. Frame enlargement from
The Gentle Sex.

mont, who joined the A.T.S. at seventeen and remained until the war ended, described it as her "first taste of life" and said that she was "learning all the time."[49] She met people "from all walks of life," including lesbians, girls that "talk posh," working-class girls, "girls that come off farms." She concludes that "it was a jolly good life because I'd never been able to mix like that." A letter to *Time and Tide* deploys euphemisms for lesbianism in describing the reasons a husband might give for not wanting his wife to join the services: he thinks "the work is too hard," "the service women are too tough a crowd," "he doesn't want to come home to another uniform," and "he thinks I should grow coarse and hardened."[50]

Lesbian relations between wartime women, an unavoidable implication of the women-in-uniform genre, are occasionally vaguely suggested in home front films, as in in the scenes on the hop farm at which Allison works in *A Canterbury Tale*. Here the embittered Miss Prudence Honeywood has given up on the idea of marriage—only one man has ever asked her, and he wanted her to live in a long, sad urban street—and she now

[49] Jean Mormont in Rowbottom and McCrindle, *Dutiful Daughters*, p. 142.
[50] Anonymous, "Women's War Service," *Time and Tide*, 11 October 1941, p. 867.

Figure 2.27. Feminine hairstyles must be mobilized
for war. "The Recruit," *Punch*, 19 September 1942,
p. 241.

lives with her sister running the farm. She heaves muck, smokes a cigarette, and stands mannishly astride. "Call me Pru," she says to Allison.
"I don't like Prudence, name or quality." In *Great Day*, an unpopular
female character, Miss Tindle, who is helping to prepare the village for
Eleanor Roosevelt's arrival, can also be read as a lesbian figure. A row
develops around an eggless cake that is to be displayed for Mrs. Roosevelt,
since this cake actually has an egg in it. The cake is described heatedly as
"a deliberate deception, a fake, a lie," and then Miss Tindle turns on the
rest of the women, scolding them as "sentimental fools thinking of nothing
but men. That's all you think of. That's all you're good for. Women! Look
at you. Standing around like a lot of sheep waiting for the butcher."[51]

The War Office was concerned enough about losing the literal definitions of femininity—the curving female form—that it announced that serving women "must be corseted, and corseted correctly," and commis-

[51] John Costello discusses lesbianism in the American W.A.A.C.'s in *Love, Sex, and
War: Changing Values, 1939–1945* (London: Collins, 1985), pp. 93–98.

sioned corset designs from Frederick R. Berlei that would "preserve the feminine line, and at the same time be practical under a uniform."[52] These corsets included a pocket tucked into the girdle waist, since serving women were unable to carry a handbag. A detailed *Picture Post* article on this aspect of legislating womanliness showed "fashion experts" scrutinizing a wartime corset (Figure 2.28). The caption read: "It's a decisive moment in the history of the corset . . . a garment designed to safeguard women's femininity for the duration." It then remembers that "in the last war, women came to look less womanly as time went on." A naval historian recently described the creation of a suitable uniform for the "Wrens" in World War II as "a unique sartorial event," and added that "it is not surprising that the combination of appropriate femininity and utility in service had been at times a major preoccupation. . . . Few would deny that these more recent efforts have been very successful since the days of ankle-length skirts, gaberdine hats and voluminous coat-frocks."[53]

IT IS CLEAR from the foregoing discussion that *The Gentle Sex* must marshal much controversial and contradictory material in its attempt to both

Figure 2.28. Safeguarding femininity in war. *Picture Post*, 2 March 1940, p. 26.

[52] Anonymous, "Wartime Corsets," *Picture Post*, 2 March 1940, p. 26.
[53] Richard Cooper and Grant Uden, *A Dictionary of British Ships and Seamen* (New York: St. Martin's Press, 1980), p. 569.

recruit women and reassure men. There is a tension between strategies for addressing a *female* audience—the primary audience for an A.T.S. recruitment film—and a *national* audience that will support the efforts represented. The persona of Leslie Howard plays a crucial role in reining in these differences in an effort to unify the address of the text.

Howard was called on to rescue the project because his personality and voice had played a central part in engaging and even constituting the British wartime audience. Heard on radio, and heard and seen in films—even shown in *The Gentle Sex* to be making and controlling a film—Howard was a well-known personality with a standard English, received pronunciation accent. He would have been familiar to contemporary filmgoers because of his B.B.C. wartime radio work and his successful acting roles in *Gone with the Wind, Pimpernel Smith, 49th Parallel, Pygmalion,* and, most recently, *The First of the Few,* as well as his recitation of the famous concluding prayer of *In Which We Serve,* the biggest home box-office success of 1942, just a year earlier.[54] He regularly spoke on *Britain Speaks,* recorded for the North American service, and occasionally sat on the B.B.C. *Brains Trust* panel. This ''mere man'' could invoke, through his mere presence, the idea of a unified nation, despite the diversity of accent, class, and character that comprised it. Guy Morgan remembered him in 1948 as ''something of a symbol to the British people'' because ''he came home from America to help us when times were bad. . . . The public liked and trusted his quiet voice and whimsical judgement; he had, and always will have, a very special place in his country's affections.''[55]

Howard's voice then must be understood in this general context of his radio reputation and radio's wartime role as the highly effective and preferred official medium for directing and linking ''the people.'' Howard's voice would have been heard with added poignancy after 1 June 1943 (*The Gentle Sex* opened six weeks earlier, in April 1943), when he was shot down over the Bay of Biscay as his plane brought him back from a lecture tour of Portugal. Peter Noble wrote in response to the death that Leslie Howard's ''presence in England constituted . . . one of the most valuable facets of British propaganda.''[56]

Howard's voice does its best to claim the A.T.S. women's activities for a male viewer by hovering somewhere between voice-off and voice-over

[54] According to the 1941 *Kinematograph Weekly* report, Leslie Howard was *the* most popular star with British audiences; other popular stars were Charles Boyer, Lawrence Olivier, Bette Davis, and Vivian Leigh. In 1942 he was still on that list, and was also on the ''British Best Director'' list, along with Lance Comfort, Michael Powell, and Carol Reed. See R. H. ''Josh'' Billings, ''Box Office Stakes Results,'' *Kinematograph Weekly,* 8 January 1942, p. 40.

[55] Morgan, *Red Roses Every Night,* p. 74.

[56] Noble, *The British Film Yearbook,* p. 74.

as he speaks from the parapet at the opening of the film. By the time his high angle viewpoint is shown again at the end of the opening sequence, his silhouette, the anchor of identification for the audience, has disappeared. His voice then resolves into a voice-over, but one without the power of the truly disembodied voice typical of documentary films. Howard's body, remembered leaning by the railings, is too bound into the film's diegesis to control it fully. In addition, the entire course of the film is marked by his disbelief or hesitation in his own project. His voice interrupts the women's activities sporadically, and he is constantly "surprised" at the capabilities of the women he seeks to represent. He "stumbles" upon them in unexpected places, saying, "Hello, where are we now? Oh! A lorry! Of course, now we're fully fledged drivers."

The shifting use of Leslie Howard's voice in relation to the images and sounds of mobile women betrays the conflicting spectatorial positions the film offers. It is a sort of tug-of-war between its women characters and a father figure who tries to hold them firmly within his purview. Howard's approach to assembling the film material—being distanced from but *within* the image—paralleled the working method of Mass-Observers, who would mingle in their local community and record the surrounding goings-on.[57] Howard, on the balcony, is a special spectator, who can watch the objects of his film scurrying beneath him, but also watch and ponder the process of his own watching. He has a double access to his material, split along the sound/image axis. The male, directorial silhouette *sees* the activity of women, but the later unseen owner of the voice-over listens in and deliberates their intentions. The director is inscribed as a privileged, elevated voyeur who can also eavesdrop. There is something about this subject matter, the gentle sex, that requires or provokes careful packaging and presentation, a double wrapping to control its war work.

Reviewers of *The Gentle Sex* were largely enthusiastic about the film; one challenged, "War is the ever present mental, emotional and physical focus of effort of millions, [yet] there is still this head-in-sand refusal to admit that war, right now, is the *norm*—and has been for eight of the last thirty years . . . Let us bring them soberly to the truth—show them the informative sincerity of *The Gentle Sex*."[58] However, these same reviewers were unable to classify the film to their satisfaction, calling it a "semi-

---

[57] Mass-Observation was founded in 1937 by Charles Madge and Tom Harrisson to study, through interviews, diaries, and note-taking, all aspects of British social life, from views on the monarchy to pub and gardening habits. They described their work as "democratic social science." In 1940 the services of the organization were placed at the disposal of the Ministry of Information to provide the Home Intelligence Department with material about wartime civilian morale. Understandably, this transfer upset many of the former Mass-Observers.

[58] K. F. Bean, "Letter to Olive Bell," *Sight and Sound* 12, no. 46 (September 1943): 38.

documentary,'' ''in the documentary fashion,'' ''almost a documentary,'' a ''girls-in-uniform documentary comedy drama,'' and later, ''one of the omnibus genre.''[59] I have proposed many reasons for this difficulty in classification.

First, there was the general context of weak genre boundaries within British cinema, and the expansion of the war genre to include women. Next, there was the incorporation of location shooting—unstaged footage of the Blitz and A.T.S. parades—into a film largely comprised of studio scenes, and the ''blending'' of seven professional actresses with real A.T.S. personnel.[60] Further, there was the attempt to address female experience directly in a realist style, while also generating a ''romance narrative'' (for Anne and David) of the feature-type film. Carrie Tarr has suggested in her work on *Sapphire* and *Darling* that ''the combination of a concern with social reality and a narrative motivated by female desire points to the potential for 'trouble in the text,' '' and that by extension, a film's documentary concerns may be rendered unsatisfactory because of a narrative focus around the ''problem'' of female desire.[61] *The Gentle Sex* undoubtedly manifests such a tension between its documentary and feature components—a trait Arnheim disparagingly called ''hybridism.''[62]

Tensions are also present in the unhappy coexistence of embroidery and the War Office in the titles; between the women's actions and the only semi-disembodied male voice-over that attempts to make the film cohere; and between the scenes of mobile women marching and driving, but also undressing, corseting, and grooming. These tensions are, at one level, a product of the film's inability to reconcile its strategies for addressing a *female* audience and soliciting women's consent for the war effort with its address to a unified national audience that must accept and support such massive social upheavals as female conscription. But at a deeper level, this very recruitment served to disintegrate the idea of nation from within; mass mobilization of real women worked against traditional notions of national stability, for women could no longer be counted on to be at home—in fact they were required by law *not* to be.

[59] *Daily Telegraph*, 2 May 1943; *Sunday Times*, 11 April 1943; *Monthly Film Bulletin*, 30 April 1943, p. 37; *Kinematograph Weekly*, 8 April 1943, p. 24; Raymond Durgnat, *A Mirror for England: British Movies from Austerity to Affluence* (New York: Praeger, 1971), p. 201.

[60] *Monthly Film Bulletin*, 30 April 1943, p. 37.

[61] Carrie Tarr, ''*Sapphire, Darling* and the Boundaries of Permitted Pleasure,'' *Screen* 26, no. 1 (January/February 1985): 50.

[62] Rudolf Arnheim, ''Fact and Fiction,'' *Sight and Sound* 8, no. 32 (Winter 1939–40): 136.

The Blackout

Peacetime dimouts are transformed by history.

James Agee, *Perfect Stangers*, 1945

THE MILITARY aim of the blackout, put into effect across Europe, was to prevent enemy navigation and bombing over the home front; the absence of external artificial light at night was intended to deny the aerial point of view. Rules for accomplishing a total blackout were legislated and enforced by the government, and depended on the cooperation of every single citizen. Unlike other disruptions of the early war that gave just a hint of the years of rationing and austerity to follow, the impact of the blackout was "comprehensive and immediate."[1] Living through the wartime dark was experienced by everyone, regardless of class, age, sex, race, or regional abode. Universal in nature, the image of the blackout became a synecdoche for war in cultural life.

This image (or lack of an image) had a special affinity for the cinema: the cinema enhanced its metaphoric power, making it a cornerstone of cinematic vocabulary. In Alexander Korda's film *Perfect Strangers*, transitions between the prewar, wartime, and postwar phases of the narrative are marked by linguistic and imagistic references to the blackout so that the blackout comes to "surround" the film's central, wartime events. Such blackout punctuation is typical of wartime films; indeed, the blackout serves as a demarcating device in all British films made and set in wartime, and has been deployed ever since, perhaps more frequently than any other code, to recall World War II on the screen.

The blackout held a nodal position at the intersection of three major axes of the institution of cinema: aesthetic, technological, and psychosocial. As a diegetic element the blackout imposed wartime conditions and thus fulfilled a key demand of British realism, namely that of addressing the entire population through the representation of a shared British reality: it signaled national experience and so spoke to its audience as a national group. The blackout also provided an aesthetic environment in which the image of the

---

[1] Calder, *The People's War*, p. 72. Food and clothes rationing were ended in 1953.

114

deglamorized, mobile woman could be reared and sustained, for the blackout symbolized both the general constraints on spectacle in wartime and the particular constraints on the most conventional filmic instantiation of spectacle, the display of women. Strategic and economic rationing of electric light militated against the exhibition of the artificial-looking, Hollywoodian screen woman whose very appearance depended on contrived lighting and who connoted at best unpatriotic wastefulness, and at worst, as I will discuss, collaboration with the enemy.

The blackout turned on a second axis: that of the technology of image production. The very possibility of a lit screen was subject to wartime shortages. The rationing of carbon rods led to a literal deficit of light, and single-projector shows (also the result of shortages) entailed a blackout between each reel. The differential exposure of light to film stock, the nature of film editing, and the necessity of darkness and light for both processing and seeing the image all chimed with the blackout's constitution. Wartime blackouts were shattered by light, as was the auditorial darkness of the cinema. Technical advances such as faster film stocks of 100 to 200 ASA, accompanied by small Fresnel-lens spots and photoflood bulbs, which were available from the early 1940s, permitted shooting at lower lighting levels—and hence a closer approximation to blackout experience—but even with these changes the reproduction of a blackout was always a knife-edged affair.[2] The blackout spelled the end of representation, the end of visual pleasure. Most films kept sequences of totally black footage down to a minimum, and continued the sound track behind them to prevent total severance of audience attention from screen fiction. Frank Launder's *Two Thousand Women* (1944) places its extended blackout scene at the end of one reel and the beginning of the next, using fictional blackness to camouflage the reel change.

The blackout intersected with a third dimension of the experience of wartime cinema—that of cinema-going itself, the audience's sensation of entering and viewing in a darkened auditorium. Barthes writes of the "more or less brightly lit sidewalk" he returns to on leaving the movie theater, the place that gradually enables him to emerge from the hypnosis induced by the cinema's dark.[3] Not so the wartime filmgoer, whose film experience was doubled in the wartime night. The blackout and cinema together mobilized the spectator for war. Blackness encased twice over the space of screen fiction: the external night and the internal darkness together

[2] The ASA speed-rating was introduced with the new stock and lighting. See Barry Salt, *Film Style and Technology: History and Analysis* (London: Starword Press, 1983), pp. 287–89.
[3] Roland Barthes, "Leaving the Movie Theater," in *The Rustle of Language*, trans. Richard Howard (New York: Hill and Wang, 1984), p. 345.

framed the aural and visual show. The blackout was a route to and from film fantasy: it ushered in, figured the fantastic.

Lying at the point of intersection of these three axes, the blackout dwells close to the heart of cinematic representation. A phenomenon that begins as government legislation finds roost in the ultimate entertainment looking-machine. The mundane habit of blacking-out spreads into a vast web of social and even aesthetic codes. But, despite its governmental origins, the tropic blackout holds to no single politics. Transformed through the medium of cinema, it becomes a metaphor for deprivation, danger, and confusion; the rent in the tyranny of vision, in the ideology of the visible (to use Comolli's term) come to symbolize the discontinuity of broken conventions in war. Its opposite—a beam of shining light, wrecker of blackness—functions multivalently too, signifying excitement, transgression, daring, extravagance, and shock. Under wartime conditions, the projection beam in the cinema holds the promise of an unfettered world, while it also formally echoes the military searchlight, that effective weapon of death. Caught in this proliferating cultural lattice are wartime's contradictory images of woman, for the metaphoric space of the blackout is also an arena in which gender distinctions blur and conventional gender roles shift ground. As a character in *Two Thousand Women* puts it, "Mata Hari did all her best work at night," again linking female sexual activity to endangered national politics, this time under cover of dark.

Diegetic blackouts both attenuate cinematic spectacle and quarantine fantasies of spectacular transformation. The blackout is a symbol of the despecularization of wartime cinematic offerings, but also the frame through which the image is seen. The crucial point is that the one figure refers simultaneously to fantasy, reality, and the material conditions of filmmaking.

A multiplicity of meanings always points to a locus of cultural importance and conflict. As Terry Eagleton argues in a discussion of Bakhtin, it is not simply a matter of what a sign means, "but of investigating its varied history, as conflicting social groups, classes, individuals and discourses seek to appropriate it and imbue it with their own meanings."[4] Fredric Jameson has suggested that the multiple symbolism of the killer shark in *Jaws* (1975), another instance of polysemy, is necessary because "works of mass culture . . . cannot manage anxieties about the social order unless they have first revived them and given them some rudimentary expression."[5] The film *Jaws* thus must partially reveal society's problems and

[4] Terry Eagleton, *Literary Theory: An Introduction* (Minneapolis: University of Minnesota Press, 1983), p. 117.
[5] Fredric Jameson, "Reification and Utopia in Mass Culture," *Social Text* 1 (Winter 1979): 144.

desires in order to diffuse them. The filmic metaphor of the blackout has such an orchestral function, like the shark, organizing and absorbing different meanings as it is borrowed and lent by different individual spectators, classes, groups, and discourses, serving as a switching point for wartime anxieties and fantasies of sexual and national identity in a peculiarly literal instance of the textual inscription of ideology through "eloquent silences, . . . significant gaps and fissures."[6]

WHAT HAPPENS in the blackout? *Perfect Strangers* provides an extraordinary set of answers to this question. The film was produced and directed in England by Alexander Korda as the first and only completed MGM–London Film. It previewed in August 1945 shortly after the restoration of peace, opening to the British public on 15 October 1945 and in America the following December under the more prosaic title *Vacation from Marriage*.[7] The opening third of the story introduces the daily routine of Robert and Cathy Wilson, played by Robert Donat and Deborah Kerr, on Robert's last day as a civilian. He works as a bookkeeper for Jones and Hargrove while Cathy stays at home starching her husband's collars. She transports herself from housewifely duties by imagining stylish trips to warmer climes, using the local travel agent's literature as inspiration; on the morning we meet her she is humming to the family wireless about "an airline ticket to romantic places."

The film's first image, displayed behind the title credits, is a frozen tableau of chimneys, skylights, trap doors, metal railings, smog and rooftops—a decidedly grimy scape with St. Paul's Cathedral just discernible among other spires. Big Ben chimes and a gentle melody fades up. The image dissolves to a medium shot of more chimneys and stepped roofs,

[6] Terry Eagleton, "Pierre Macherey," p. 138.

[7] Roger Manvell's notes on the production, drawn up for the British Council Overseas Press Department for 7 October 1945, are available in the British Film Institute Library, and are published in part in Karol Kulik, *Alexander Korda: The Man Who Could Work Miracles* (London: W. H. Allen, 1975). The notes contain the following information: "*Perfect Strangers* has been made under considerable difficulties, since the bulk of the studio work was in progress during the flying-bomb attacks on London. Korda had his script torn to ribbons by jagged glass when a flying bomb fell in the studio grounds and blasted the office block and dressing rooms. Other difficulties, which were also experienced by every British studio, had to be overcome. Plywood for sets being no longer obtainable, set walls were constructed of composition board, often made of salvaged newspapers, or of papers pasted over old wooden frames. In addition, tons of plaster, cardboard, brown wrapping-paper, reused timber and miles of wall-paper were all assembled into the sets. Costumes and uniforms had to be borrowed; the Government's allowance of materials for costumes in films is scarcely sufficient. The unit, however, gained greatly from assistance from the Admiralty, so that scenes were shot at Naval and WRNS establishments with the cooperation of naval personnel."

presided over by a tethered barrage balloon. The shot then cuts to a moving image of Cathy peering out of her garret home, her face lost in chimney-pot reflections on the glass window. Three more blimps come into view overhead. The combined iconography promises a story of lower-middle-class life in wartime London, a frequent British realist theme that had already been treated in *Waterloo Road* (1945) and *The Bells Go Down* (1943). The film will not deliver on this promise.

A closer shot, still from the exterior, now shows Cathy as a pasty-faced woman with unkempt hair, draped in a shapeless dressing gown as she draws back the morning curtains. A cut to a medium close-up reveals a fireplace, mantelpiece, and arc of surrounding photographs. Steam from the collar Cathy is pressing spreads over the window and she sneezes, claiming the first diegetic sound of the film. At last the camera "enters" the flat, panning to the right and then to the left across the interior as Cathy carries out her daily chores. On the mantel are photographs of summers spent on bicycles, and two paperweights, one a snowstorm containing the Eiffel Tower, a metonym for Cathy's dream destinations. She sneezes again, and as she turns her back to the camera, heading away from the fireside to the bedroom, a male voice-over begins an ironic commentary:

It may seem to have happened ages and ages ago, but it was really only a few years back that our story of the adventures of Robert and Cathy Wilson started. To be exact, on a gloomy spring day in London, in the year 1940. Look at them as they start the most wonderful chapter of their lives on this very exciting morning.

The subsequent close-up reveals a calendar leaf printed with "3 April 1940"; Robert's hand peels it back to uncover the fourth.

This film, like so many other British home-front films produced before the war's end, makes certain that its audience will not mistake the screen's fictional events for those of their own present, even though the subject matter explored is still thoroughly relevant. The film's promoters depended on the audience's recognition of that relevance despite the temporal displacement, advertising their commodity as "one of the most timely productions in screen history" because it "envisioned the switch-over from war to peace in the life of the country in general and in the lives of a typical married couple in particular."[8] Through the disembodied voice-over narration and the calendar device, the 1945 audience is invited to recall a specific moment in the early war, April 1940, whose identity and signifi-

[8] Publicity material, British Film Institute Library, London. Sir Alexander Korda announced in February 1945, "We have now consolidated our plans for a long term production programme of important British films. The first of these is *Perfect Stangers.*" See Noble, *The British Film Yearbook* (1946), p. 78.

cance had become representable only in retrospect. From the perspective of 1945, the date of April 1940 now conjured up a memory of national malaise, of the last calm before the storm, of the period before the May election of Churchill, the late May evacuation from Dunkirk, the summer Battle of Britain, and the onset of the Blitz in September.[9] It spoke of the "phoney war," the months of routinely observing the blackout and hoisting barrage balloons with no clear signs of aerial attack. In fact, the whole of the next sequence of the film, until Robert departs for the Navy that night, is devoted to establishing the monotony and predictability of this couple's married existence, tempting the audience to extrapolate, retrospectively, to their own "phoney war" lives. Robert and Cathy's morning patterns are so fixed that they hardly need speak. Robert eats eggs, drinks tea, reads *The Telegraph*, knocks the barometer, and picks up his torch, gas mask, and briefcase; as Cathy hooks his umbrella over his arm, he leaves. She prohibits a departing kiss on account of her perennial and sexually metaphoric cold. (Even at the station that evening they are denied a farewell kiss when rushing, uniformed soldiers buffet them apart as the engine pulls out.)

Later this same day, after a number of scenes in which Robert fails to obtain a company salary for his war service while Cathy dreams of distant resorts, the couple is together at home again, preparing for Robert's departure for HMS *Bembo*, the dubious name of his future home in the Forces. The couple repeats much of the morning's routine, even though Robert ultimately classes his umbrella as superfluous baggage in war. He slips a souvenir photograph of Cathy into his pocket, which will later remind him of her prewar aspect. Just as they are setting out for the troop train he exclaims, "Oh! The curtains!" and rushes to ensure a successful blackout for Cathy when she returns home from the station. The curtains are closed over the floating balloons, the couple shuts the door, and the camera is left lingering in the empty apartment. The reference to the blackout marks the end of Robert and Cathy's humdrum existence and the beginning of their wartime lives (Figure 3.1).[10]

---

[9] Arthur Marwick writes that in the early months of 1940 there was much talk in the press of the " 'creeping paralysis' affecting the British war effort under Neville Chamberlain's Government." On 10 May 1940, Churchill formed his National Coalition Government and Chamberlain's Conservative Government was disbanded. Arthur Marwick, *The Home Front: The British and the Second World War* (London: Thames and Hudson, 1976), p. 30.

[10] It is interesting to note a mirroring echo of the blackout's power to signify war in Rainer Werner Fassbinder's *The Marriage of Maria Braun* (1978). While the war phase of *Perfect Strangers* begins with a blackout, *Maria Braun* opens with Maria's marriage during an air raid, and the transition to postwar Germany is then effected through a "bleach-out" to total whiteness behind the credits, plus the sound of the all-clear. In other words, in *Maria Braun*

Figure 3.1. The dreary couple: Robert accepts Cathy's gift of a sponge bag as she sees him off on the troop train. *Perfect Strangers*, production still.

Robert and Cathy both respond to their government's call to duty: after Robert has joined the Navy, Cathy opts for the Wrens. For three years they live as "single" adults on a veritable vacation from marriage. War answers Cathy's desire for a more exciting life. Through Wren Officer Dizzy Clayton she encounters lipstick, hair perms, gin, and sartorial style, adopting a jaunty angle for her military cap, straightening her shoulders, and tightening her uniform belt for feminine contouring. Her masculine outfit seems to empower her to carry out a brave Blitz mission along the Thames. She also contemplates having an affair with a naval architect. Robert too is transformed through his encounter with war. He overcomes seasickness, shaves off his moustache, and falls vaguely in love with his convalescence nurse, Elena (Ann Todd), after he is injured off the coast of North Africa.

After three years both characters have become glamorous and confident in equal measure, but each is unaware of equivalent improvements in the other, since they have not yet seen each other's metamorphoses. They both independently conclude that only divorce can resolve such rapid evolution. Besides, the prospect of sexual intimacy after so long a parting is obscene

the opposite strategy, a white-out, conveys the opposite historical state, the move to peacetime, while the same logic is at work.

to Cathy. She falteringly discloses her anxieties to Dizzy while also providing the film's all but oxymoronic title: "He'll expect me to . . . Well, I mean he's very fond of me. . . . Well, what I mean is, I think it's downright immoral to treat a husband *as* a husband when you haven't seen him for three years. Robert and I are perfect strangers. I can't just resume married life without any preliminaries. I can't just . . ." She is now utterly unable to return to the flat, to that space with which the film opened, the space of the phoney war. She phones Robert from the local telephone box to request a rendezvous on "neutral ground" at the bus stop down below. Her turn of phrase is doubly apt, for the ground is neutral not only in being away from the Wilsons's home territory, but also in being a place of almost total blackness. Here visible sexual differentiation is lost, replaced by a condition of neutrality—indeed, a potentially neuter condition in which neither sex is identifiable.

Staging the meeting in this way temporarily withholds the characters' newly acquired good looks from each other; as Robert puts it, "D'you realise, I haven't seen you for three years? Not that I can see you now." He recognizes Cathy not by her appearance but by the sound of her familiar cough, now mutated to a smoker's hack. After a brief altercation they agree to a divorce and head for the Coach and Horses to settle matters over a lemonade. The tracking two-shot in the blackout barely reveals their silhouettes. Only the glinting naval braids of their uniforms help to distinguish them from the grey rippling reflections in the emergency water-storage pool beyond them and the blitzed buildings around them. The sole strong illumination is from searchlights, which beam vertically upward and sway to pinpoint enemy aircraft. A few barrage balloons are mirrored in the pool, while the drone of airplanes, apparently overhead, adds yet one more wartime marker to the scene.

After Robert's comment, the screen goes black for an extended period of time. The length of blackness begins to signify more than a simple cut between shots. By the time another image appears, the camera has been repositioned behind Robert and Cathy: we now see their outlines as they push aside a heavy blackout curtain and emerge into the blinding, glittering light of the saloon bar. The blackness of the edit has slid across into the narrative blackness of wartime fabric. Two axes of the cinematic apparatus, the mechanical and the fictional, have merged: narrative darkness has coalesced with the splice between exposed shots. The blackout has functioned as the perfect narrative elision, for literal and figurative blackouts are indistinguishable.

The parting of the saloon curtain presages, just as cinema screen curtains do, the impending revelation of a fantasy, a world in which ordinary Britons (the wartime audience) metamorphose into "perfect strangers" (their ego-ideals). The image of Robert and Cathy's silhouettes against the light redoubles the audience's relation to the flickering screen, staring out at its brightness while imbibing its fictions. As they enter the pub both players hold their hands over their eyes and search for a place to sit in a gesture curiously reminiscent of that used to cut out glare when stepping into strong sunshine. It is only then, as their eyes grow accustomed to the light, that Robert and Cathy first *see* each other, after three years, and that the narrative can rapidly move toward closure in their reconciliation and return to married life. It is the spectacle of visual beauty, both male and female, that resolves the plot and dispels wartime anxiety over changed relations between the sexes (Figure 3.2). Robert and Cathy recognize that they are permanently different, as all war citizens are, but that they are different to the same extent. Reattracted to one another, confirmed by Robert's ejaculatory drink-spilling, they fall in love again, their marriage reinvigorated by world bloodshed. As James Agee commented, it is "good to see war credited with one of the few things it can possibly be credited with."[11]

The technical difficulty of shooting the reunion scene was appreciated

Figure 3.2. Robert and Cathy admire each other's new, star image after three years apart in the Forces. *Perfect Strangers*, production still.

[11] James Agee, "Vacation from Marriage," *The Nation*, 23 March 1946, p. 355.

by an American reviewer: "Mr. Korda . . . does something . . . that only a few Hollywood directors would dare do. Many of the scenes are taken against the London wartime blackout with the consequent blurring of the players against the background. The method is effective."[12] It was effective both in presenting wartorn Europe and in marking, by an absence, the different national origin of the film. The scene momentarily signaled a non-Hollywood product to the reviewer through its flattened, low-contrast, lackluster *mise-en-scène*. Via international comparison the screen blackout has become a component of British national identity, its murkiness directly interfering with the visual display so central to the reviewer's standard notion of American film.

The players are blurred not only against their background but also against each other: the two sexes cannot be told apart at a visual level.[13] There is total dependence on the sound track to carry sexual distinction. The question of lost gender boundaries, endemic to wartime as I have argued, is explored in *Perfect Strangers* through the figure of the blackout, and can be answered only when the blackout lifts and sexual differentiation is visible again—in other words, when the war is over.

In *Perfect Strangers,* the release from wartime uncertainties is celebrated in a proliferation of mirrors and other reflective surfaces, which have hitherto been largely absent from the *mise-en-scène* and which surround Cathy and Robert's entry into the pub. Both characters become a spectacle for each other, for Dizzy Clayton, for Robert's Naval colleague Scotty, and above all for the home front audience. As if to hammer home the message, Cathy checks her appearance twice, first in her compact and then in the pub glass. The orgy of light is recapitulated in the camera's final tracking shot, which moves past the embracing couple at home and out into the shining dawn through the flat window by which it first entered. Light abounds because the Blitz has removed the surrounding buildings that, as Cathy sighs, "used to make the room so dark."

IN *Perfect Strangers* two central characters are transformed from dowdy, workaday citizens in the phoney war to radiant, eager lovers in the victorious present. There is also an implicit class mobility at work here; the image the couple projects is also one of greater status and wealth. For Cathy it is a migration from British realist woman to American film star, a micro-history of Deborah Kerr's career from *Love on the Dole* to *Quo Vadis*, but for Robert too specularity abounds, confounding the asymmetry

---

[12] Joe Pihodna, "Vacation from Marriage," *Herald Tribune*, 15 March 1946.
[13] See Chapter 2 for a discussion of how wearing a uniform also impedes the signification of sexual difference, precisely because of its tendency to make similar, or "uniform."

Mulvey described in her formulation "'Woman as Image, Man as Bearer of the Look."[14] The wartime cure must include the display of men as well, as the dialogue makes clear when Robert apologizes for not being exactly "Clark Gable" in his pre-service days and being "just a little lacking in star quality." Glamour in Robert is a sign of virility; forgotten is his queasy timidity in the crowsnest, and the shots of his fellow sailor stitching a tapestry by him below deck. Only as a Gable can Robert share postwar prospects with his now worldly wife. Cathy, replying to Robert's apology says: "I don't suppose I was exactly a pinup girl, but how could I help it?" She is plainly contradicted, both by her own image and by Scotty, who is shocked into calling her a "pinup girl" when he too first sees her in the pub.

The visual transformations of Robert and Cathy suggest the distance between British realism and dominant American film style. Their hair becomes Brylcreemed and gleaming, their skin unwrinkles, their speech quickens, their posture straightens, and the camera work and lighting that make them visible shift, too, enhancing the glow of their features. Their old realist raiments are shed, too transient and unsustainable a mirage for the postwar world. *Perfect Strangers* proposes that that which constructed national identity on the screen in wartime must now be excluded by the reconstitution of stable sexual identities in 1945.

The film's plot mirrors its hybrid, Anglo-American funding history and the blended expectations of its intended binational audience. This kind of internationalism ran counter to the project of establishing an indigenous film identity, a goal in which Korda, his eye always on the American market, had little interest. To the question, "What effect does the war have on life between the sexes?" the film seems to reply, "It turns couples into movie stars."[15] Given British cinema's uneasy Oedipal relationship to Hollywood, recently intensified by war, such an answer was deeply displeasing to patriotic critics. The formula of two well-known, high-quality British actors presenting wartime life brought success at the box office, but critics wedded to the notion of British realism decried such a fantastic solution to the serious wartime problem of separation.[16] The apparent frankness toward marital relations inspired modest support from some quarters, but for Roger Manvell the film diminished the significance of war to "an almost prewar conception, . . . a phenomenon in the plot of a romantic

[14] Laura Mulvey, "Visual Pleasure and Narrative Cinema," *Screen* 16, no. 3 (Autumn 1975): 11.

[15] James Agee writes, "In an easy travesty of a generally uneasy problem, they [Robert and Cathy] confront each other looking like movie stars." *The Nation*, 23 March 1946.

[16] See R. H. "Josh" Billings, "Good News for Britain," *Kinematograph Weekly*, 20 December 1945, pp. 50–51.

comedy."[17] His phrase "prewar conception" denigrates the film for repressing historical facts to the background. By this prewar perspective, the war is reduced to mere backdrop against which stardom is displayed, made even more dazzling by contrast to the setting of urban destruction with which *Perfect Strangers* ends.

Critics rejected *Perfect Strangers* because it inverts the ethos of realism: it engages with a pervasive wartime problem and then mythically solves it. The film straddles the fence between British realist picture and Hollywood romance. It incorporates documentary footage of blitzing and raiding, but its characters emerge spotless and utterly extraordinary. It starts with despecularized characters, but then specularizes them through their encounter with war, not vice versa. The *Monthly Film Bulletin*'s reservations were in just this vein: "This is a superficial film, which assumes that all that is needed for marital happiness and success in life is physical well-being and glamour."[18] Robert and Cathy's glamour is too obviously the kind that exists only on celluloid, by dint of artful lighting, *mise-en-scène*, and makeup, elements of the Hollywood aesthetic eschewed by those rooting for a national film style.

Elspeth Grant preferred "the business of civilian adjustment to the military way of life" in *The Way Ahead* and *The Gentle Sex*, in which no miraculous solutions are offered.[19] In these two films only a modicum of narrative closure is brought about, through characters' resignation to loss, enabled through Forces' solidarity. These films do not focus on a single couple en route to romantic union; on the contrary, they track several characters throughout, and at least two lose their loved ones to the enemy on the way. For Grant the incompleteness of the endings and the rambling structures of these narratives far better approximate British experience than does the fabulous pairing of Korda's film.

However, even *Perfect Strangers*, with its more conventional structure, leaves questions unanswered about Robert and Cathy's postwar lives. Its narrative and imagery still registers the ideological difficulty of making films in Britain on the cusp between war and peace; the gravity of war's effect still prevents total narrative unity and cohesion.

If the mobilized spectator knew that the war was almost over, neither he nor she nor any producer knew what lay ahead; indeed, no one knew what

[17] Roger Manvell, "The British Feature Film from 1940 to 1945," in Balcon et al., *Twenty Years of British Film*, p. 88.

[18] Anonymous review, "Perfect Strangers," *Monthly Film Bulletin* 12, no. 141 (30 September 1945): 106.

[19] Elspeth Grant, "Perfect Strangers: A New Film's First Night," *Daily Sketch*, 31 August 1945, p. 5.

narratives to brew for the armistice.[20] Although the expected Allied victory was already won when *Perfect Strangers* was released, the studio had not been certain of this in production. The splinters of this ignorance lie scattered in the text. As the film ends, each character still has only ten days' leave, while Britain remains to be "built up again."[21] The relation of the future to the past lies undecided; Cathy still wants to be a housewife, she says, but of a different sort to her pre-Wren days. What kind will that be? The film cannot respond. Is the early life of the couple, before the film begins, to be written off? Cathy and Robert provide different answers: for Cathy, photographs of their annual holiday at Clacton-on-Sea trigger nostalgic reminiscences of pre-1939, while Robert looks at these relics of their past with scorn, his rhetoric casting doubt on any capacity of the photograph to represent the real. He notes to Scotty, "Funny how photographs let you down. You know this was quite good of me at the time. If a man can change so much in four years . . ."

The transformation of Robert and Cathy hinges on cosmetic manipulation and a gravitation to the Hollywood star system, but it is the figure of the blackout that establishes the space in which such changes can occur. Their "improvement" results from the extraordinary circumstances of wartime, contained, cinematically, within the blackout. The blackout is the crucial organizing aesthetic by which a "dull bookkeeper . . . and his equally unspectacular wife" can grow into spectacular partners[22]—it is the "history" about which Agee quips when he writes of "peacetime dimouts . . . transformed by history." According to the logic of *Perfect Strangers*, before the war, and in the "phoney" war, gender was not sufficiently demarcated in visual terms. Although Cathy and Robert conformed to traditional divisions of labor as housewife and bookkeeper, their public appear-

---

[20] *Kinematograph Weekly* explained the producers' dilemma in the changeover to peace: "With an ill-suppressed sigh of 'here it comes,' Hollywood stepped back cautiously with all its production plans and began to meander uncertainly. Only one rule seems to have been grasped with any confidence. War films would have to stop! 'What to put in their place?' That was, and still is, the great question. . . . Three months before V-E Day any Hollywood production boss would have bet his shirt that the end of military action would signal a safe course for a long series of screenplays dealing with various phases of reconversion and international rehabilitation. Three months after V-E Day, the same man knew that in the absence of any clear signs, he could easily lose his shirt on any film which attempted anything like prophecy in the field of international reorganization." W. H. Mooring, "Anglo-American Film Relations: Conflict as Well as Cooperation," *Kinematograph Weekly*, 20 December 1945.

[21] The last lines of the film are, Cathy: "Poor old London." Robert: "We've just got to build it up again. Well, what does that matter? We're young!"

[22] Red Kann, "Vacation from Marriage," *Motion Picture Herald*, 1 December 1945, p. 2733.

ances were largely similar, shapeless clothing and plodding hats betraying a lack of healthy narcissism.

With the war, filmic powdering and remodeling are possible, emphasizing, as the blackout lifts, the new cultural importance of establishing gender boundaries in visual terms. The blackout signposts, first, a transition to wartime and hence to unstable sexual relations. In the "diffused eroticism" of the metaphoric dark, even affairs are possible.[23] But once the Wilsons have emerged from the blackout for the last time (as they enter the pub) their sexuality is fixed for the future in the form of Hollywoodian femininity and masculinity. Anxieties over sexuality, which had resulted from the real wartime blurring and breakdown of sexual roles, have been channeled into an acceptable form in *Perfect Strangers* in the intimation that the war has been a good thing, even though it has changed people a great deal, because it has precipitated more strongly defined, more visually verifiable monogamous heterosexuality, as well as fantastic class mobility.

BY 1945 THE blackout had evolved into a metaphor for both probity and prurience. The elegance of the trope for films about national life was that it gave credence to the fantastic within the bounds of realism, for while it stood for the nitty-gritty of wartime Britain, it simultaneously typed this experience as aberrant, temporary, and extraordinary. Through the blackout, fantasies about war could become commodities of popular culture contained within patriotism.

The blackout accrued its triple wartime status in part through the exchange of one blackness for another endemic to wartime filmgoing. In Roger Manvell's words, "The war started with closed cinemas and shaded lights, with people quiet and serious in the expectation of a new and unknown violence. When the violence did not come during the first few weeks, the cinemas were soon reopened and people learned that their need for entertainment exceeded their dislike of the black streets and unlit pavements."[24] The dark of the cinema and the social dark overlapped, so that social and textual networks bled into one another in the viewer's double experience of consuming films and fumbling through the wartime night. The cinematic blackout's power resonated for the viewer across the fields of genre, of economic and military need, of social discourse, and of private subjectivity, participating in the construction of the national subject both inside and outside the auditorium.

Brownouts, social but unlegislated responses to war, had existed in

[23] Roland Barthes, "Leaving the Movie Theater," in *The Rustle of Language*, trans. Richard Howard, p. 346.
[24] Roger Manvell, "The British Feature Film from 1940 to 1945," in Balcon et al., *Twenty Years of British Film*, p. 81.

World War I as far away as New York, but the blackout was a phenomenon specific to World War II. The noun "blackout" referred to the fabric or paint used to cut out light, and to the government regulation of blacking-out. It also designated, in an older use, the condition of being without information or news, and the temporary, complete failure of memory or loss of consciousness. In the context of flying, it referred to transient blindness resulting from centrifugal force incurred when a sudden turn was made. As a verb, it meant to obscure or obliterate, particularly light escaping from windows. *Everyman's Guide to the War Regulations* defined "blackout" as a period of time extending "from half an hour after sunset to half an hour before sunrise," and cautioned that "lights are not effectively screened unless it is impossible for an observer outside the premises to know whether the lights inside are on or off."[25]

Additional symbolic meanings accreted to the blackout during the phoney war, before air raids began. Harrisson and Madge's collection of Mass-Observers' material, *War Begins at Home*, published four months into the war, included a chapter entitled "Black-out." Several accounts here equate the last hours of peace with blackout installment:

> Gone into quicksand. Fed up with astrologers. Black-out speed-up in town. General depression. Goes to bed feeling it's a dream (man 49). Tries to read sports page, but ends up reading news. One girl does bad piece of work in mill. Immense black-out purchasing in town (man 45). Black-out purchase. Angry at price. People thought thunderstorms of night before, an air raid (man 32).[26]

Many diarists complain of adhering to blackout regulations without any evidence of enemy aggression to the British mainland, and women in particular resent the constraint of blacking-out, which prevented them from meeting friends and from going out, or staying out at night.[27] One Observer explicitly distinguishes between the male and female predicament: "To men the black-out is mainly boring, to women it is frightening."[28] A perceptive Leeds shopkeeper complained that the blackout was strategically quite unnecessary, but ideologically invaluable: it was "only done to inconvenience the public and make them realize there's a war on."[29]

[25] Evelyn Thomas, *Everyman's Guide to the War Regulations: An ABC of Essential Information for the Ordinary Citizen* (St. Albans: Donnington Press, November 1939), pp. 9 and 27.
[26] Diaries for 2 September 1939 in *Mass-Observation, War Begins at Home*, edited and arranged by Tom Harrisson and Charles Madge (London: Chatto and Windus, 1940), p. 36.
[27] Ibid., p. 190.
[28] Ibid., p. 220.
[29] Ibid., p. 190.

The blackout was a social menace, causing the total number of people killed in road accidents to rise in September 1939 by nearly one hundred percent. Other people "walked into canals, fell down steps, plunged through glass roofs and toppled from railway platforms" in the dark.[30] A poll taken in January 1940 showed that "one person in five could claim to have sustained some injury as a result of the blackout," while no one had been killed on the home front as a result of enemy action.[31] (The first home front casualty was not until April 1940, in the Orkneys.)

After 1943, when G.I.'s arrived to carry out daytime raids on the Continent, and especially after June 1944, when first the pilotless, jet-propelled V-1 aircraft and then the silent V-2 rocket missiles flew over both day and night no longer relying on sight (albeit only for a few weeks), the blackout became a symbol of the early part of the war—the worst part, from the Allied point of view.[32] In Autumn 1944, the blackout was changed to a dimout, celebrated in a Sobranie cigarette advertisement captioned "Brighter dim-out." The ad suggested taking "down the black-outs from social life," and more openly enjoying pleasures such as smoking.[33] It reinforced a developing myth that, in retrospect, the early war had been the time of most inhibition, deprivation, and constraint, an idea dramatized in the opening sequence of *Perfect Strangers*, in April 1940, when Cathy refuses to let Robert kiss her good-bye, ostensibly because of her cold. Alice McLean, a young member of the A.T.S. and also a Mass-Observer, gives a more positive version of life in the blackout. When it was changed to a dimout she vividly recounted the fervent complaints of her colleagues for whom the blackout had facilitated sexual encounters:

Lighting conditions along Knightsbridge and Kensington Road are such that the Albert Hall is now surrounded by light after being surrounded by gloom after all these years. The stretch of the pavement from the corner to the door of our billet is shining bright and completely deserted. Ever since the A.T.S. descended on this quiet Kensington backwater at the beginning of the war, countless swains of all nationalities have bidden a fond farewell to their Khaki-clad Juliets along this strip of pavement. Now the lights have gone up along this paradise, and the couples will be forced to seek some less public rendezvous for their goodnight kisses. Among many of the girls in my

[30] Calder, *The People's War*, p. 73.
[31] Ibid.
[32] V-1's were also known as buzz bombs, flying bombs, and doodlebugs.
[33] Advertisement for Sobranie cigarettes, "Brighter dim-out," *Time and Tide*, 10 March 1945, p. 212.

unit the lifting of the black-out at this particular spot is most unpopular, and they say so with feeling.[34]

Just as the blackout became a synecdoche for war, shining light figured the longed-for peace. The end of hostilities was described as the time "when the lights go up," and light bulb manufacturers eagerly fueled the new association.[35] Mazda lamps guaranteed their customers advances in domestic lighting "when the 'cease fire' sounds," while Osram promoted their bulbs by associating light with health (Figures 3.3 and 3.4). Osram's advertisement showed two small girls on rocking horses, one scowling in dim light and the other grinning in bright light. As the caption explained: "Light up—and smile! . . . Happy, healthy homes are more important now than ever. Then why not have good cheerful light? Your black-out should be all right." Royal Ediswan Lamps kept women well lit and alone at home in their advertisement (Figure 3.5). With fetal resonance, the shape of a light bulb encloses the image of the female reader while the words "Forget the Black-out Side" ring the bulb, floating in darkened surroundings pierced only by the moon. Light cocoons and protects women against the terrifying events of war, invoked in the double entendre of the phrase "Black-out Side," meaning not only the literal darkness outdoors, but also the depressing and distressing aspects of wartime life. Even Kiwi Boot Polish and Crooke's Halibut Liver Oil found ways to refer to the blackout in their advertisements. The reference enabled them both to address their customers as specifically wartime folk, and to imbricate themselves in the war effort by implying that as manufacturers they too were patriotically observing wartime measures.[36] In the Kiwi advertisement a cone of torchlight shines down on a dazzling pair of polished shoes capped by the slogan "brightest black-out!" Crooke's uses a black cat with glowing eyes to sell its product, reminding buyers that liver oil contains Vitamin A for nighttime vision.

Ghilchik used the phrase "the light is let in" to encapsulate the war's last, crepuscular phase (Figure 3.6). His cartoon contains a sketchy outline of an emaciated body huddled in a bare interior. A monumental woman personifying Truth draws the blackout curtain to expose a swastika and the

---

[34] Leonard Moseley, *Backs to the Wall: London under Fire, 1939–1945* (London: Weidenfeld and Nicholson, 1971), p. 367. Moseley does not specify the precise source of the diary, except to say that it is from a Mass-Observation report.

[35] Editorial essay, "When the Lights Go Up," *Time and Tide*, 9 October 1943, p. 1. This inverts Edward Gray's characterization of the post–World War I world as one in which "the lights go out in Europe," a reference to the end of monarchies, among other things. I am grateful to Wolfgang Schivelbusch for this comparison.

[36] Advertisement for Kiwi polish, *Picture Post*, 2 March 1940, p. 58; advertisement for Crooke's Halibut Liver Oil, *Picture Post*, 17 February 1940, p. 7.

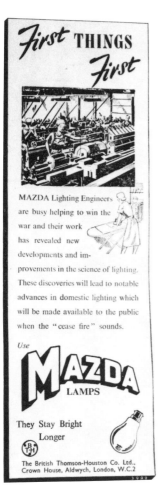

Figure 3.3. Mazda speaks of lighting improvements to women at home and in the factory. Advertisement in *Time and Tide*, 23 October 1943, p. 867.

words "horror camp" inverted on the window. With her free hand she holds up a mirror to a rotund man, himself a metaphor for the German nation, positioned not outside but within this camp. He stares incredulously at his ghastly, fanged reflection. Here the blackout curtain is a metaphor for the concealment of atrocities in the concentration camps, but it is also the interface between war and peace, and between ally and enemy. With an Allied victory (also condensed onto the massive female body) the period of news or information blackout is ended. To make an invidious comparison, this echoes the construction of Robert and Cathy's wartime experience, for only when they draw back the *Coach and Horses'* curtain as they enter the saloon is the "truth" of their attraction for one another

Light up — and smile!

The little ones are just as quick to react to bright lights and good spirits as everyone else in the house—and happy, healthy homes are more important now than ever. Then why not have good cheerful light? Your black-out should be all right. Your electricity isn't rationed. Light up then—and smile, let Baby's home be the bright and happy place it used to be. Pearl Osram Lamps, 40 and 60 watt, 1/7; 100 watt, 2/-.

Osram
A G.E.C. PRODUCT

THE WONDERFUL LAMP

Figure 3.4. Osram light bulbs contribute to the
nation's healthy future. Advertisement in *Picture Post*,
2 March 1940, p. 6.

revealed, and only then can the "aberration" of their wartime affairs be ended.

V-E Day, 8 May 1945, was celebrated in a literal blaze of light. Bonfires and fireworks, which had been illegal after dark since 1939, were lit with abandon. A Forces doctor remembered the lights of London "going on in their thousands, illuminating the public buildings and monuments. . . . There were fireworks galore . . . searchlights swept overhead . . . torches flared . . . and London, after six years of Stygian darkness, was luxuriating in an orgy of light."[37] Another recalled that "on the night of V-E Day

[37] This doctor, Dr. Rollin, added, "Nelson's column, Admiralty Arch, the National Gallery, and the palace itself glowed rose-red in the newfound light." Stephen Lock, ed., *As You Were: VE Day—A Medical Retrospective* (London: British Medical Association, 1984), p. 144.

Figure 3.5. Royal Ediswan Lamps provide an insulating womb of light for their female customers. Advertisement in *Picture Post*, 10 February 1940, p. 10.

the lights, switched on all over the city, somehow symbolized the heart of the people.''[38] Government officials used the end of blackness as ''a symbol of the successful defense of freedom.''[39] On 24 April 1945, after the last of the V-1 and V-2 sites were captured, the Speaker of the House of Commons illuminated the parliamentary tower by solemnly announcing, ''I now switch on our lantern light.''[40]

WARTIME British films are peppered with textual blackouts. They (dis)appear prominently in *The Spy in Black* (1939), *In Which We Serve* (1942), *Millions Like Us* (1943), *Two Thousand Women* (1944), *Waterloo Road* (1945), *Perfect Strangers* (1945), and *Piccadilly Incident* (1946), and even occur in the later *It Always Rains on Sundays* (1947) and *The Small Back Room* (1949), as well as in the costume melodrama *The Man in Grey* (1943). In Alberto Cavalcanti's *Went the Day Well?* (1942), a violent and chilling fantasy of German invasion, the hostage villagers finally overcome their captors when the lights fail in the church in which

[38] Ibid., p. 83.
[39] Ibid.
[40] Ibid.

133

The light is let in

Figure 3.6. The news blackout is lifted on German concentration camps. Ghilchik cartoon, "The Light is Let In," *Time and Tide*, 28 April 1945, p. 353.

they are imprisoned. The natives are more successful at maneuvering in the blackness than their enemy, a skill acquired, it is implied, through habituation to the wartime darkness. *In Which We Serve*, made and released during the worst Allied disasters, does not make explicit, verbal reference to the blackout; it is simply *there*, a commonplace of wartime life. In scenes of Walter and Kath Hardy's household, two overhead lamps draped in blackout always intrude into the top of the film frame, haunting the discussions of the three knitting and ironing women left behind, women who symbolize the nation for whom the crew of HMS *Torrin* fight. When the air raid begins, these shaded lamps jangle wildly, a visual register of the physical impact of falling bombs. The arrival of the fatal missile that will kill Kath and her mother is represented by loud booms on the sound track, but by total blackness on the screen: blacking-out is the most expedient way to represent their deaths.

The narrative blackout became increasingly able to locate a film's diegesis in the definite, albeit immediate, past, establishing in the viewer an informed sense of superiority and knowledge of the nation's recent history through remembrance of the early war. By 1944, films always refer to the blackout at the outset, as in *Perfect Strangers*, drumming up patriotic memories of difficulties overcome. This gateway separating off the earlier home front as a distinct space was often guarded by a male voice-over: Alistair Sim's in *Waterloo Road*, a judge's in *Piccadilly Incident*, an unknown patriarch's in *Millions Like Us* and *Perfect Strangers*. *Millions Like Us* begins as a male voice asks, "Remember that summer before the war?" After glimpses of peacetime life in which the main characters are introduced, a montage sequence shows doused lights on the entertainment pier, and a storefront notice warning "No black-out material. No drawing pins." The following long shot of crowds milling at a blacked-out station displaying the signs "Dieppe/Dunkirk" confirms the film's early-war diegesis. *Waterloo Road* also begins with a narrational preamble. Doctor Montgomery (Alastair Sim) reminisces about the Blitz days just as a passing steam train effects the flashback. The very next words are those of a mother arriving home with her daughter: "Take down the black-out, Ruby, while I light the stove." The spectator concludes that the women had left the house before daybreak, but the reference also provides a dark and demarcating "tunnel" through which the early war will be reexperienced in the cinema, a tunnel echoing the auditorial frame.

In the postwar film *Piccadilly Incident*, the blackout functions even more explicitly as a passageway to the past. According to Jympsom Harman, the denouement of the film was suggested to the producer in a "conversation overheard in the black-out at Piccadilly."[41] The film's credits appear over a high-angle establishing shot of traffic circulating at Piccadilly Circus around the boarded-up statue of Eros, a succinct cliché of wartime deprivation.[42] As the scene dissolves to a long shot of the Old Bailey, a "legal" voice-over sets the story in motion. With a further dissolve, this voice is synchronized to the image of a judge: "As you have heard, this case started in 1941, during the height of the Blitz. It was one of the casual things that go with that period. An incident in Piccadilly between a man and a girl."[43] The camera dollies in to the judge's face, but on the word "girl," the image dissolves to a tracking shot of running feet. They scurry

[41] Jympson Harman, "Film to Have First Radio Preview," *Evening News*, 20 July 1946.

[42] In fact, the statue of Eros, London's first aluminum statue, was removed to Egham at the outbreak of war, and only reinstalled at the Circus in 1947. In other words, the opening shot was true of 1946 when the film was released: that reminder of the war was still in place. What one sees in the film is the boarded up *base* of the fountain below the statue. See Arthur Byron, *London's Statues: A Guide to London's Outdoor Statues and Sculpture* (London: Constable Press, 1981).

[43] The opening speech starts in medias res, as follows: ". . . and excite the widest comment. This case is unusual but unfortunately not unique . . . and no legal machinery exists to meet the circumstances of this and many similar cases arising out of the war period. Until this legal defect is remedied and provision made to meet such cases, the innocent will continue to suffer the embarrassment of social stigma and even ostracism." The speech continues as quoted in my text. The film script is housed in the British Film Institute Library, London.

down a dark, urban street, incendiary flares occasionally accentuating their female nature. Suddenly the legs collide with a male pair rushing in the opposite direction, and Wren Diana Fraser (Anna Neagle) falls downward into the frame along with Captain Alan Pearson (Michael Wilding). Alan shouts, "Ow! Why don't you look where you're going?" to which Diana replies, "Why don't you?"

The impaired vision of the nighttime blackout leads to a chance "incident," a "casual thing" of "that period," which in turn generates romance (Figure 3.7). Within three days the couple will be married, but their future is fated. In a "reverse Enoch Arden" maneuver, as one reviewer put it, Diana is separated from Alan for three years, marooned on a desert island when her ship is sunk off Singapore.[44] She eventually returns to London and the tale ends with her death in one of the last V-2 raids in 1944, after Alan, who has long since given her up for dead, has married an American Red Cross worker who has borne him a son (Figure 3.8).

Figure 3.7. The couple who collide in the blackout are doomed: Wren Diana Fraser (Anna Neagle) and Captain Alan Pearson (Michael Wilding).
Piccadilly Incident, production still.

[44] *Reynolds Weekly*, 25 August 1946.

Figure 3.8. The new international family: American Red Cross worker
(Frances Mercer) marries British Captain Pearson and bears his illegitimate son.
Piccadilly Incident, production still.

While bigamy is eventually avoided through Diana's demise, the Anglo-American child will always be illegitimate.

The blackout functions not only to locate the flashback from the court undeniably in the Blitz, but also to undermine the value of the relationship established there: blackout conditions subtly justify the later loss of the heroine. In addition, the very title *Piccadilly Incident* would also have cast doubt upon the permanence and validity of the romantic liaison for a contemporary audience.[45] Charles Gillen, a G.I. stationed in Europe, remembered that G.I.s' favorite places for pickups were the pavements near Rainbow Corner, Piccadilly, the chief West End recreation center for off-duty American troops. He graphically records that "after darkness in the blackout, the pavements were a seething mass of girls and men grabbing each

[45] The cover of the book *Piccadilly Incident* (London: Book-of-the-Film Series, in World Film Series, 1946), published after the film's premiere, and after the end of the war, illustrated the couple embracing in front of the *winged* Eros. The image amounts to a further wartime indulgence and transgression, since at the time the couple were pursuing their romance, the statue was nothing but a boarded-up base.

other, shrieking, shouting, laughing and then pairing off and leaving for a Soho club or a bomb site in a back street.''[46] Further, in a draft article on streetwalking, Tom Harrisson refers to a long-extant category of prostitute as the "Piccadilly Flash" or "taxi girl."[47] Piccadilly, while at the heart of London (as commemorated in the famous World War I song), was a marginal area and an important site for blackout assignations. This wider association is additional cultural poison for Diana and Alan's fictional relationship.

The film addresses its audience as a jury that must look back from 1946 to the Blitz, and judge. As far as gender relations go, this jury should remember "that period" as an eccentric phase, a time when rapid and unwise relationships were formed in extremis, which could not later be adapted to peacetime conditions. There would always be a residue, a price to pay, symbolized in this film in rather an oblique moral as an illegitimate child of the later marriage. The film is able to mount this version of history with any clarity only because the war had already ended when it went into production. Its mythmaking is a form of demobilization.

Frank Launder cleverly inverts the strategic cleft between light and dark in *Two Thousand Women* by setting his narrative behind enemy lines inside a women's internment camp in Occupied France.[48] Blackouts and beams of light organize the narrative here too, but the rules are reversed in that this is a British enclave within axis territory—"the only British colony not inhabited by man," as one of the characters explains. Two interns, Miss Muriel Manningford (Flora Robson) and Miss Clare Meredith (Muriel Aked), throw open their windows to cast a guiding beam of light for a distressed British plane overhead. The light bulb in their room is promptly confiscated, and later both characters are sent to a camp in Germany and are never heard from again. It is their uncovering of the blackout that here is an act of patriotism. As Muriel says, "I feel we struck a blow for England tonight, in our own small way of course."

One other character in *Two Thousand Women* breaks the blackout: Rosemary Brown (Patricia Roc), an ex-singer who, as one of the British pilots puts it, "got mixed up with a married man who tried to poison his wife. Chamberlain had to fly to Munich to knock her off the front page." Rose-

---

[46] Moseley, *Backs to the Wall*, p. 290.

[47] Tom Harrisson, "Article for *Polemic*," Sussex Mass Observation Archives, file report no. 2465, p. 27. Subject index: Sexual behavior.

[48] Launder recalls: "The idea came to me through two show girls who visited Shepherd's Bush. They were escapees from the women's internment camp at Vittel, where approximately two thousand women, caught at the time of the Fall of France, were held captive. From the anecdotes they related, and their method of escape, I built the story." Geoff Brown, *Launder and Gilliat*, p. 109.

mary has been a novice since those days, burying her murky past. In the film's opening shot, set just before the Fall of France, she runs through the darkness of a French wood and out onto a road, where she lights up a signpost to find her way. French troops immediately impound her torch and arrest her in her nun's garb for "signaling to the enemy." This, we later learn, is a misinterpretation of her actions—she was actually looking for food—but the torch beams certainly signal that something is awry: her sexuality. Such spectacular lighting displays jar with religious celibacy, alerting the audience to the discrepancy between her character and her clothing. Her flashing light is the earliest sign of her active sexuality, which cannot be repressed. At the film's end Rosemary has fallen in love with a British pilot, having decided never to take her vows.

It is possible to argue that all British films made at this time, realist or otherwise, probed the war's effect on gender roles through the blackout trope. Even the costume melodrama *The Wicked Lady*, Gainsborough Studios' 1946 box office winner in which Lady Barbara Skelton (Margaret Lockwood) plays a noblewoman by day and a masked, armed highway robber by night, invokes wartime optics (Figure 3.9). Because of her com-

Figure 3.9. The armed woman: Lady Barbara Skelton (Margaret Lockwood) confronts wartime audiences. *The Wicked Lady*, production still.

139

petence and daring, her mask, and the darkness, Captain Jackson (James Mason) mistakes her for a man when he finds her conducting a holdup on his terrain. When Barbara uncovers her face back at the Leaping Stag he is shocked to find "it's a skirt we have in the saddle!" Of course, misrecognizing sexes in disguise is a recurring cultural motif with a long theatrical and literary history, but in *The Wicked Lady*, ostensibly set in the age of Charles II, a *wartime* issue is textually inscribed through the lighting code. A woman acquires masculine talents, and consequently loosens her ties to femininity under cover of darkness, which in the contemporary cultural vocabulary has come to stand for the conditions of war in which real women do indeed carry out tasks traditionally performed by men. The fantasy the film entertains is that women wield guns—a prohibited act, for while women guided the searchlight beams, men released the ack-ack fire. The choice of an era in which male and female costumes were similar (albeit ornate) in style, just as in World War II, the attenuation of historical markers in darkness, and the wartime associations of night all compound the film's effectiveness in addressing contemporary experience through a campy camouflage, all qualities contributing to its immense box office popularity.[49]

The memory of the blackout still resonates in *It Always Rains on Sunday*, released and set in 1947. Domestic crisis sets in when Rose Sandigate, a London mother, goes out to the Anderson Shelter for some blackout material to patch a broken window.[50] In the dark hut, defunct vis-à-vis air raids but now a makeshift garden shed, she is surprised by escaped convict Tommy Swann, who was once her fiancé, before the war. It is the revival of this romance, linked narratively and visually to the blackout, that threatens the Sandigates' postwar family life. The film ends with Tommy Swann's death and Rose's repentant reconciliation with her husband after her failed suicide attempt.

The efficacy of the blackout metaphor was recognized in Hollywood, too, where it was used to emphasize spatial rather than temporal displacement. British films never included the term "blackout" within their titles,

---

[49] Sue Harper has convincingly argued that the film also draws contemporary analogies "in the area of sexual pleasure" by staging the only visually explicit sexual scene by a river, a location "stripped of any historicising mise-en-scène." Sue Harper, "Historical Pleasures: Gainsborough Costume Melodrama," in Christine Gledhill, ed., *Home Is Where the Heart Is: Studies in Melodrama and the Woman's Film* (London: British Film Institute Publishing, 1987), p. 180.

[50] Anderson Shelters were named after Sir John Anderson, Home Secretary and Minister of Home Security at the outbreak of war. One and a half million of them were issued to protect against air raids. Rose refers to it simply as "the Anderson," counting on the recent memories of the audience.

and American films were retitled to avoid its use: *The London Blackout Murders* became *Secret Motive*, and the film's release was delayed in Britain. *Pacific Blackout* (1942) stayed the same, presumably because the adjective ensured a remote location. *They Met in the Dark* (1943) was the closest British cinema came to verbal advertisement of a film through association with the blackout. Hollywood, however, retitled *Contraband*, *Blackout*, and used early references to the blackout to transport American spectators across the Atlantic to London in *Ministry of Fear* (1944), *Tonight and Every Night* (1945), and *To Each His Own* (1946), among other films.

The latter film opens with a leftward panning shot of a rowdy nighttime crowd. A superimposed text introduces "Miss Norris . . . a middle-aged American woman, walking down a London Street on a blacked-out New Year's Eve." Carrying her tin hat, she clumps along until a G.I. shines a torch directly into her eyes, revealing her to be Olivia de Havilland, the star promised in the credits. Her clipped reprimand, "Put that light out!" initiates the film's dialogue track but extinguishes her image: Britain's national need cancels the radiance of stardom for a moment. In *Tonight and Every Night*, the dancer Tommy Lawson beams a flashlight to illuminate his London theater's blacked-out neon sign. When the warden shouts, "Put that light out! Don't you know there's a war on?" Tommy apologizes, explaining, "I just wanted to see our name in lights," a satisfaction also suspended for Britons in the emergency. Immediately afterward Tommy fails the Forces eye test [!] and so remains a dancer. In a subsequent scene three R.A.F. members accompanied by a G.I. approach the theater; the American complains, "It's hard to get your bearings in this bottle of ink." The U.S. audience is again entertained with the peculiarities of British lighting, to which American G.I.'s had to adapt.

In *Ministry of Fear* the last few minutes before blackout time coincide with the first few moments of freedom for Steve Neale (Ray Milland). The film opens with a pan to the right across a clockface showing 6:00 p.m.— a time close to blackout—past a window of fading evening light, and then through a slow reverse pan back to Neale, who is being released from an asylum. Neale does not heed the warden's warning against going to London, which is "being heavily bombed." Biding time before catching a train to the city, he ambles toward the local fair, where he will win a fateful cake. A woman hurries by with a group of children, urging, "Come along. Getting on to blackout time." Cake in hand, Neale returns to the station and enters a blacked-out railway carriage as the stationmaster barks, "There's no reading with them 'dimout' lights." A Nazi criminal, pretending to be blind, joins Neale in the carriage. He mutters, "It seems strange to hear people tell of the blackout. I guess I'm better off than most at getting about in the dark.'' As Neale looks down to cut and share his prize, the spy brains him with his white cane, literally blacking him out. He absconds with the cake, which is later revealed to have contained secret information.[51]

These American films introduce England, and specifically London, as the site of the blackout, a place where human relations are unpredictable, confused, or deceptive, and where ''normal'' social exchange is impossible. Blind men see, and the seeing are blinded. The repeated motif of dazzling a character with torchlight works as a visual and narrative cliché, reinforcing, by redundancy, the restrictions on vision that protection of the nation necessitated.

IN DISCUSSING *Perfect Strangers* I argued that while the technique of blacking-out was initially deployed in defense of the national boundary, it came to encapsulate the wartime destabilization of gender roles in cultural representation. In an exemplary case of the way sexual and national differences are reciprocally eroded and constructed in wartime, the shoring up of national identity through the blackout jeopardized the representability of sexual difference. A sample of other wartime artifacts—two cartoons, a dance, an official poster, an article illustration, and an advertisement— demonstrate further how these two sets of differences displace and shift in relation to one another, and emphasize once more the importance of archival investigations of gender construction in the cinema and other media.

The two cartoons were published in *Punch*, the conservative weekly magazine aimed primarily at a middle-class, male audience. They present cinema-going as a leisure activity for couples, and, as mentioned in Chapter 1, this was indeed the main available form of leisure in wartime. ''Let's Go to the Pictures'' illustrates, in sixteen frames accompanied by captions, the potential of darkness for sexual mix-up (Figure 3.10).[52] A couple enters a blacked-out auditorium and looks for a seat, but as the man's eyes grow accustomed to the dark, he realizes he has sat among ''Perfect Strangers.'' The eleven central frames, which mark the couple's progress, are entirely black except for small splashes of white light, conflations of the projection

---

[51] A series of further misfortunes befall Neale, until the film closes as he forms a happy bond with the leading lady in an ''explosion of light,'' as Vernet describes it. The print I have studied does not end in this way, but with the couple driving along in a breezy convertible. See Marc Vernet, ''Blinking, Flickering and Flashing of the Black-and-White Film,'' in Theresa Hak Kyung Cha, ed., *Apparatus, Cinematographic Apparatus: Selected Writings* (New York: Tanam Press, 1980), p. 368.

[52] Cartoon by Fougasse, ''Let's Go to the Pictures,'' *Punch*, 27 August 1941, p. 183. Fougasse (meaning a small, unpredictable land mine in World War I) was the pseudonym of Cyril Kenneth Bird. He worked throughout the Second World War designing books, pamphlets, advertisements, posters, and, interestingly in view of this example, a film strip.

LET'S GO TO THE PICTURES.

" Here we are . . .

through this door . . .

and—look out, there's a step. . . .

Better keep perfectly still till we get . . .

accustomed to——look, there's a light ! . . .

There it is—I think it wants our tickets. . . .

Now it's away again— wants us to follow it. . . .

Oh, I'm so sorry—I say, there's a body here . . .

and—oo, look out, there's a sheer precipice on our right ! . . .

Now where's the light ? Great Cæsar, it's right below us—oops, steady !

Hullo, that's someone's hat—I seem to be in among a lot of people and feet and . . .

coats and umbrellas and —so sorry—faces . . .

and—ah, here we are : an empty seat . . . .

and the darkness really does seem to be getting better. . . .

I shall soon be able to . . .

see where—Good Heavens, I'm among PERFECT STRANGERS ! ! ! !*"*

Figure 3.10. The cinema doubles wartime blackness. Cartoon by Fougasse, ''Let's Go to the Pictures,'' *Punch*, 27 August 1941, p. 183.

beam and the usher's flashlight, and resonant of the wartime night. "I think it wants our tickets," remarks the cinema-goer on seeing the usher's lit hand, emphasizing the fact that in the dark, people are genderless or of unidentifiable gender. In the cinema auditorium the sound track can keep these differences intact, soldering the textual, sexual identities together in adversity: the human voice rather than the human body becomes the primary signifier of gender. In this cartoon, however, in which there is no sound track, no gendered voice, and, temporarily, no human image, the splash of flashlight conceals the body beyond, and the owner of the beam is culturally neutered.

Like Korda's version of "Perfect Strangers," this cartoon describes the disorientation of sight deprivation in socio-sexual terms: it pictures the risk, even likelihood, of losing your partner and ending up with a stranger. The cartoon displaces the real erosion of gender categories onto the fictional space of moviegoing. Two years later, in 1943, just before the Allied North African victory at El Alamein, Fougasse used the motif of frames in the cinema again, and told once more the story of mis-recognition in the dark, across six frames, only this time it was of the film itself.[53] The couple creep into the murky auditorium, silhouetted in front of the lit screen. As their eyes adjust, and as they begin to assemble the narrative, they realize that, in a double bill, they have mistakenly caught the tail end of the film they came for, and have paid for the whole of the film they wanted to avoid. In playing on the misfortune of being "in the dark" about the film, the cartoon doubles "blacknesses"—that of the theater with that of perception. In fact, both cartoons pun on the relation between the theater dark and the cultural equation of sight with knowledge: in a medium in which the only senses deployed are seeing and hearing, the comprehension of both gender and narrative are at risk without light.

A wartime poster printed in red and black on white, for the Royal Society for the Prevention of Accidents, amplifies the blackout's relation to sexuality (Figure 3.11). Mostly dark but for two pools of white light, the surrealist imagery of this poster fetishizes a pair of parted, rouged, somewhat Grecian lips, and a high-heeled shoe. The poster cautions, "Wait! Count 15 Slowly before Moving in the Black-out." Since it includes the image of parts of a woman, the poster might address those wartime women described by female Mass-Observers who were frightened to venture abroad at night. However, I would suggest that this poster is addressed to men. The kind of accident envisaged here is sexual seduction of a male by this shady, dismembered woman, somewhere along the circling, dashed red line that connects her scarlet lips and sexualized foot. The meaning of the lit circle around her foot slides across two registers: is it the beam from

[53] Cartoon by Fougasse, "As Far as I Can Make Out," *Punch*, 7 April 1943, p. 287.

Figure 3.11. The erotic potential of the blackout.
Poster designed by G. R. Morris for the Royal Society for
the Prevention of Accidents, circa 1940.

a personal flashlight, a commonplace of wartime equipment, or the icon of
the prostitute's lamplight? In the process of cautioning citizens on blackout
behavior, the poster discloses the wartime night as an eroticized, hypnotic
space, one that shares those properties Barthes, Pasolini, Kristeva, and
many other writers attribute to the cinema auditorium.

Wrens had to wear "blackouts," their nickname for regulation black
underwear, for attending dances aboard Royal Navy ships, presumably to
deter sexual encounters. This name again associates the wartime pitch with
eroticism, if only by censorship.[54] The first new dance of the war depends

---

[54] Paul Fussell, *Wartime: Understanding and Behavior in the Second World War* (London: Oxford University Press, 1989), p. 108.

145

on the sexual energy of wartime darkness outright. Playing from late November 1939, the routine of the "Blackout Stroll" had only four simple positions, and, as the exploitation sheet explained, anyone who could walk could dance it:

At the end of the second chorus, the lights dim and those who wish, turn and find a new partner. It's just like walking up the street in the black-out—you might meet anybody. But this time it's gay and bright, and dancers have an opportunity of meeting new friends, while enjoying themselves in the gaiety of the dance.[55]

The events of the dance echoed, but tamed and contained, disturbances in the sphere of wartime sexuality. It licensed revelers to pursue their fantasies in a socially acceptable form. New romantic encounters were limited to brief exchanges after choruses, in dimmed light rather than full black-out, after which the lighting was made "gay and bright" again. By incorporating the threat of wartime promiscuity into a social event, a sense of community and national unity is promoted while the very real tensions and excitements of the wartime night are diffused.

The publicity sheet for the dance perpetuated a memory of peacetime gendered divisions of sight—the division between male looking and female appearance—by noting the advantages plain women might derive from the selection of partners in the dark: "You ladies called 'wall-flowers,' fated to sit out all the dances, because perhaps your face isn't your fortune, or you aren't too good a dancer, or your figure isn't the cuddly kind . . . HERE'S YOUR CHANCE TO DANCE THE 'BLACKOUT STROLL,' LONDON'S LATEST STEP IS YOUR GODSEND."[56] These sentences paper over the ideological clash between wartime patriotism and traditional notions of femininity. The war demanded attention to communal rather than individual matters. Private labor for a public appearance of effortless feminine loveliness had to be officially de-emphasized; the toning down of artificial female beauty often functioned as visible evidence in cultural representation that a woman was doing her patriotic duty, as discussed in Chapter 2.

However, many wartime texts betray a fear of the consequences of a de-emphasis on female appearance, of the validation of women's social role

[55] Mass-Observation, *War Begins at Home*, p. 231.
[56] Mass-Observation, *War Begins at Home*, p. 231. Tommy Connor's lyrics to the dance were: "There's no more cuddling in the moonlight, / There's no more petting in the park. / But why let's worry over moonlight? / For when we're strolling in the dark IT'S LOVELY. / Everybody do the 'Blackout Stroll'; / Laugh and drive your cares right up the pole. / Whisper 'see ya later' to your baby doll, / For now we change our partners in the 'Blackout Stroll.' "

on the basis of other criteria—those reserved for men—which would and do lead to a breakdown of the structures that maintain sexual difference. Some texts construct the blackout as a direct threat to conventional femininity. In *Piccadilly Incident*, for instance, Bill, abandoned on the tropical island with Diana, woos her with assurances that he would not be distracted by any newfangled woman—"a blonde, a not-so-blonde, nor a blacked-right-out."[57] A *Picture Post* article on "Shelter Life," written as if seen by a "Martian," describes the "strangest sight in London—strangest scene of all our time" (Figure 3.12).[58] The article reflects on the fate of the nuclear family during the Blitz: "Here all one's life is public. Privacy, so highly cherished by Britons, is gone. . . . Here nothing is inti-

Figure 3.12. Maintaining femininity underground.
Picture Post, 26 October 1940.

[57] *Piccadilly Incident* (London: Book-of-the-Film Series, in World Film Series, 1946), p. 26.
[58] Anonymous, "Shelter Life," *Picture Post*, 26 October 1940, p. 9.

mate. One talks, eats, sleeps, lives with a hundred, a thousand others.'' The ''strangest sight'' is that of a young woman applying makeup in an underground passageway, ignoring the bodies collected around her. A woman applying her mask of femininity represents metonymically all those other activities that the British would prefer to perform in private. But this one *must* be shown to be taking place, must be photographed, despite the Blitz, for wearing makeup is one of the most culturally embedded signifiers of sexual difference. The image of this woman looking in the mirror reassures the reader that femininity *is* innate, that even in total war a woman is compelled to consume makeup and ''do'' her face.

A contemporary *Picture Post* promotion for toilet soap invokes the blackout to accuse women of slipping in their duty of maintaining femininity, which, of course, if innate should require no effort at all. Below the caption the text reads: ''Cause of Ugly Skin Seen in BLACK-OUT TEST'' (Figure 3.13).[59] On closer inspection, the message female readers are given is that those among them not putting enough maintenance into their appearance will be obvious even in the wartime gloom. The test is to remove an application of luminous makeup supplied by the manufacturers. If using a toilet soap other than that being promoted, makeup traces will remain on the face; these will then light up as a telltale ''shine in the dark.'' This failure in female responsibility amounts to collaboration with the enemy, an assistance of his navigation through the glow of her untended visage. Patriotism for women means washing with a particular brand of soap.

In this convoluted attempt to sell toiletries, women are told that even in the dark they can be seen. Capitalism needs to preserve the importance of woman's image in the face of her wartime actions. Familiar definitions of male and female roles, in which men look and women appear, as John Berger succinctly wrote, are commensurate with the profit motive. But if

[59] Soap advertisement: ''The Girl Who Shines in the Dark,'' *Picture Post*, 2 November 1940. The rest of the caption reads: ''You see above a picture of a girl as she appeared in a darkened room under an ultra-violet ray lamp. This is what happened before the picture was made. First, she used vanishing cream and powder to which a luminous substance had been added. Under the ultra-violet ray lamp, her whole face glowed. Then, she washed her face with ordinary toilet soap in the usual way, and was seated under the lamp again. The photograph above shows what she looked like. Traces of make-up were seen in many places on her skin. Beauty experts say that ordinary face-washing too often fails to get the skin clean and the dirt left behind soon clogs the pores, causing a dull, pasty complexion. But when the girl in the test above used the luminous make-up again and washed her face as before, but with Lux Toilet Soap this time, there was no make-up left on her skin. Her face was completely clean. The technical explanation is: the quick and abundant lather of Lux Toilet Soap is 'active.' Only this active lather can remove make-up, stale powder and the dust which gets clogged in it. That is why Lux Toilet Soap is able to keep the complexion so clear and smooth.''

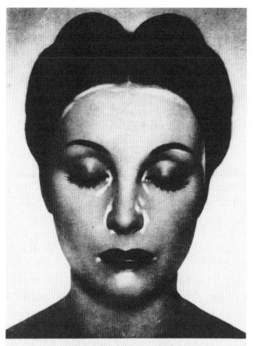

The Girl Who Shines in the Dark

After using luminous make-up, this girl washed her face with ordinary toilet soap. She thought her face was clean, but in the dark it looked like this, showing cream and powder in many places on her skin. It's this kind of face-washing, done day after day, that gives so many girls dull, pasty complexions spoiled by ugly blemishes.

Figure 3.13. Lapses in female toiletry assist enemy navigation. *Picture Post*, 2 November 1940, p. 40.

the war is symbolized through the blackout, as here, surely woman's attention to her visual appearance becomes irrelevant and unnecessary since, metaphorically at least, the entire visual register has been lost; the looker/looked-at relation has expired in the dark. In its struggle to repair the economic havoc this will wreak, this advertisement is forced to invoke the enemy's hidden gaze to sell its product, just as the government must in inspiring citizens to obey its blackout regulation. Both the advertisement and government propaganda incriminate the unauthorized voyeur, the aerial enemy, to whom the cinema spectator is cousin.

THE WARTIME crisis produced conditions of vision never again to be repeated. Even by the end of World War II, military technology had advanced to the point at which the blackout no longer served a strategic purpose: pilotless missiles reached their targets without human eyes. These extreme circumstances infected all cultural codes of looking, including those of cinema-going.

In wartime Britain the government legislated axes of sight by controlling lighting. Under this new arrangement the most crucial demarcation was between private and public looking, activities that operated at literal right angles to one another. At ground level, interpersonal, horizontally directed viewing at night was severely curtailed. Individual torch lamps had to be pointed downward, car headlamps were shuttered, windows were blocked off, neon signs were extinguished. A fashion sprang up for large white organdy collars attachable to women's dresses, in response to this new, dangerous invisibility of the body, and there was a run on white canes, normally the province of the blind.[60] The only external illuminations allowed were the swaying vertical searchlights turned on during raids to track planes slated for destruction by ack-ack fire, as dramatically restaged in *The Gentle Sex*.[61] The success of the state-controlled vertical system of looking depended on the suppression of the horizontal, private realm. This was the only way to eliminate the specter of the returned look from the nighttime sky, the only way to deny the enemies' perpendicular, vertical gaze, a gaze that hid under cover of darkness and thrived on the slips of citizens beneath. To be fanciful, when lights burned below it was as if the nation became a vast cinema screen, vulnerable to consumption. The scarcity of aerial views of the country in British wartime films, discussed in Chapter 1, is a corollary of this visual reorganization: there maps did the job of picturing the territory without giving form to this threatening, omniscient bird's-eye view.

The daily darkening and undarkening of windows in wartime constituted a peculiar form of government intrusion into everyone's lives, amounting to an orchestration and manipulation of spectacle and private vision. The only place where seeing in darkness was permitted was inside the cinema auditorium, where the display of horizontally beamed patterns of light and dark were firmly sealed off from the military, vertical display staged every wartime night. However, the meaning of the latter infected the former, and vice versa. The film spectator's pleasure of viewing unseen in the dark—a voyeuristic pleasure as has been so often noted—was refracted through the

[60] Wolfgang Schivelbusch drew my attention to these alterations in fashion.

[61] The romantic couple dwarfed by searchlights was a recurring wartime image. We see it in *Perfect Strangers* as Robert and Cathy return home, and in *The Gentle Sex* in the form of a postcard received by Maggie Fraser from her Scottish corporal. The card shows the backs of a couple sitting together on a bench, the searchlights beaming upward beyond them. The postcard's fitting caption is "New Light on an Old Subject."

prism of wartime in such a way as to give a heightened consiousness of that pleasure, precisely because it was banned outside. In more specific terms, the synecdoche of the blackout forced the spectator to recall extra-cinematic experience while simultaneously encountering the fictional screen world: the figure of the blackout reproduced the conditions of film viewing, but also worked to remind the spectator of war—in short, to mobilize her. This combination of a necessary recollection of reality and a sanctioned experience of fantasy (of viewing horizontal light shows in the dark) makes wartime film spectatorship exemplary of spectatorship in general. It throws into relief cinema's general contradictory habit of invoking reality while staging a fiction.

In his article "The Apparatus," Jean-Louis Baudry explores this capacity of cinema. He describes the cinema as a place that transforms perception into a quasi-hallucination; in the cinema we perceive, but it is a perception of images, or, to quote Baudry, "a real perception takes place in the cinema, if not an ordinary perception of reality."[62] He further suggests that the physical conditions of cinema-going—"The darkness of the movie theater, the relative passivity of the situation, the forced immobility of the ciné-subject, and the effects which result from the projection of images, moving images"—produce in the spectator a pleasurable state of artificial regression, reminiscent of infant experience in which reality was "enveloping" and there was a lack of differentiation between subject and environment.[63] Because in the cinema, as opposed to during every other waking adult experience, the separation of the spectator's body from the exterior world (including the screen world) is not well defined, argues Baudry, the spectator is less conscious of the obvious discrepancy between reality and the two-dimensional screen supporting projected images. This leads to a "partial elimination of the reality test" by the spectator—only partial because films are not dreams or hallucinations, those most powerful of fantasies because they appeared to *be* reality.[64] Baudry reminds us that spectators willingly go to the cinema and partially suspend their disbelief; "the subject has always the choice to close his eyes, to withdraw from the spectacle, or to leave," unlike during the dream state.[65]

Baudry's thesis is appealing as an explanation for cinema attendance reaching an all time high during the war in Britain. It was horrible being a wartime adult; the condition was accompanied by immense fear and guilt,

[62] Jean-Louis Baudry, "The Apparatus," trans. Bertrand Augst and Jean Andrews, *Camera Obscura* 1, no. 1 (Fall 1976): 123. I am grateful to Richard Allen for discussions we had on this section of the chapter.

[63] Ibid., p. 119.

[64] Ibid., p. 120.

[65] Ibid.

hence those images of young children, and unanswered questions to them, in the films of the later war that I have discussed in Chapter 1. How soothing was the cinema if it provided an escape to the relatively unburdened life of infancy. A less controversial aspect of Baudry's argument, and one that has broader explanatory power, is his account of the dual nature of film spectatorship. This duality was dramatized by the condition of war. If the cinema was a site of psychic regression, it also functioned to remind the spectator of his or her particular, and critical, historical place. Above all because of shifts in the meaning of light, dark, and vision in wartime, the film spectator never fully forgot her existence in front of the screen, and before and after the show, while she also took special delight in the sanctioned light displays in the dark.

Wartime audiences viewed with a heightened sensitivity to optical politics, and a heightened awareness of cinema's precise function of providing a cultural place for fantasies and for instruction. The danger of light display outside the cinema was well known to this new, mobilized spectator—outside the cinema the enemy might be watching too, and this could result not only in the loss of an individual, but in the loss of the nation too. To look unseen, in wartime, was now to be a fifth columnist. To scatter light in the external darkness was to be a collaborator, or to invite sexual attention which, for women, according to cultural representation, amounted to the same thing. Such rearrangements in the connotations of vision ricochet through wartime film images, so that diegetic light cones take on a new criminal and sexual significance. In the diegetic blackout, at ground level, the flash of a torchlight gives visual form to a character's look. Light metonymically signals looking, foreclosing the possibility of a concealed voyeurism in the dark. A fictional character can no longer see in blackness without indicating that she is looking: she has to illuminate that which she sees.

These new cultural codes, produced through the peculiar, universal experience of the wartime blackout, illuminate the spectator's understanding of his or her activity. Caught in the beam of wartime, the cinema spectator becomes acutely aware of being an authorized voyeur, of looking unseen in the dark in the only place it is legally possible; outside, this activity had become the prerogative of the enemy, of the spy. Cinema's voyeuristic pleasures became intensified by this recognition; the vast numbers of wartime cinema viewers delighted precisely in being fifth columnists, truly appreciating, for the duration of the war (of the blackout), the unique power of the cinema.

Processing History: The Timing of a *Brief Encounter*

We have all made up our minds . . . that we
are not simply going back to the so-called peace and
civilization of 1939. If it really is the case
that wars are turning points between epochs,
then we are standing on the threshold of
a new epoch whose character we have yet
to discover—or, better still, create.

Editorial, *Britain Today*, July 1945

The concept of a ''woman's film'' and
''woman's fiction'' as a separate category of art . . .
does not exist in Europe. . . . *Brief Encounter*
and *The Seventh Veil* are not without their
soap opera elements, but they are on a slightly
higher plane than their American counterparts.

Molly Haskell, *From Reverence to Rape*

THE AMERICAN film *Mildred Pierce* (Curtiz, 1945) has become a canonical text for feminist film criticism. In perhaps the best known article about it, Pam Cook describes the abutment of two conflicting genres in the film—melodrama and film noir—and argues that switches between their styles, and between the past and the present, demonstrate that ''the ideological work of the film is to articulate the necessity of the drawing of boundaries and to encourage the acceptance of the repression which the establishment of such order entails.''[1] The most important boundary, formally embedded as genre and temporal distinction, is that which maintains the sexual division of labor. In the case of *Mildred Pierce* it is a question of encircling the category motherhood, to work for a new clarity of that term.

[1] Pam Cook, ''Duplicity in Mildred Pierce,'' in E. Ann Kaplan, ed., *Women in Film Noir* (London: British Film Institute Publishing, 1978), p. 68.

The problem in wartime, as both Mary Ann Doane and Linda Williams have pointed out, is that the very idea of motherhood becomes a "fractured concept" through exactly the kind of reorganization of sexual roles that *Mildred Pierce* dramatizes.[2] On closer inspection of the film, we see that the contrast between melodramatic and film noir lighting styles is in fact far from distinct, but instead breaks down as the narrative develops, noir imagery seeping into the increasingly recent past. It is the *failure* of boundary maintenance that is expressed through the lighting code, for *Mildred Pierce* has bitten off more than it can chew and is finally unable to resolve the contradictions between the cultural ideal of motherhood and the demands that 1945 makes upon it. *Brief Encounter*, released in the same month as *Mildred Pierce*—December 1945—finds itself grappling with a similar conflict.

In an essay that ranges across a panoply of historical and mythological texts, ancient and modern, Nancy Huston describes the "striking equivalence" of maternal and military service. She reminds us of the mutual exclusiveness of these "jobs," each being the particular preserve of one of the sexes: "It is the act of giving birth itself which is considered to be profoundly incompatible with the act of dealing death."[3] Huston is describing the same kind of division as Cook, a gendered division between the public and the domestic. While this division has historically been at its most conspicuous in times of war, the conditions of 1939–45, of total war, were to have the reverse effect, questioning and undermining the separateness of military and maternal service.

The British War Office refused to conscript mothers outright, but nevertheless pulled them explicitly out of the traditional maternal orbit. (The rising practices of contraception and conscientious objection were to further erode the distinction between male destructive and female reproductive spheres.)[4] Maternal wartime service in Britain diverged conspicuously from the ideal. As more women worked at a distance from home, and many middle-class women worked for the first time, the government began to provide nurseries, thereby relieving mothers of a burden central to ideal motherhood.[5] Family feeding and caring were upset by rationing and bombing. Mothers (and fathers) lost children through evacuation, drafting, enemy action, and by being forced, by the difficulty of daily conditions as

---

[2] Doane, *The Desire to Desire*, p. 78; Linda Williams, "Feminist Film Theory: *Mildred Pierce* and the Second World War," in E. Deidre Pribram, ed., *Female Spectators: Looking at Film and Television* (New York: Verso, 1988), pp. 12–30.

[3] Huston, "The Matrix of War," pp. 153 and 162.

[4] Huston, "The Matrix of War," p. 168.

[5] Denise Riley, " 'The Free Mothers': Pronatalism and Working Women in Industry at the End of the Last War in Britain," *History Workshop Journal* 11 (Spring 1981): 59–118.

a single parent, to give them away for fostering. Such cleavages from the maternal ideal are strewn through contemporary advertising: health tonic and vitamin slogans swelled the pages of *Picture Post*, addressed to older married women suffering "Separation, Darkness, Loneliness, Money Worries."[6] Wincarnis Tonic claimed to build up stamina against "the war on women's nerves."[7]

Besides the syndrome of "the double life," discussed in Chapter 2, rising illegitimacy tarnished traditional conceits of female sexuality. War prevented many births from being legalized through marriage during pregnancy, and the illegitimate birthrate almost doubled between 1940 and 1945 (whereas seventy percent of illegal conceptions were regularized before the war, only thirty-seven percent were in 1945). In addition, a Birmingham Health Officer observed from his local survey, "during the last two years of the war one third of all illegitimate children in the city were born to married women."[8] These changes were accompanied by a soaring divorce rate: in the years 1936 to 1938, 22,188 petitions were filed, as against 60,294 in 1943–45. Of these, fifty-eight percent were filed by husbands, and seventy percent of those on grounds of adultery. The married woman as icon of "decency and stability" was no more.[9]

While illegitimacy was increasing, the total birthrate was dropping. The ensuing climate of pronatalist opinion lead to prompt closure of government nurseries at the end of the war, and to the introduction of the 1945 Family Allowances Act by which mothers received weekly monies for their second and subsequent children. Denise Riley describes the "odd twilight" of the immediate postwar years in which the expression "free mothers" referred both to the right of mothers of the Free Nations to be freer of the drudgery of home responsibilities, and to the idea that this should only be in order to be better at the job of motherhood.[10]

This is the history to which David Lean's *Brief Encounter* inevitably belonged as it presented a mother's choice between emotional and sexual fulfillment outside marriage, and obligation to her husband and family: a choice between risk and security. The film describes the affair of Laura Jesson, a middle-aged, middle-class housewife and mother, and Alec Harvey, a middle-aged, married doctor. His class comes with his profession, hers with her marriage, while their dress and accents support their class

---

[6] Advertisement for "Wincarnis Quick Action Tonic," *Picture Post*, 10 February 1940, p. 10.

[7] Ibid.

[8] Ferguson and Fitzgerald, *Studies in the Social Services*, p. 98.

[9] Riley, " 'The Free Mothers,' " p. 65. Riley describes the married female factory worker in these words vis-à-vis single women on the same job.

[10] Riley, " 'The Free Mothers,' " pp. 60 and 63.

position in both cases. Their relationship develops from a chance meeting one Thursday in Milford, their local, unremarkable market town. After five weeks of Thursday rendezvous the couple are riven with guilt, though they have not technically become lovers, their only opportunity for sexual intimacy having been disrupted by the return of Alec's colleague Stephen to his flat. Discovered, the couple agrees to part forever. The film ends as Alec leaves to move his family to a new medical post in distant Johannesburg, while Laura returns to her husband, Fred, described by her (in contrast to his counterpart, Mrs. Madeleine Harvey) as "kindly, unemotional and not delicate at all."[11]

Brief Encounter and *Mildred Pierce* both take on motherhood and female identity in the wake of war. Both stories are told as a sequence of flashbacks, introduced by a female voice-over and interrupted periodically by the diegetic present. The central characters, Laura and Mildred, have two children each. Mildred's younger daughter, Kay, dies of pneumonia after Mildred returns from committing adultery, whereas Laura's son Bobbie is only mildly concussed while she is away merely contemplating an affair. Furthermore, Laura explicitly recognizes Bobbie's accident as "punishment," whereas Mildred does not openly register that she has "killed" her daughter through her liaison. Earlier in the film, Bobbie is otherwise healthy, but Kay already has a cough, which is aggravated by Mildred's romance. The connection is made ironically when Mildred's lover Monty says, "You take my breath away," as he and Mildred relax at his beachhouse while Kay's young life is dangling in an oxygen tent, back at Mrs. Biederhof's, a "friend" of Mildred's husband.

Laura and Alec declare their love in a boathouse rather than a beachhouse, but it is similar in being a watery, informal location where family ties are loosened and privacy is more readily available. Mildred actually divorces her first husband, Bert, halfway through *Mildred Pierce*, and becomes a successful breadwinner, while Laura just leaves her husband on Thursdays and has no obvious means of support besides his income. She lacks the economic independence to underwrite her affair, nor has she any dependable friends equivalent to Mildred's Ida: her female acquaintances are gossips and flirts.

Mildred marries Monty, who is then murdered by her elder daughter, and ends up back with Bert. Alec, in *Brief Encounter*, survives the film

---

[11] *Brief Encounter*'s scenario lives on. Its successors include *Passionate Friends*, a 1948 film that restars Trevor Howard, with Ann Todd, and *Staying On*, set in India, restarring both Johnson and Howard and thus almost playing out a fantasy ending of *Brief Encounter*— that Laura followed Alec to a new continent. In *Falling in Love* (1984), two middle-class characters, played by Meryl Streep and Robert de Niro, unexpectedly fall in love on a Connecticut commuter train.

but emigrates to Africa, leaving Laura still with Fred. Both women contemplate suicide, and by similar methods: plunging off a railway platform (Laura) and a bridge (Mildred). Laura desires to end her life in desperation over the loss of Alec, Mildred because she has discovered her daughter's crime. Both women finally return to their unexciting husbands, and the suburbs, for the continuity and normalcy they represent, and because, in the films' terms, there is no other alternative.

I do not mean to collapse the differences between the two films. *Brief Encounter*'s engagement with the middle-class woman's bind is magnified because Laura is not only married but has children, but the theme of mothering is far more important in *Mildred Pierce*. The events of the latter film are more extreme, supported by more radical switchings between visual styles and more severe punishment of Mildred—the loss of her entire family and career. There are other significant stylistic and thematic differences: Mildred's voice-over takes the form of an explanation for the police, not a private but unheard confession to her husband, as is Laura's in *Brief Encounter*. A policeman has to scold Mildred away from suicide, while Laura cannot, in the end, bring herself to take her life—she backs away from the platform without assistance. *Brief Encounter* exhibits a variety of high- and low-key lighting styles, like *Mildred Pierce*, but these work not to mark off distinct genre categories but to contribute to the imbrication of fantasy and realist elements within the presentation of a woman's memory.

Such comparison of two films reminds us that specificity of socio-cultural and national milieu militates against the assignation of fixed meanings to aesthetic codes: these films share a historical moment, but different national spaces. *Mildred Pierce* and *Brief Encounter* are simultaneously produced accounts of a mother's experience, arising in an era in which the iconography of motherhood is sorely unable to reconcile the forces circulating around and within it. The question here must be to what extent differences between the two films can be understood as consequences of different local wartime needs and pressures.

SEVERAL feminists have noted the inability of aesthetic forms to image a mother as "something else besides a mother."[12] The sexual mother has always lacked a secure iconography, because she occupies such an intricate complex of social positions. As E. Ann Kaplan has noted, although

---

[12] Her situation is closely scrutinized in Sirk's *All That Heaven Allows* (1956). The desire to be "something else besides a mother" is falsely spoken by Stella Dallas in *Stella Dallas*, and the expression has been given its best advertisement in Linda Williams, "Something Else Besides a Mother: *Stella Dallas* and the Maternal Melodrama," *Cinema Journal* 24, no. 1 (Fall 1984): 2–27.

female sexuality has generally been co-opted and transformed for the pleasure of the male spectator, this has not been totally true for motherhood. In an argument that echoes that of Huston concerning the mutual exclusiveness of maternal and military service, Kaplan writes that "the extremity of patriarchal domination of female sexuality may be a reaction to helplessness in the face of the threat that motherhood represents."[13] Motherhood is a preserve utterly unavailable to the male. This dichotomy, she suggests, has led to an incompleteness of the iconographic record, a failure of full representational colonization of motherhood.

Brief Encounter accomplishes a particularly hesitant figuring of the mother, consonant with the atmosphere of Britain's uncertain move from war to peace. This image of a mother is built, as I have argued for the blackout and for other key wartime imagery, at the crossing point of foundational axes of the cinematic apparatus: technological, aesthetic, private, institutional. She functions in the mesh of differences of nation, class, and gender, here organized as a highly baroque set of spatial and above all temporal coordinates.

The establishment of a logical, albeit fictional, temporal order was a crucial aspect of addressing the wartime spectator as a national subject through film. As with the invention of gendered identity, this temporal position could never simply be stated, or taken, once and for all. As Metz understood so clearly, there is no fundamental unity to filmic temporality: film is a matrix of times past and present, of filming, editing, viewing, and diegesis. Instead, a specific temporal moment for a fiction can be defined only through the kinds of omissions, links, and elisions that also generate a gendered and national place. Films produced in the transition from war to peace had to combat the rapidity of historical change with the offer of a stable temporality for their viewers. The acute problem for representation, and above all for film, was the organization of time in such a way as to close off the traumatic past of the war while also making sense of it. Audiences should recognize their position, on a threshold, in the way that *Britain Today* demands in the epigraph to this chapter, and films need to find a stationary point from which to inspect and patch the damage, ostensibly looking back, but in fact looking nervously forward.

The question of temporal moment is paramount for *Brief Encounter*, for the film negotiates the war's legacy for concepts of femininity through an intricate temporal lattice. Its diegesis is fastened both to that "so-called peace and civilization" of the winter before the outbreak of war, and to

---

[13] Kaplan argues that the apparent difficulty of representing sexual mothers within existing ideological forms points to a crucial weakness in patriarchal discourse, which could be exploited by feminist film theory and practice. E. Ann Kaplan, *Women and Film: Both Sides of the Camera* (New York: Methuen, 1983), pp. 205–6.

the time of the audience's present, that is, 1945. But the film raises social and aesthetic issues (from adultery to the use of stroboscopic lighting) germane to the wartime and immediately postwar home front and the place of British filmmaking within it. The combination invites the audience to experience nostalgia, distance, and recognition, and even, for some, alienation. In addition to this chicanery of historical times, the film summons up the routine rhythms of cinematic realism alongside the timelessness of film fantasy, which contributes to the displacement of the historical dilemma of mothers onto myths and memories. *Brief Encounter* could produce no single, stable temporal point for the investigation of a mother's desire, certainly not the point of 1945; it could, however, air the problem by turning to the prewar world. This world also allowed the film's fantasy of harmonious class relationships, given the postwar election of a Labour Government.

Brief Encounter's mixed temporality gives textual form to the overall predicament of filmic representation at the war's end. Such films have no nameable epoch, but are nevertheless burdened with the task of initiating one. Linda Williams has written on the question of temporality in *Mildred Pierce*, and has noted that while that film is set mostly during the war, it makes scant direct reference to the war's events and effects.[14] It is this loosening of Mildred's story from history that permits a glimpse of the way history shapes her life: the film is able to "reflect the problems encountered by women under patriarchal rule precisely because it does not reflect the historical conditions that made that criticism possible in the first place."[15]

Like *Mildred Pierce*, *Brief Encounter* keeps the war outside its text, a choice that lets it too catch sight of contemporary social strictures on middle-class women in British society. However, *Brief Encounter* adds an extra layer of insulation to the system Williams describes: the time of the diegetic present is not that of the audience's present as it is in *Mildred Pierce*. Instead it is a past that opens into a multitude of further pasts, framed by female memory. It is the topic of adultery that keeps the war, the present, very much in the spectator's mind.

Facing the problems of 1945 was centrally within the stated purview of cinema's venture into new realism. The future socio-economic and cultural position of women was clearly a central problem of 1945, as the cover of *Picture Post* had inadvertently declared (Figure 2.2).[16] But *Brief Encounter*'s temporal conniptions speak of the inability of realism to reconcile itself with the very subject it so needed for its own identity. The film's

[14] Williams, "Feminist Film Theory: *Mildred Pierce* and the Second World War," p. 25.
[15] Ibid.
[16] Cover, *Picture Post*, 6 January 1945, vol. 26, no. 1.

temporal blankets—including the timelessness of the fantastic—are there to insulate the presentation of a woman's problems, but they also erode the film's realist status. As the film invests further and further in female identity, it is forced to abandon the realist style.

TO MOVE toward the new, egalitarian society that Labour promised in May 1945, on Attlee's unexpected defeat of Churchill, the events of the war had immediately to be consigned to the past. The peremptory rapidity of this procedure was Mervyn Wilson's source of humor in a contemporary cartoon that bears a striking relation to the opening moves of another film of 1945, *The Way to the Stars* (Figure 4.1). An important ideological function of cinema has always been to process and package the past for current

"Last year there was nothing here except an American bombing station."

Figure 4.1. The rejuvenescent powers of nature consign the war to the distant past. *Punch*, 17 October 1945, p. 329.

160

consumption, but this was especially difficult in 1945. The recent past of Britain was hard to formulate, for its heritage of rationing, illegitimate births, strikes, and urban destruction and its memories of deaths and partings were still very much of the present. It was difficult to secure any clear delineations between the past and the present.

One solution was the filmic fabrication of a very distant era. As far back as 1939 Ezra Goodman had noted the economic efficacy of this for Hollywood: "Period pieces and costume films are coming into favour again because it is felt that, no matter what tomorrow's headlines may report, such productions will not date."[17] *The Wicked Lady* adopts this tactic. Like *Mildred Pierce* and *Brief Encounter*, it was released in December 1945, and also dealt with a woman's desire for a more exciting and better-financed life. However, its setting was in the Age of Charles II, a remote, peacetime era, though of particular cultural resonance.[18] The Restoration was not some vague, amorphous eon but one that spoke to the audience's present. The return of the monarchy in Charles II's coronation, after Cromwell's republic and the civil war, represented the resolution of a period of turmoil and instability, parallel in its effects to that of invasion.[19] The era of Charles II in *The Wicked Lady* had a parallel temporal and conceptual status to the winter of 1938–39, the historical setting for *Brief Encounter*. However, *The Wicked Lady*'s remoter past held the promise of a more fantastic release from wartime austerity. It permitted greater aesthetic richness and flamboyance in its heroine, the rapacious Lady Skelton, with her firey, consuming eyes, delirious at the awfulness of murder as she suffocates the most recent witness to her crimes. These extreme close-ups of her eyes were excised from the American-release print of the film, along with the deeper cleavage shots; both were deemed controversial. Such appetite in female spectatorship is largely absent from *Brief Encounter* in its more recent setting—Laura's eyes glaze over, both when she listens to Alec's discourse on preventive medicine and when she retreats from suicide at the end. These differences, among others, caused *The Wicked Lady* to beat *Brief Encounter* at the box office for 1946.[20] Laura Jesson, thema-

---

[17] Ezra Goodman, "Hollywood Is Worried," *Sight and Sound* 8, no. 31 (Autumn 1939): 106.

[18] See Harper, "Historical Pleasures," pp. 167–96.

[19] Cromwell was referenced as often as 1066 in wartime popular culture, both as a traumatic influence on British history that had been survived, and as a military leader of extraordinary talent. The narrator in *Desert Victory* introduces General Montgomery as "a man who lives as sternly as a Cromwell, and who is much a part of his modern ironsides," while the Cromwell was a make of British tank during World War II. See my essay "The Female Spy" in Sklar and Musser, eds., *Resisting Images*, for discussion of Cromwell's contradictory status.

[20] Since both films were released at the end of 1945 they were included in box office

tizing realism in her earnestness and sincerity, was the antithesis of the scheming and murderous Lady Skelton who vigorously pursued her every desire, sartorial and sexual, until her gunshot death. As one feminist critic wryly remarked, "Bad Girl Makes Good Box Office."[21]

Other films released between 1944 and 1946 processed the recent past by lacing their narratives with a quasi-historical discourse: calendar leaves in *Perfect Strangers*, a judge's preamble in *Piccadilly Incident*, and bold introductory dates in *The Way Ahead* and *The Way to the Stars*. An opening sequence was added to the latter film late in production to accommodate the fact that the war had ended while it was still being made. Such temporal complexities undermined the desired purity of new British realism, frustrating one particular critic who described the pollution in the following way: "One of the attributes of a first class director is his use of restraint to gain force; camera trickery can destroy this by misguided abuse of its powers. Lately I notice, for example, a revival of the flashback to a degree which almost amounts to a mania. . . . Now an increasing number of stories are being launched by a narrator going back into the past, resuming and reappearing. This purely mechanical dodge is even throwing dust in critical eyes."[22]

The difficulty of securing temporal fixity in *The Way to the Stars* warrants further discussion. After the opening credits, in which the R.A.F. and U.S.A.F. are thanked for their enthusiastic cooperation, there is an exterior shot of a wired-off, neglected R.A.F. station. The camera pans right, scanning the wires, while blowing paper catches on the barbs. A male voice-over adumbrates the image, "This was an airfield. Control tower derelict. Crew room no more." Several interior close-ups of the abandoned station follow: a wall defaced with the scribbled words "Golden Lion"; a telephone number and a pencil sketch of a pinup girl, the name "Johnny" drawn down her leg; a cut to a shot of stale cigarette butts. These are all that remain of a wartime community. This spoor is the evidence of its history: human relations reduced to their debris.

A medium shot follows in which two sheep-farmers study a foreground plaque which reads "Halfpenny Field—Recorded in the Domesday Book," a shot identical in meaning to Wilson's cartoon (Figure 4.1). Through this shot we understand that since 1066, the last invasion, their piece of England has been a field, and thus that its recent life as an air base

---

statistics of 1946. See "These Were the Box Office Hits of the Year," *Kinematograph Weekly*, 19 December 1946, pp. 46–47.

[21] Catherine de la Roche, "That 'Feminine Angle,' " *Penguin Film Review* 8 (Harmondsworth: Penguin, January 1949), p. 32.

[22] L. Mannock, "We Critics Have Our Uses," *Sight and Sound* 10, no. 39 (Autumn 1941).

is a passing aberration. World War II is merely the most recent disturbance on a terrain that had seen many changes but whose nature has remained fundamentally the same. At this point a male voice-over suddenly announces, "It was very different in . . ." and as the soundtrack swells with strident military music the date "1940," in austere wartime lettering, fills the screen. The spectator has been shifted back several years to begin the narrative. The first synchronous sound follows as a new pilot arrives at the now functioning airfield. The film will be segmented twice more when the dates 1942 and 1944 flash up, dividing the text roughly into thirds.

At the release of *The Way to the Stars* in June 1945, such an airfield could only have been closed for three months at the most: it would still have been operating during the massive Dresden bombings by R.A.F. and U.S.A.F. planes on 13 and 14 February 1945, that is, before all U.S. planes were directed to the Pacific theater after V-E Day in May. Thus the deft transition to the recent past, 1940 in this film, depends on the audience's present knowledge; it depends on a present that can be precisely measured as a distance from the past of the diegesis. In *The Way to the Stars* this present is embodied in the figures of the two farmers, at home during the war, over recruitment age, who offer the viewer a stable initial location from which to interpret the representation of anterior events.

Unlike *The Way to the Stars*, *Brief Encounter* is unable to open from the here and now and look directly backward because of the greater ideological challenge of its material. *Brief Encounter* can offer no equivalents to these farmers, and in fact it can only *imply* a platform of the present, obliquely, for while the American airfield is indeed no more, the "problem" of women persists.

Brief Encounter WAS welcomed with open arms as a splendid example of the new British school of filmmaking. Critics, their vocabulary honed over the war years, selectively established the significance of the film at the apogee of the new realist style by proclaiming its qualities of sincerity, honesty, and transparency. It offered "creatures of flesh and blood, drawn in the round, with all their faults, impulses, hopes and fears like ourselves."[23] It seemed "to catch in words and pictures, so many things that are penetratingly true."[24] "How simple, commonplace, uncomfortably true and fascinating is this story of not-so-young, not-so-illicit love."[25] "The merit of the film, and its charm, is to be found in its simplicity and

[23] A. L. Vargas, "British Films and Their Audience," *Penguin Film Review* 8 (Harmondsworth: Penguin, January 1949), p. 75.

[24] C. A. Lejeune, *The Listener*, 29 November 1945.

[25] *The Chronicle*, clipping, *Brief Encounter*, microjacket, British Film Institute Library.

sincerity."[26] Even for feminist E. Arnot Robertson, the film was a "glorious exception . . . blessedly adult, truthful and contemporary."[27]

The trade press shared the realist lexicon. *Kinematograph Weekly* rated *Brief Encounter*'s merits in terms of a "human, true-to-life story, fine acting, tender and morally secure climax, title and author," while the *Motion Picture Herald* thought the film was "shot through with sincerity . . . integrity is this picture's watchword."[28] *Today's Cinema* appreciated its "realistic and unforced narrative angles."[29] British critics consistently downplayed the importance of the film's "feminine angle," and seemed blind to the reasons for the displeasure that many regional, working-class, and more recent spectators have expressed.[30] They were unable to acknowledge the baroque temporal construction of the film, nor its many other qualities that reeked of melodrama: its theme of guilty love, a focus on female experience, a narrative arranged as female memory, a dramatization of the failure of human communication, and a concomitant struggle to express meanings through music and *mise-en-scène* rather than via verbal exchange.

The only scathing review was published in *Documentary News Letter*, as part of a retrospective article on the films of 1945. This review described *Brief Encounter* as "a sorry affair. Impeccably directed and photographed, this slight story of two middle-aged people in search of a bed became vaguely comic instead of being noble or pathetic."[31] This journal was founded expressly to debate, define, and propagate documentary realism throughout British cinema. It could not condone what it recognized as a bowdlerized version.

There was a clear discrepancy between films sanctioned by privileged, largely male, middle-class critics, and those that became box office successes—in other words, those that were favored by the largely working-class and predominantly female audience, that "great mass of cinemagoers who don't know ham from spam."[32] This divergence was especially

---

[26] *Shell Magazine*, clipping, *Brief Encounter*, microjacket, British Film Institute Library.

[27] E. Arnot Robertson, "Woman and the Film," *Penguin Film Review* 3 (Harmondsworth: Penguin, August 1947), p. 32.

[28] *Kinematograph Weekly*, 15 November 1945; *Motion Picture Herald*, 15 December 1945.

[29] *Today's Cinema*, 14 November 1945.

[30] Catherine de la Roche, "That 'Feminine Angle.' "

[31] Editorial essay, "The Films of 1945," *Documentary News Letter* (1946/47), p. 10.

[32] Richard Kayne in Ion Hammond, comp., *This Year of Films: What the Critics Said* (London: British Film Institute Library, 1948), p. 9. R. H. "Josh" Billings wrote that the success of *Piccadilly Incident* and *The Wicked Lady* over *Brief Encounter* "revealed . . . as in previous years . . . the strained relationship existing between highbrow critics and the

distressing for critics in wartime because it contravened ideologies of national unity and flew in the face of their efforts to define a national film style as one that, because it represented ordinary people, would be popular. Why was it, they asked, that the first big winners of peacetime were not *Brief Encounter* and *The Way to the Stars*, but *The Seventh Veil* and *The Wicked Lady*?[33]

The gap between the critical and the public evaluation of *Brief Encounter* took on a significance disproportional to the film's box office weakness; after all, it did fairly well in Britain, brought Celia Johnson an Oscar nomination, and won her the 1946 New York Film Critics' Best Actress Award.[34] The poor correlation was bothersome because it evidenced the fallibility of critical writing: its powerlessness to constitute and control its object's life and the inadequacies both of the definition of realism and its use. In the years following *Brief Encounter*'s release the film took on totemic status as an instance of the chasm that might open between audience and critical opinion.[35] Bazin, among others, was eventually to renege on his initial, positive evaluation of the film.[36]

Catherine de la Roche provides the most perceptive contemporary cri-

---

box office.'' See R. H. ''Josh'' Billings, ''These Were the Box Office Hits of the Year,'' *Kinematograph Weekly*, 19 December 1946, p. 47.

[33] Ibid., pp. 46–47.

[34] In addition, *Brief Encounter* was the first big success of Rank's Prestige Pictures deal, set up with the cooperation of Universal to distribute British films to art houses in America.

[35] Richard Kayne writes, ''Noel Coward's *Brief Encounter* was a financial flop in Scotland and elsewhere and yet the critics are agreed that it was one of the best films ever to come out of any British studio.'' Richard Kayne in Hammond, comp., *This Year of Films: What the Critics Said*, p. 9. In retrospect director David Lean felt compelled to venture reasons for the film's financial failure. He thought that the film went ''too far'' in espousing realism in that there were ''no big-star names. There was an unhappy ending to the main love-story. The film was played in unglamorous surroundings. And the three leading characters were approaching middle-age.'' David Lean, ''*Brief Encounter*,'' *Penguin Film Review* 4 (Hardmondsworth: Penguin, October 1947), p. 31.

[36] In 1949 Bazin wrote that *Brief Encounter* would ''probably have been impossible'' without the tradition of ten years of documentary filmmaking in England. ''The English, instead of breaking with the technique and the history of European and American cinema, have succeeded in combining a highly refined aestheticism with the advances of a certain realism. Nothing could be more tightly structured, more carefully prepared, than *Brief Encounter*; . . . yet can we imagine a more realistic portrait of English manners and psychology?'' Returning to his manuscript seven years later in 1956, Bazin adds a footnote to the text: ''This paragraph [quoted above], which redounds to the glory of the English cinema but not to that of the writer, has been retained to bear witness to critical illusions about English cinema which I was not the only one to entertain. *Brief Encounter* made almost as great an impression as *Roma, Città Aperta*. Time has shown which of the two had a real cinematic future. Besides, the Noel Coward–David Lean film owed very little to the Griersonian school of documentary.'' André Bazin, *What Is Cinema?*, vol. 2, p. 49.

tique of *Brief Encounter*. In an article written in 1948, she numbered *The Best Years of Our Lives*, *The Rake's Progress* (U.S. title *Notorious Gentleman*), *Mine Own Executioner*, and *Frieda* as among the few recent films that had "conquered new ground thematically" in their attempts to interpret "modern characters and ideas in modern idiom."[37] *Best Years*, *Mine Own Executioner*, and *Frieda* all tackled the long-term impact of the war on domestic life. *Mine Own Executioner* presented the tragedy of a shell-shocked, ex-ace pilot who becomes psychotic, eventually killing his wife; *Frieda* dramatized the inability of a postwar English community to accept a blond German woman as the wife of a local schoolteacher; and the American *The Best Years of Our Lives* compared the difficult reintegration of three war veterans returning to their home communities.

De la Roche shared with her colleagues the general view that British film should address the issues of modern life, but she cautioned against films that used realism merely as a "mask." Such a mask, she argued, was insufficient to camouflage any work that had a fundamentally "unreal nature" stemming from "detachment, evasion or distortion." She could not wholeheartedly endorse *Brief Encounter* because it wore such a mask, and only included it on her list of good recent films with the proviso, "within the limits of its detachment."[38] Her reaction signals the mechanism by which *Brief Encounter* deals with its controversial subject. The "detachment" that intervenes between the potent subject and its wartime audience is one of temporal distance, buoyed up by class difference. The diegetic displacement to the prewar period permits a reemphasis on class division which wartime pressures to national unity had worked to elide. Whereas in the earlier, midwar films—*The Gentle Sex* and *The Way Ahead*, for example—class divisions were explicitly challenged, or lessened, via the motif of the crowded train compartment, or, in *The Way Ahead*, Davenport's invitation that Parsons need not observe his superior peacetime "status," *Brief Encounter*'s representation of class jars with the ideal of egalitarianism. Laura has a maid, Ethel, and an upper-class accent, and fears having an affair because it will make her "cheap" and "low"—in effect, lower class. She also comments that lying is "degrading" and remembers that Fred, her husband, would consider her common if he knew she were smoking alone at night in the town square. In *Brief Encounter* working- and middle-class lives are conducted separately, even though they intermittently share the same space—the station waiting room of

[37] Catherine de la Roche, "The Mask of Realism," *Penguin Film Review* 7 (Harmondsworth: Penguin, September 1948), p. 43. Before 1943, de la Roche had worked in the story department at London Films, but then became head of Russo-British film exchanges based in London.

[38] Ibid.

course—and certain aspects of Laura's life and needs parallel those of Myrtle Bagott (Joyce Carey), the working-class waiting room proprietress. Myrtle has left her first husband, as Laura contemplates doing, and both women are humiliated and shaken in the film, calming their nerves with a nip of three star, Myrtle's emergency supply of brandy. *Brief Encounter*'s presentation of clear class divisions contradicted the new Labour government's optimism for class harmony and was responsible for audience alienation from the film, which I shall discuss below.

By adopting de la Roche's "mask of realism," *Brief Encounter* appeared to deal sincerely with a woman's dilemma, but the codes of realism worked to make that which was actually controlling a woman's choice invisible. Through a veneer of realism, the events that overtake Laura seem so inevitable that even with the hindsight of two to three years, Catherine de la Roche was alone in sensing the device. The woman's problem remains distanced from its audience, and in converting a social problem into entertainment, the film wears not only a mask of realism, but also one of social comment.

Brief Encounter PREMIERED at the New Gallery, London, on 26 November 1945. The show was held to aid the Royal Naval War Libraries, and the program sellers were Wrens and Naval ratings.[39] Before the screening, screenwriter and producer Noel Coward publicly congratulated the Navy on its "wonderful" wartime service, renewing his bond from the days of *In Which We Serve*. Coward adapted the script for *Brief Encounter* from his play *Still Life*, which belonged to an evening-long trilogy and was one of a collection of ten such playlets written in 1936 titled *Tonight at 8:30*. The structural differences between *Still Life* and *Brief Encounter* leave a fascinating record of the way war can reshape aesthetic and narrative form.

Coward retained the play's central theme of guilty love, but he tempered the screen couple by comparison with their stage forerunners, who were far more flirtatious, scheming, and definitely adulterous. Coward removed such lines as "I feel like a prostitute," spoken by Laura to Alec. The play had taken place on one set, the refreshment room at Milford Junction, such confinement suiting the practical constraints of theatrical presentation. The Junction remains the central focus of the film, but space is expanded from that site into other environments inhabited by additional characters, so that the running time of the piece grows from less than an hour on stage to eighty-six minutes on screen. Conversely, diegetic time is shrunk, from several months in the case of the play to only five weeks in the film. (One could argue that diegetic time in the film is shrunk to merely an afternoon

[39] *Today's Cinema*, 14 November 1945.

and evening, spent mainly in the Jesson living room.) This temporal reduction accentuates both the brevity of the encounter and the couple's relative innocence by comparison with their stage predecessors. Time is further manipulated in the film by the use of two flashbacks and a fantasy sequence. These make it structurally more convoluted than the temporally linear play.

The addition of Laura's voice-over to the screen narrative converts her into the central character; on stage Alec Harvey had been equally important. This emphasis on Laura also helps to define wartime breakups as women's business rather than matters of concern to men and women alike. The new date chosen for the film's action is winter 1938–39, a few months before the European outbreak of war, rather than April 1936, the beginning month of the play. The wintry, pollarded willows and off-season boating expedition enabled by the change of season contribute to the general bleakness of Milford life and Laura's predicament in the film.

It was no easy matter to concoct a convincing prewar atmosphere when the film went into production in late 1944. Materials for costumes, props, and sets were still scarce, and the severest rationing was yet to be introduced. The station scenes, shot at Carnforth in the Lake District, had to be filmed between 10:00 p.m. and 8:00 a.m. to reduce troop and supply-train disruption.[40] The cast and unit of seventy were separately lodged in five different districts because most hotels were filled with refugees from Southeast England where "it was the days of the heavy rocket raids."[41] The crew almost lost its equipment and supplies one evening in a fire at a nearby petrol dump, and "the production might have been held up indefinitely owing to the shortage of camera gear."[42] In fact, shooting was completed in about eight weeks.

The solution of these production problems was a matter of some pride to Cineguild, which explained in its publicity bumf, "Dummy packets of chocolate were borrowed . . . cakes were covered with mock icing, and apples and oranges were moulded in the plasterer's shop." Such efforts were greatly appreciated by precisely that kind of realist critic who objected to *The Wicked Lady*'s "nonsense of period."[43] *Theater Arts* congratulated Coward and Lean on their "extraordinary feat of projection [i.e., backward from the present!] by setting the picture in pre-war days and providing—out of the rigors and shortages of post-war life—all the proper accoutrements of the past, including chocolate buns and a peculiar

---

[40] The Forces frequently used this route to the South of England, especially since Liverpool and Glasgow were the main ports through which American G.I.'s entered Britain.

[41] Cineguild, *Brief Encounter*, microjacket, British Film Institute Library.

[42] Ibid.

[43] *The Tribune*, 23 November 1945, p. 41.

brand of pre-war soldier."[44] The *Daily Mirror* appreciated the "interludes in the local cafe with its typical ladies' orchestra of pre-war days."[45] Isabel Quigly, writing in the 1960s, remembered that audiences, recognizing the peacetime clues, enviously giggled at "Laura's purchase of large bars of chocolate without coupons."[46]

Props aside, other elements of dialogue and *mise-en-scène* would have left contemporary viewers in no doubt as to the film's prewar setting. With alarming naiveté Fred and Laura discuss entering their son for the Navy on the grounds that "it's a healthy life . . . a good life . . . he'll have a wife in every port and be able to see the world." Dolly Messiter, Laura's gossiping friend, draws attention to the radical changes of wartime when she banters in necessary ignorance: "Wild horses wouldn't drag me away from England, and home, and all the things I'm used to." The Jessons' living room curtains are left wide open at night, broadcasting to the audience the peacetime absence of legislated blackouts, and Laura sits embroidering at home in the evenings, an activity associated with peacetime luxury as opposed to the make-do-and-mend knitting and darning of wartime. Lastly, Alec whispers in the cinema of Donald Duck's immunity from the universe going up in flames and the world crashing around him, a joke divested of its humor by 1945.

These linguistic and stylistic precautions tether the film in the prewar period. Locating the action in a nonstrategic, nonspecific fictional inland town further distanced the narrative from contemporary audience experience. (The town's fictional nature derives in part from its hybrid, North/South character: while Alec, Laura, Fred, Dolly, and, above all, the children have Southern accents, the Ketchworth policeman sounds very Northern, and Alec's interest in mining diseases, the dark stone architecture, and occasional glimpses of signs of Hellifield, Keighly, Bradford, and Leeds on the station platform suggest a Northern setting.)[47] Catherine de la Roche criticized the omission of any reference to the political events of the film's own already distanced era. *Brief Encounter* "didn't achieve complete realism, because there wasn't a hint of the familiar events and anxieties" of the year in which it was set.[48] By early 1939 the Spanish

[44] *Theater Arts* 30 (October 1946): 596.

[45] *Daily Mirror*, 23 November 1945.

[46] Quigly, *Brief Encounter*, microjacket, British Film Institute Library.

[47] Critics provide further evidence of the setting's regional ambiguity: a *Movie* review locates the action in the Home Counties; the *New Yorker* puts it in the Midlands; and contemporary publicity material insists on the North. See Adrian Turner, *The Movie* 27 (1980): 536; the *New Yorker*, 22, no. 48, 5 July 1946.

[48] Catherine de la Roche, "A Director's Approach to Filmmaking: David Lean," unpublished script of interview, broadcast on B.B.C. Radio 3, 18 August 1947. Script at British Film Institute Library.

Civil War and the German annexing of Austria and Czechoslovakia had already generated a pessimistic and tense atmosphere in Europe, no part of which impinges on Fred and Laura's world. The absence of such political references alongside the presence of rare luxuries (champagne, Nestlès nut-milk, oranges) encode nostalgia and romantic otherwordliness in the plot. The contemporary audience member could view the film with a sense of historical superiority that appealed to his or her sense of place, knowing that the constructed epoch on the screen had a definite and catastrophic endpoint. Paradoxically, the documentary force of cinematography proved that the precious peacetime objects had once existed in the past, but *not* that they must have been co-present with the camera when they were photographically recorded in 1944, and must therefore have been either plaster-made or from the black market. The items acquire integrity through being both recognized and lost, meshed into the past through narrative.

The presence of Banburies and palm-court orchestras, even of the naiveté of Laura herself, are part of the process of fixing the past as separate from the present, a process dependent on the backward glance from the present for its significance and interpretation. These objects and character traits become temporally significant only as a result of their negation through the events of the war. *Brief Encounter*'s insistently prewar *mise-en-scène*, and the narrative per se, serve the purpose of the aorist, or story tense, closing off the events of the narrative from the spectator.[49] The prewar objects are an inscription of the past in the text of the film, and the ensuing displacement isolates the past from the present to serve a present need. The years 1938–39 were a more appropriate setting for a romantic epic than 1945, and it was more compelling and plausible to present a story in which adultery was resisted in a bygone era.

---

[49] In his *Problems in General Linguistics*, Emile Benveniste notes that the diverse tenses of French verbs are distributed across two planes of utterance: "histoire" and "discours," or "story" and "discourse." The unrivaled tense for writing history is the aorist, the simple, or definite past, a tense excluded from the system of discourse. The aorist is used only in the third person as the specialized tense of the historical event. According to Benveniste, in an historical account events are set forth chronologically, as they occurred, and seem to narrate themselves, without the need of a formal narrator. The tale is posited as simply true, as objective history, and apparently unstructured by surrounding forces. Christian Metz has adapted Benveniste's theory for his discussion of film narrative, and argues that the efficacy of film, as a discourse, is that it effaces all marks of its enunciation and disguises itself as story. See Emile Benveniste, *Problems in General Linguistics* [1966], (Miami: Miami Linguistics Series, no. 8, 1971), especially p. 208, and Christian Metz, "History/Discourse: A Note on Two Voyeurisms," trans. Susan Bennett, in *Psychoanalysis and Cinema: The Imaginary Signifier* (Bloomington: Indiana University Press, 1975), especially p. 21.

ORANGES AND chocolates were not the only components of the film to enforce a temporal disjunction from the spectator. The entire narrative is structured by temporal separations, both between diegetic past and present and between systems of time, themselves overlaid with gendered connotations. The regular, linear time of train schedules contests the irregular, convoluted time of Laura's memory and romance. From the title's reference to brevity to Laura's extravagant three-dial barometer/clock present for Fred, *Brief Encounter* is saturated with visual and verbal images of time. The first shot shows Mr. Godby (Stanley Holloway) checking his fob watch and grinning at the punctuality of the second express train after the first has rushed into blackness behind the titles. As he crosses the tracks to the brightly lit refreshment room, he passes under a massive platform clock. The murky, speeding thrill of the railway exterior is here shown to be under the thumb of time and order.

Myrtle, the refreshment room proprietress, has no "time" for idle gossip, and closes her first scene saying "Time and tide wait for no man, Mr. Godby." Shortly afterward the spectator is introduced to Laura, whose desperate thoughts in the railway carriage also run along temporal lines: "This can't last, this misery can't last. . . . Nothing lasts really, neither happiness or despair. Not even life lasts very long." During Laura and Alec's first admissions of love, Laura exhorts them to caution by sobbing, "There's still time, if we control ourselves and behave like sensible human beings, there's still time to . . . to . . . ," to which Alec replies, "There's no time at all." The couple's whole affair is constrained and regulated by a system of precision timing. "No, I can't on Thursday. That's my Milford day," answers Laura, refusing a lunch engagement with Mary Norton on the grounds that her shopping habit cannot be altered. Alec too can do his Milford locum only on Thursdays, the day Stephen Lynn vacates his hospital post for trips to London. When Laura arrives home later than usual on a Thursday, there has inevitably been a domestic disaster—squabbling children or an injured son—events that underscore the necessity of limiting her time away from home, of maintaining a regular schedule, a temporally predictable and bounded life.

Each Thursday's meeting between Alec and Laura is itself terminated by the London Midland and Scottish (L.M.S.) timetable: as Alec's 5:40 departs for Churley, Laura has just enough time to cross under the tracks and catch the 5:43 for Ketchworth. Within these programmed parameters, Laura and Alec's time together is constantly interrupted by train whistles, platform bells, and station announcements. In the opening seven minutes of the film there are no less than three whistles, three bells, and two public addresses. At home, later the same night, it is Laura's memory of a screaming whistle, heard again on the soundtrack, that causes her to break

171

down in front of Fred: the sound of the temporal regimen tolls for Laura, and the viewer, the demise of her affair.

Timetables and bells persist up to the film's last image. In contrast to the opening shot, this is a still of empty tracks, unpunctuated by the railway's rhythm. The railway's pulse is no longer needed—no trains need pass. Instead time passes, the tracks remain empty, the encounter is over, and Laura is left with nothing, no evidence, just a void, and the dubiously desirable permanence of Fred. The temporal disruption of "feminine" fiction has run its course.

This regular, tyrannical timetabling of Laura and Alec's affair is continually countered by an internal jumbling of diegetic time within the winter of 1938–39. The compelling force of "the realistic setting of the life of a British provincial town with its super cinema, its cafes with luncheons and teas to orchestral accompaniments, its streets and its dark, prosaic station" is forever being challenged by the nonconsecutiveness of narrative events, a mélange of temporalities rooted in Laura's subjectivity through her possession of a voice-over.[50]

The story of *Brief Encounter* takes place on six successive Thursdays, spanning five weeks and presented as two flashbacks remembered by Laura from her fireside at home. The film opens and closes on the sixth and final Thursday, the day on which Laura has agreed to separate permanently from Alec. Each Thursday is marked by at least one scene in the Milford Junction refreshment room, locus of the couple's first meeting and last parting. In this way the waiting room becomes their home away from home, the spatial focus of the film, all the more poignant for its public and temporary nature. The waiting room surrounds the affair with impermanence but is preferable to other meeting places—the Kardomah Cafe, the cinema, The Royal Hotel, a street corner, the municipal boating pond—which do not offer the relative cosiness of Myrtle's cake-laden counter and wiped tables. Only the boathouse will afford the couple a comparable space of informality; Stephen's pristine service flat, ostensibly the most private site they have, eventually proves the most uncomfortable and inaccessible.

The rendezvous spots in Milford and its environs are balanced in the film against Laura's home in Ketchworth, where she is always seen with Fred and her children. Indeed, these secondary characters appear only within the Jesson household. Alec's dependents are never shown, a fact that not only perpetuates the imbalance of Laura and Alec's relative responsibilities during their affair, but also reinforces the idea that men are

---

[50] Roger Manvell, review notes, *Brief Encounter* microjacket, British Film Institute Library, p. 3.

freer of their families than women, and that married women are umbilically tied to their families and home. Here is another subtle instance of the way in which cultural representation is instituting marriage and reproduction as ''specifically female spheres,'' to quote Huston again, even though these processes require the cooperation of both sexes.[51]

It is from the Jessons' domestic setting that the story is told, and here that it ends in an enclosing embrace after Laura has remembered and expunged the scene of her final 5:40 parting from Alec at Milford. The action of the film therefore shifts between Milford and Ketchworth, like the trains, and while the first scene is at Milford, the last is at Ketchworth, echoing Laura's return to her marriage and family.

Laura's journey is not quite this simple, however. The Thursdays are not presented in chronological order, and while the two locations are usually alternated as the narrative unfolds, this is not always the case. For example, the transition from the third to the fourth Thursday is effected through a straightforward fade from an image of Laura on the evening Milford platform, to her next meeting with Alec in the cinema the following Thursday; there is no ''return'' to Fred in Ketchworth. This is actually the only pair of Milford Thursdays *not* separated by a reference to home/Ketchworth, either through an actual scene or through the sound of Laura's voice-over, emanating from the Ketchworth fireside. It is as if to rectify this breakdown in the film's spatial and narrative system of alternating between two locations that Fred rudely ''interrupts'' the narrative flow during the fourth Thursday, just as Laura and Alec are engaged in their first kiss, thereby forcing Ketchworth and home literally back into the picture. On this fourth Thursday, the couple has prematurely left the cinema and has returned from the boating pond to Milford Station. As they embrace in an underpass, Fred forces the flashback to a halt by shouting, ''Don't you think we might have that down a bit, darling? . . . Hoy, Laura! Do you mind if I turn that down a little? It really is deafening.'' He refers to Rachmaninov's Second Piano Concerto blasting from the living room radio. His voice rings out over the couple's lovemaking long before his image is seen. The sound wrenches both Laura and the audience back to Ketchworth, reminding them of the romantic melody's diegetic source. Laura had earlier selected Rachmaninov over more popular offerings on the radio, but by this point the music has become disengaged from its fictional source. Fred's interruption reminds the audience that Rachmaninov has always belonged to the diegetic track, even while supporting Laura's fond imaginings: it has functioned both for realism and for fantasy.[52]

---

[51] Huston, ''The Matrix of War,'' p. 166.

[52] Rick Altman attributes this quality of straddling two realms above all to the American

Fred's voice reinstates the logic of realism, while foregrounding the way the strong female focus of the film is pulling away from that logic. Laura can only resume her nostalgic reminiscence once the Rachmaninov volume has been mechanically lowered.

Because of this "break" in her account—Fred's "Hoy Laura!"—the Milford Thursdays appear in the sequence 6,1,2,3,4,6,4,5,6, 6 being the final Thursday, which appears first in the present, then as a rupture in the past, and lastly in the present, as Laura ends the film sobbing in Fred's arms. By the end of the film diegetic time has been so segmented and reversed that the spectator is left bewildered about how many Thursdays have passed, how many times the narrative has returned to the "present"—that is, winter 1938–39—from the past, how often it has traveled from Ketchworth to Milford. For one thing, *all* the Milford Thursdays are overlaid with moments of the diegetic present in that Laura's voice-over is emitted from the film's present. All this temporal mixing would be less troubling were it not for the extreme care that Laura takes in recalling each precious Thursday of her lost affair. Laura's supposedly illuminating remarks such as "We only met a week last Thursday," "All that was only last week," or "That was only this morning" simply prove all the more disorienting to the spectator.

SO FAR I have argued that *Brief Encounter*'s events were distanced from a contemporary audience because they occurred, indubitably, in the winter of 1938–39, and secondly because they were presented as flashbacks, recalled from a slightly more recent but equally prewar domestic setting. As if this jostling of time and memory were not dispiriting enough for a reviewer who wished to claim that the film was "simple" and "unforced," temporality is further complicated by the irregularity of the flashback mechanisms, and by two instances in which Laura's voice-over does not serve the purpose of giving access to her past memories.

Brief Encounter's flashbacks are usually triggered by a combined package of Laura's voice-over and sequences of Rachmaninov, but the two aural codes do not always perform this duty. For a start, the classical concerto also doubles as title music. Its dramatic opening chords resound over the still shot of Milford Junction while trains thunder through and credits roll up. As Fred embraces Laura in the film's penultimate shot, the music wells up again and spills over onto the final image of the film, the empty nighttime station. In framing the narrative, the music's function is to pre-

---

film musical. His general argument is valuable, but his citing of *Brief Encounter* as an example of the opposite tendency oversimplifies the deployment of music in the film for it too straddles two realms. Rick Altman, *The American Film Musical* (Bloomington: Indiana University Press, 1987), p. 63.

figure the story's wrenching emotion, and then to seal off the experience from Laura and the spectator who, in ways I will suggest, are figured together. The music is all the more affective through its contrast to the dank surroundings: its fabulous richness and high culture status are peculiarly at odds with the film's wintry, municipal exteriors.

Rachmaninov is first associated with Laura in the first railway carriage scene, as she returns to Ketchworth with Dolly Messiter after what is later revealed to have been her final parting from Alec. A slow pianissimo passage accompanies Laura's voice-over as she murmurs of Dolly: "I wish I could trust you. I wish you were a wise, kind friend instead of just a gossiping acquaintance that I've known for years casually and never particularly cared for . . . I wish . . . I wish . . ." She goes on to deliver her "This can't last" speech. The voice-over technique immediately confirms Laura's position at the center of the film, long before her flashbacks complicate its structure. The point here, however, is that this is *not* a flashback, and *not* part of the confession that Laura will begin later, but rather an overheard expression to the audience of her desire both to overcome the unexpected experience of falling in love which has led to such suffering in the subsequent agony of parting, and also her desire to hang on to that pain as the only trace of the past she has. Her voice-over does not speak her memory here, but rather her current preoccupations and her frustration at Dolly's chatter, which she is too well-bred to quash directly.

There is a second occasion on which Laura's voice-over departs from the confessional mode. As she wrestles with her conscience in the refreshment room on the fifth Thursday, knowing that Alec is alone in Stephen's bachelor rooms, she listens repeatedly to her own voice alternating with Alec's: she hears herself insist, "I really must go home," to which he replies, "I'm going back to the flat." This new use of Laura's voice-over introduces the most precarious part of her story, the point at which adultery is most surely in the cards. From this moment of fearful indecision at Milford Junction—whether to repress her desire to go to Alec, or transgress the bonds of marriage—and throughout her rush to the railway carriage from the waiting room, her subsequent haste away from the carriage to Alec, the fiasco of Stephen's return to the flat, and in fact until she regains the nighttime streets, her voice-over is not heard. The voice which throughout has made the audience privy to her inner feelings, and which has thus ensured their "auditory mastery" of her thought, goes silent; it is as if radio contact is lost.[53] Her lurch toward infidelity "breaks" the sound track convention, cutting off the audience from her informing commentary.

[53] Kaja Silverman, *The Acoustic Mirror: The Female Voice in Psychoanalysis and Cinema* (Bloomington: Indiana University Press, 1988), p. 53.

It is during this sequence, when the spectator's "receiver" has gone dead, that Laura is first active in prizing open a private space and time to be with Alec; it is her first practical step toward "giving in" to her sexual desire. Needless to say, creating this space upsets the previously established routine of the Thursday timetable: she misses the 5:43 to Ketchworth and has to catch the 10:10. During this interlude, Laura is in fact oblivious to the passing of time. After her flight from the flat she walks "without much purpose" and recalls, "I realized that I had been wandering about for over three hours, but it didn't seem to be any time at all." She just makes the last train, just conforming to the technological schedule, a narrative correlation for just remaining within the vows of marriage.

The use of the same aural code to a new end, contradictory to the one previously established, breaks that code's habitual signification of honesty and soul-searching, upsetting the spectator's habitual relation to Laura's status, and indeed upsetting the textual workings of the film. But it is not only the aural track that shifts at this point: all previously established codes of the film, aural and visual, adjust with Laura's decision to return to the flat. Changes in the textual fabric convey the crisis in the social fabric, the questioning of a married woman's commitment to marriage and family. As Laura scurries through the streets, Milford is transformed from a humdrum, daytime shopping center into a rain-slicked, nighttime no-man's land. At this climactic point of transgression, aesthetic restraint is abandoned and a punishing, *noirish* style takes over, replete with extreme camera angles and high-contrast lighting, reminiscent not only of American urban crime films, but of blackout representations of British films set in wartime.[54]

As Laura digresses from "normal," prescribed behavior, the imagery slips into blackness, in conformity with the blackout paradigm: disturbance in the realm of sexuality is clearly visually coded. The schema has actually been triggered much earlier, at the outset of the affair, when Laura is blinded by a cinder and meets Alec, who retrieves the mote. The incident, a blackout in miniature, provides yet another instance of the way so much cinema has presented female vision as faulty.[55] From the cinder incident on, Laura's perceptual capacity is put into question for the audience.

Darkness is first linked to Laura's desire from the seventh minute of the film, as she travels with Dolly on the railway carriage. The volume of Dolly's gossiping sinks down while the framing of Laura shifts from a

---

[54] I do not mean to suggest that high-contrast lighting originated in wartime cinema. Of course it has always been a powerful device of representation, but its coincidence with the blackout gives it a crucial historical significance as argued in Chapter 3.

[55] Mary Ann Doane examines this trope in *The Desire to Desire*, especially in Chapter 6 in her discussion of *Caught* and *Rebecca*.

close-up to a choker shot. The light around her fades, as if an iris were contracting, and she voices, as voice-over, her first feelings of misery at the end of her affair. On arrival at Ketchworth, as Dolly wakes her, the scene lightens again and the interlude of melancholic reverie is ended. Light marks the return of everyday reason and responsibility.

Laura's desire is imaged through darkness and threatening shadows in several subsequent scenes typical of melodrama's mode of representing narrative meaning through exaggerated visual style. After her accidental encounter with Alec at the Kardomah, and her assent to a meeting the following week, she reflects on the implications of the afternoon and wonders whether Alec will tell his wife. As she paces up and down the platform in time to a slow recapitulation of the musical theme, her face is cast mostly in shadow. Half of her face then emerges into the light as her voice-over trembles, "Then suddenly I knew that he wouldn't. I knew beyond a shadow of a doubt that he wouldn't say a word, and at that moment the first awful feeling of danger swept over me." Her recognition of the social prohibition on her sexual desire is doubly registered at the word "danger": the Rachmaninov comes to an abrupt halt and a blast of hissing steam clouds the screen. The scalding steam both images and sterilizes passion.

The rising intensity of Laura's passion is regulated not only by steam, train timetables, and engine whistles, but by an increasingly obvious series of cagelike images which frame and "cut" her body, and which are often combined with descending slopes! The first grid coincides with the first moment of physical contact between Alec and Laura, on the third (Kardomah) Thursday. The couple have been to a matinee showing of *Love in a Mist*, a title imbued with not a little Coward humor. Laura's voice-over recommences at the dissolve between the cinema and the steps leading down to Milford Junction. On the words, "Just as we were passing the gate, he put his hand under my arm," the couple enters a tunnel of iron bars whose shadows dissect their bodies. Laura reflects, "I didn't notice it then but I remember it now," guiding the viewer's attention to the all but imperceptible glimpse of Alec's physical touch. As the couple emerges from behind the bars into platform light, the lip-synchronized sound returns.

The second obvious cage image ends their day in the country the following week. As they park Stephen's car in his garage, Alec and Laura's heads are framed by the grid of garage windows. The audience sees them through glass, mouthing words inaudibly, while yet again Laura's voice-over is heard, explaining the romantic significance of a moment from which the audience is literally barred. She remembers that Alec suggested she come up to the flat: "I refused rather too vehemently." This scene prefigures the most spectacular and compelling cage of the film, a cage that surrounds Laura's entry into Stephen's apartment later that night, a cage incorporated therefore into the film's passage of most serious transgression.

The camera ''lurks,'' waiting for Laura on the public landing inside Stephen's modern ''service'' building, with its metal frame windows, elevator cages, and cold floor and wall surfaces. It is raining outside as Laura enters. First seen beyond the glass and metal swing doors, she walks through the lobby, up the left-hand stone steps, turns on the half landing by the camera and crosses between it and the elevator shaft. She passes now away from the spectator, walking up the steps by the right of the lift cage, and then behind the fragmenting lozenges of its gate, moving now to the left. The camera pans with her, losing her as she slips behind a wall and regaining her as she reaches the door of the flat, on her second turn to the left. By now she is seen through two successive layers of gridded windows, across an inner courtyard of the building, and bordered by walls, sheet-glass, and metal. At this point, Laura rings the bell and the shot cuts to a close-up, slicing through the intervening glass and metal layers. The shot just described is the longest and most complicated of the film, composed of a tilt-up, pan right, tilt-up, and then a very long pan left. Laura's path doubles back on itself within the shot so that her very tracks are convoluted. The apartment complex takes on the character of a trap or maze, with its many turns and layers of superimposed grids.

Except for its unorthodox use in her dilemma about returning to the flat (previously described), Laura's voice-over is not heard from the moment of her embrace with Alec as the express train passes, throughout this grid sequence, until after she has fled the apartment on Stephen's unexpected return. When her voice-over recommences it is accompanied by a sequence of elevated, high-contrast shots of rain-wetted streets alternated with close-ups of her running, splashing feet. The high camera angles drastically diminish her size. A high-angle shot of a glistening monument to the First World War, with two slanting guns, frames her small mass huddled far below on a town bench, exhausted after running. The image reverberates with the history of the more recent war, that just experienced by the audience, especially since a new wreath has been laid on the monument, keeping the memory of military deaths alive.

The entire sequence, from the embrace to the war memorial, is the most varied and dramatically shot of the film. It represents the frustrated climax of the couple's relationship, encoded visually with the sense of disruption that would have ensued had they broken their other attachments. *Brief Encounter* corroborates Kaplan's observation on the difficulty of representing sexual mothers within Western culture, for when the ''problem'' of the sexual mother is most directly addressed, in and around Stephen's apart-

178

ment, the filmic codes shift into blackness, symbolic cages crowd in, and aural contact is lost.

ONE WAY in which the "problem" of the sexual mother is contained and managed in *Brief Encounter* is through the suggestion that the problem is somehow solely a woman's problem, separate from larger political and cultural concerns. This suggestion is made in various ways. First of all, the film invites identification by specifically female audience members—and an audience of Mrs. Jessons above all—by imaging several moments of female spectatorship, a common trope of American melodrama of the period, including *Stella Dallas*, *Rebecca*, *Daisy Kenyon*, and *Caught*. Laura's spectatorship takes a number of diegetic forms, of varying temporal and spatial complexity. She is a filmgoer, studies her image in the mirror, and looks into fantasized reflections in her railway carriage window as she travels home from Milford on the fourth Thursday.

This last example occurs after the splitting of the flashback into two parts by Fred's interruption. Laura's fantasy takes place within this flashback, thus deranging film time even further, while a fragment of her character persists at each temporal and diegetic level, sometimes on both image and sound track. In the carriage Laura imagines being with Alec "in all sorts of glamorous circumstances . . . in Paris, in a box at the Opera . . . in Venice . . . leaning on the rail of a ship . . . on some tropical beach in the moonlight." The different exotic destinations Laura's voice-over narration describes dissolve into one another, superimposed on her own carriage-window reflection, which also fades in and out as her fantasy waxes and wanes. In her imagination she accompanies Alec in a bare-shouldered, nay risqué evening dress, reminiscent of those adorning the more traditionally spectacular cinema of Hollywood. The scene is stylistically distinct in its inclusion both of glamorized femininity and of other reflective surfaces that enhance its visual lavishness.

In the only bedroom scene in the film, as Laura lies to Fred for the first time, her face is reflected simultaneously in her dressing-table mirror and a hand mirror. This configuration, an echo of Hollywood's conventionalized use of the same figure to represent the duplicitous woman, inscribes Laura's "ordinary," habitual self watching her other self invent and scheme, that self which is indeed closer to the emerging femininity of American film noir. Later, in her voice-over commentary, Laura remembers that she was doing her face at the time of lying to Fred, making the dressing-table a site of both cosmetic and marital deception.

These instances of Laura's concentration on her own reflected image are two of many in which she appears to watch herself having the experience of an illicit affair, as if she were both in a movie theater *and* experiencing

179

the narrative first hand. These scenes present in microcosm the film's narrative structure of a woman producing remembered mental images from her living room and the condition of the film's external audience watching the movie screen. Such spectators believe in the fiction while always knowing themselves to be outside it as spectators.

The theme of Laura watching herself, of being visually and aurally distanced from herself, is given vivid introduction with the first flashback. In the shot prior to the commencement of the flashback, Laura is sitting in the foreground of the living room with her embroidery, positioned against the light, with her silhouetted back outlined near the camera. As the living room fades to the past of the waiting room, two images of Laura coexist for several seconds, the one still in the foreground in silhouette, the new one in the background in profile, sitting at one of Myrtle's tables. For several seconds the first Laura looks as if into the screen, duplicating the position of the external female spectator.

This doubling is repeated within the diegetic past in Laura's cinemagoing habit. She and Alec are members of two matinee audiences—*Love in a Mist* and *Flames of Passion*—and Laura refers to filmgoing on two occasions in her voice-over account. She tells Alec that every Thursday she does the week's shopping, changes her library book, has lunch, and goes to the pictures. On the second Thursday she recalls: "I went to the Palladium as usual. It was a terribly long film"; on the third Thursday she remembers: "I hadn't enjoyed the picture. It was one of those noisy musical things and I'm so sick of them."

An explanation for Laura's lack of pleasure in going to the cinema is suggested elsewhere in her voice-over commentary, when she refers to her discomfort at being the object of other people's sight. She wonders if passengers are watching her on the train, and she senses uneasily the policeman scrutinizing her by the war memorial as she smokes. She remembers Fred's dislike of the *sight* of women smoking in public. Her knowledge of being both viewer and viewed—the particular condition of the female cinema-goer, as Gertrud Koch has argued—both draws her back to the cinema, and makes her want to leave early.[56]

Another device through which *Brief Encounter* builds association with a female audience is references to contemporary women's fiction: Laura is a reader as well as a filmgoer. She is shown reading at the Kardomah, though with little assiduity, and pretending to read on the train. The Boots' librarian reserves Laura the latest novel by Kate O'Brien (which in 1939 would have been, appropriately, *Prayer for the Wanderer*). According to the film, this novel is in great demand: the librarian has hidden it under the

---

[56] Gertrud Koch, "Why Women Go to the Movies," *Jump Cut* 27 (July 1982): 51–53.

counter to safeguard it for Laura. A female spectator of the forties might well know that such novels dealt with similar subjects to *Brief Encounter* itself. In contrast to Laura, this novel's heroine, Una, is "a symbol of a perfect wife and mother": she stands for "one ideal of love, a love which transcends passion to find itself in domestic bliss."[57] In fact it is precisely the equivalent aspect of *Brief Encounter*, Laura's rejection of temptation despite wavering, and her final resting place within the middle-class home, that is redolent of the narratives of glossy women's literature. As *Today's Cinema* wrote of *Brief Encounter*'s treatment: "Even illicit romance may remain wholesome when untainted by sordidness."[58]

Lastly, the presence of a female voice-over surely implies an address to a female viewer, as it does in *Letter from an Unknown Woman, Mildred Pierce*, and a handful of other films from the nineteen-forties. Manny Farber went as far as to say that because of the voice-over, "the whole movie takes on the quality of sensitive dignified femininity."[59] The question is, to what extent does this voice provide material on which female fantasy can work, and to what extent does it betray or compromise the representation of female subjectivity? For the most part we must understand this voice as self-incriminating and self-indicting. It facilitates flashbacks which, in their temporal anteriority, modify Laura's past actions, making them passive and over-fictionalized. Laura Mulvey suggests that having "a female point of view dominating the narrative produces an excess which precludes satisfaction" for its audience. The kind of fantasy escape such a film offers "is so strongly marked by recognizable real and familiar traps that the escape is closer to a daydream than a fairy story."[60] Such fantasy is of a temporary, truncated character, as is Laura's inner fantasy in the train, which amounts to a longed-for future set in the past, a future utterly irreconcilable with that which actually transpired for the film's 1945 audience. In Mulvey's terms, the illusion is marked by a trap.

Laura describes herself through her voice-over as "neurotic," "hysterical," and "that kind of woman," categories of femininity then substantiated in the very structure of the film. According to Freud, the hysteric "suffers mainly from reminiscences," and her physical symptoms, often of muteness, are traceable to these repressed memories. Laura's voice-over and its relation to the rest of the narrative largely recapitulates this psychoanalytic conception of femininity. Her voice-over takes the form of a reminiscence while it also coexists with muteness toward Fred in the

[57] Nicola Beauman, *A Very Great Profession: The Woman's Novel, 1914–1939* (London: Virago, 1983), p. 223.

[58] *Today's Cinema*, 14 November 1945.

[59] Manny Farber, "Middle-Aged Fling," *The New Republic*, 21 October 1946.

[60] Laura Mulvey, "Notes on Sirk and Melodrama," *Movie* 25 (Winter 1977–78): 56.

present. Laura is shown to be completely pliable under medical scrutiny, and indeed in need of such scrutiny from the moment a cinder lodges in her eye. She becomes hypnotized by Alec's intonement of medical terminology, her eyes glazing over with love as he drones "silicosis, ternecosis, anthracosis, pneumoconiosis." Her reminiscence also originates from daydreaming over embroidery, one of the factors that Freud felt "rendered women particularly prone to hysteria" because it induced "dispositional hypnoid states."[61]

Laura's voice-over does not parallel the all-knowing, disembodied male voice-over of the wartime documentary (*Desert Victory*, for example) with its masquerade as a "point of textual origin"; the ironic, disembodied voice-over of *Perfect Strangers*; the anxious, semi-disembodied voice-over of Howard in *The Gentle Sex*; nor Doctor Montgomery's assured, though embodied, voice in *Waterloo Road*.[62] Her voice-over is not only embodied but firmly tied to the story's "interior," to use Silverman's term, taking the form of a compulsive confession.[63] In this respect it can be associated with many films made in the transition from war to peace— *Mildred Pierce* and *Double Indemnity* (1944), for instance—in which the embodied voice-over frequently misleads, negates, or exhausts itself by the end of the film. This is exactly what happens in *Brief Encounter*.

As the narrative unfolds, the momentum of Laura's voice subsides. Fred adopts the "movie" seat in their living room on the third Thursday—the seat that mirrors the external spectator's seat (Figure 4.2)—and from then on shots of him glancing at Laura indicate that he is watching her watching herself until, as he engulfs her in his arms in the final scene, hiding her face and stifling her voice-over forever, he thanks her for "coming back" to him. This phrase implies that, despite her muteness, he has "heard" her confession all along. Fred effectively performs the task of the analyst of Laura's hysteria. One critic admired Cyril Raymond's performance as "the homely husband" precisely because he had "masculine" control enough to listen to Laura's tale without revealing that he heard it: he "suspected more than his emotions showed."[64]

By adopting a quasi-documentary formula, through the use of a female voice-over, but altering its effect, the film subtly presents Laura as vulnerable and lacking control by contrast to a patriarch such as Alastair Sim in *Waterloo Road*. As one writer commented, "Miss Johnson has the diffi-

[61] Joseph Breuer and Sigmund Freud, *Studies on Hysteria, 1883–1885* in J. and A. Strachey, eds., *The Complete Works of Sigmund Freud*, volume 2 (London: The Hogarth Press, 1932–36; Penguin Books, 1974), p. 12. Cited in Parker, *The Subversive Stitch*, p. 11.

[62] Silverman, *The Acoustic Mirror*, p. 53.

[63] Ibid.

[64] Lionel Collier, "Brief Encounter," *The Picturegoer*, 2 February 1946.

culties of interpreting with her face close to the camera the audible progression of her secret thoughts—a clumsy device conspicuously out of place in a technically competent film.''[65] The correlation between Laura's facial expressions and her spoken thoughts results from subtle and skilled editing, but even so, two other writers found the voice-over to be excessive. The first wrote, ''I do not like the technical trick of telling the story in the form of an off-screen commentary. To my mind Miss Johnson's face, and her walk, and her eyes, can tell a story or impart a mood, or reveal a confidence without the help of any narrative,'' while the other echoed, ''This running commentary of the 'I felt dreadful' variety seems wholly expendable and *Brief Encounter*'s one serious error of judgement.''[66]

Perceiving the voice-over as redundant precludes recognizing its important function in the film of hystericizing the woman, thus reducing her problem to a consequence of feminine sexuality. While it lends the character of Laura more weight, it simultaneously deals her more responsibility in the affair and constructs her involvement as pathologically obsessive. I would not want to claim, however, that there was nothing other than masochistic pleasure or value attached to the female voice-over by female spectators. For a start, the very existence of a female voice-over in the cinema represented a recent expansion of territory for female expression, consequent to recent social change. And while the voice-over reinforced dominant social constructions of gender—of woman as hysteric—it also exaggerated that construction, making it perhaps intermittently conspicuous. Further, although Laura's narration ends, smothered in the convolvuli of floral upholstery, it has never been synchronized to her body in the way that, for instance, Walter Neff's is in *Double Indemnity*, through the device of a dictaphone. There are also moments when her voice-over does not form part of a reminiscence, as when she wishes Dolly ''were dead'' in the first train carriage scene. There is then a degree to which the space of Laura's mind remains free from medical colonization, by not being tied to her body, and it still remains conceivable that this fictional female thought is not fully circumscribed by the form of the film, even if female action is.

THE COMBINATION of multiple temporalities, a central female character with a confessional voice-over, and a banal setting in prewar Britain worked against any clear genre classification for *Brief Encounter*. It was

---

[65] Anonymous, ''Brief Encounter,'' *The Daily Telegraph*, 22 November 1945.

[66] C. A. Lejeune, ''The Films,'' *The Observer*, 25 November 1945. Jerry Vermilye, *The Great British Films, 1933–1971* (Secaucus, N.J.: Citadel Press, 1978), p. 93.

part "Woman's Film," part new British realism, part period piece. It raised the question of women's status in peacetime in the realist style, but also diffused it though its designation solely as a woman's problem. Official critical response to the film evidences just this kind of tension between definitions of realism and the matter of how much the representation of female experience could be included within its walls. This is the significance of the word "though" when *Today's Cinema* calls the film "first rate general entertainment, though appealing predominantly to a female audience."[67] Female experience could not readily be categorized as being of central importance, of general interest, even if Howard, Launder, Gilliat, Priestley and others had professed that it was when imaging the mobile woman in 1943. This is why another critic predicted of *Brief Encounter* that "all women and most men will love this film."[68]

American critics were most ready to speak of the difficult balance between realism and a woman's fantasy as they praised the film for its frankness and sincerity, and then slighted it for its address to women. James Agee suggests in his review that fiction for women, however good, can never be quite as good as fiction for men: "It is my impression that the same story, with fancy variations, is told once or twice in every issue of every magazine for housewives. . . . If . . . the movie at its best suggests *merely* all that women's magazine fiction might be at its own best, that is not intended to be a back-handed compliment."[69] John Mason Brown took less trouble to conceal his patronizing opinion, resenting in particular the clash of popular culture with high romantic music: "It may be set to Rachmaninov's Concerto No 2, but it is keyed to daydreaming, the Dodie Smith of 'Call it a Day,' and women's glossy magazines."[70] Manny Farber resolved the same contradiction as follows: "The film sometimes suggests women's magazine fiction, but Celia Johnson's performance . . . takes it way out of the *Ladies' Home Journal* class."[71]

Despite the film's blackened subterranean passages and canted angles, and despite its narrative structure formed from fractured female memory, and its inclusion of two protagonists who are ignorant of (or at least ignore) the events of 1939, most British critics still perceived *Brief Encounter* as

[67] *Today's Cinema*, 14 November 1945.

[68] Joan Lester, "New Coward Film Is Good," *Reynolds Weekly*, 25 November 1945.

[69] James Agee, "Brief Encounter," *The Nation*, 31 October 1946; my emphasis. American publicity for *Brief Encounter*, held at the Lincoln Center for the Performing Arts, New York, described it as "a story of the most precious moments of a woman's life—it could happen to you."

[70] John Mason Brown, "Seeing Things: The Midas Touch," *Saturday Review of Literature*, 12 October 1946, p. 36.

[71] Farber, "Middle-Aged Fling."

"simple" and "straightforward." Memories of the cinematography of Laura's fantasies, her run through the nighttime city, her suicide attempt, and the overall centrality of her consciousness are repressed in critics' minds. Edgar Anstey can write, "To the realism of the excellent dialogue the camera adds the pictorial detail most likely to reinforce it. No extravagant 'subjective' camera angles, no 'interpretive' movements of the camera, but a simplicity of technique in keeping with the story of three commonplace people finding a dramatically unspectacular solution to a commonplace situation."[72] The film's association with the aesthetic of new realism, and the discourse of patriotism linked to it, was far more apparent to British critics, which lead to this dimorphism of response vis-à-vis their American counterparts.

The attention to prewar detail to avoid anachronisms, plus the location shooting, promoted the film's aura of national style, as did the effort to correlate wide variations in lighting levels to logically appropriate venues. The affair is conducted in cinemas, underground passages, and night streets which would in reality be artificially lit with consequently deep shadows. The more "morally secure" locations of the refreshment room, daytime streets, and Laura's home in Ketchworth are shot with high-key lighting and are usually filmed from eye level, and framed as more balanced two- or three-shot compositions than the exterior night scenes. As in *Mildred Pierce*, the potential disruption of the lovers' actions is visually insinuated through the seepage of low-key lighting, distinctive shooting styles, and off-balance compositions into "safer" locations, such as the railway carriage, the waiting room, and the Jesson sitting room. The *Guardian* critic was vaguely aware of this lighting code which discriminated according to subject: "The one noticeable flaw is indifferent lighting for the principals. If the stars were photographed as subtly as the railway waiting-room, this film would be a visual wonder."[73] He discerns a correspondence between contrasty lighting and the acceleration of the couple's relationship.

Another compelling reason for critics to define the film as frank and straightforward was the patent dullness of the subjects' lives, and the generally unexciting presentation of middle-class living in solid, more or less Northern locations, supported by the understated cast of the acting. In Laura's words: "I'm an ordinary woman. I didn't think such violent things could happen to ordinary people. . . . It all started on an ordinary day, in the most ordinary place in the world—the refreshment room in Milford Junction." Laura's routine of traveling to Milford on Thursdays is equaled

---

[72] Edgar Anstey, "Brief Encounter," *The Spectator*, 7 December 1945.
[73] Anonymous, *The Manchester Guardian*, 22 November 1945.

by Fred's routine of doing the evening crossword (Figure 4.2). It was the ordinariness of the protagonists that appealed to Manny Farber: "The film deals, as few films do, with limp, orderly, repressed, unexciting middle-class people, and carries them through the most exciting event of their lives in a limp, orderly, repressed, unexciting way, the only way of which they would be capable. . . . It is highly unorthodox for movies to handle colorless people, and almost unheard of to leave their lives ungilded, yet it is this very naturalism that makes *Brief Encounter* a haunting work."[74] The age of the protagonists also fed into the film's realist designation: critics euphemistically referred to the "A" certificate film as "adult," or as an "eternal love-triangle," which it clearly was not since both parties were married. The *Chronicle* reviewer described four spectators who had remarked separately to him after the preview that "*Brief Encounter* was more like a French film. . . . What they meant is that the film, among other things, is emotionally grown-up."[75]

Figure 4.2. Flames of passion at the Ketchworth fireside. Laura has earlier contributed "romance" to Fred's crossword puzzle, fitting the adjacent solutions "delirium" and "Baluchistan." *Brief Encounter*, production still.

[74] Farber, "Middle-Aged Fling."
[75] Anonymous, "Grown-up Love," *Chronicle*, 24 November 1945.

Despite the setting of the diegesis in the immediately prewar period, many elements of the film resonated with 1945 and this too deflected attention away from its fantasy scenes and complex temporal structure.[76] In the late war discussion of adultery was so pervasive that the film would have to have been understood in relation to current debates. The problem of adultery was too large and disturbing to be ignored. Felix Barker remembers the connection in this way: "With its forced separations, war breeds adultery; and when it appeared in 1945, *Brief Encounter* had such a topical poignancy that many people found it unbearable."[77] Besides the subject of adultery, the film's theme of snatched opportunities in bleak surroundings gave it a wartime flavor, as did the low lighting of the nighttime exterior scenes and the frequent train whistles that pierce Laura's consciousness with an equivalent perforative force to other films' air raid sirens. The station refreshment room and platform were staples of British wartime film iconography: consider the Crewe refreshment room in *The Way Ahead* and the platform farewells of *The Gentle Sex*, *Perfect Strangers*, and *Piccadilly Incident*. With its constant comings and goings, Milford Junction surely echoed wartime good-byes. The theme of subterranean romances in tunnel discomfort redounded on wartime shelter life in the London underground, while the Milford boathouse is also mindful of wartime, with its atmosphere of making do, and making tea, in ramshackle turmoil (Figures 4.3 and 4.4). Laura's plain attire echoed women's wartime wear, giving her a practical and austere air commensurate with realism while also helping to root her image in the audience's present. The film even ended with another kind of blackout: Laura buries her head in Fred's far shoulder and the screen fades to black, before fading up to a final shot of the station again.

Finally, it is through comparison with Hollywood that the film's native character is secured in critical discourse, and the matter of Laura's appearance is of utmost importance to this process. Once weighed against Hollywood, the film's visual and temporal excesses are quickly eclipsed, as the film itself suggests in its juxtaposition of a movie trailer for a steamy jungle picture, *Flames of Passion*—"stupendous!" "colossal!!" "gigantic!!!" "epoch-making!!!"—both with a local store's uneventful screen advertisement for prams, and with *Brief Encounter* itself. The *Flames of Passion* trailer appears exaggerated through being shown within the high-class super cinema in *Milford*—by appearing in the wrong environment—and by its contrast to the banal pram. Alec Harvey mocks the same American film when he and Laura go to see it two weeks after seeing the trailer.

---

[76] It is a process of the present constantly implicating the past, as Pierre Sorlin describes it in his work on historical understanding, *The Film in History: Restaging the Past* (Totowa, N.J.: Barnes and Noble Books, 1980), p. 143.

[77] Felix Barker, "Programme Notes for *Brief Encounter*," microjacket, British Film Institute Library.

Figure 4.3. The underground romance: low-key lighting, Northern stone architecture, and the railroad's steam accompany Laura and Alec's affair. *Brief Encounter*, production still.

(The stark juxtaposition of the *Flames of Passion* trailer to the pram signals Coward's humor again, and possibly raised the question of illegitimate children for contemporary audiences, if they made the connection.)

According to the critics, the national distinctiveness of *Brief Encounter* lay in its anticlimactic pace and nonfetishized lead players: "Here is no Hollywood glamour, but warm and sympathetic insight into a real world, into real emotions."[78] American critics even contrasted the film to their own output: "What is most exceptional about it is that it dares to allow its average characters to remain average . . . it can claim an honesty and a nearness of life almost unknown in Hollywood offerings."[79] And in the *Manchester Guardian*'s words, "*Brief Encounter* is a shining example of how good a film can be when all idea of making it smart, snappy, glamorous has been discarded from the start."[80] Campbell Dixon wondered how the public would react "to this study of life as it is, a world where

[78] Patrick Kirwan, "Star . . ." *Evening Standard*, 23 November 1945.
[79] John Mason Brown, "Seeing Things," p. 36.
[80] *The Guardian*, 19 February 1946.

Figure 4.4. Laura and Alec ''make do'' in a boathouse whose ambience
echoes the bomb-damaged, wartime *mise-en-scène*.
Brief Encounter, production still.

obstacles to romance are not all painlessly removed by a celestial scenario
writer?''[81] Stephen Watts of the *Sunday Express* was the most brutally
frank when he wrote that the film makes ''no attempt to hit you over the
head with the Hollywood bladder labelled romance.''[82]

Their responses confirm the central value of the female image in defining, if not British cinema, then at least non-Hollywood cinema: national
specificity can be established only through difference, and here, through a
reciprocal arrangement with sexual difference. As the female image becomes less distinct from the male, in abandoning sequins, satin, strappy
gowns, and bare shoulders (those signs of femininity Laura leaves in the
railway carriage glass), national screen specificity is established. Attenu-
ating the visibility of sexual difference builds the possibility of signifying
national difference, under these particular historical conditions of cinema.
The repeated focus by critics on both sides of the Atlantic on the appearance of Celia Johnson, whose everyday garb contrasted so strongly with

[81] Campbell Dixon, ''Pathos of Frustrated Love,'' *The Daily Telegraph*, 26 November
1945.
[82] Stephen Watts, ''A Seat in the . . .'' *Sunday Express*, 25 January 1946.

the floral-saronged, screaming woman in the *Flames of Passion* trailer, evidences that this reciprocal system of national and sexual differentiation was at work (Figure 4.5). "The greatest departure from an American film in handling this story is the casting of the two principal characters. Neither of them is particularly handsome or buried under romantic appeal," and Celia Johnson plays just a "plain woman."[83] She is "portrayed as sufficiently attractive to win our sympathy, but not so glamorous as to be incredible."[84] Celia Johnson, "without manufactured glamor or conventional good looks, magnificently portrays the wife and mother."[85] She has

Figure 4.5. The restraint of Laura Jesson's costume serves the national interest, not least through its difference from that of the half-naked woman in *Flames of Passion. Brief Encounter*, production still.

[83] Philip T. Hartung, "The Screen," *The Commonweal*, 13 September 1946, p. 36.
[84] Lester, "New Coward Film Is Good."
[85] Anonymous, "Grown-up Love," *The Chronicle*, 24 November 1945.

been "touched by life rather than retouched by the ever-hovering make-up man."[86] She has "a clammy hairdo, little makeup, [and] looks over-worked."[87] "She has . . . a few undisguised wrinkles, often gets caught in unflattering camera angles, and appears more than once in the same old none-too-chic hat": she "in no way resembles what U.S. moviegoers have learned to expect from a suburban matron."[88] Mason Brown extrapolated her sartorial style to virtuousness: "She has one tailor-made suit. . . . She wears the same hat more than once; and is compelled to wear it as often and as proudly as most wives must wear their hats."[89] He concludes, "In short she is a wife, not a moll; a woman instead of a magazine cover."

The multiplicity of hat observations are utterly to the point. Laura wears her hat every time she meets Alec—at the Kardomah, in the cinema—until their first planned rendezvous, their trip to the country. Alec makes a special point of taking her hat when she reaches Stephen's apartment on that fateful evening, and as she later flees through the wet streets she clutches it, crushed in her hand. It is only Fred who always sees Laura without her hat, and always at home. In fact, there it is his hat that is emphasized, dominating the foreground of the first interior shot of their household. As the film develops, Laura's hat becomes an icon of the formality and morality of middle-class breeding. Laura's appearance, and by association, her narrative status, are subtly varied by moderate adjustments to her hat decoration. A stiff bow in the early flashbacks becomes a softer plume in the last one, and an almost identical suit now appears edged with a soft mink collar. The literal softening of her image in the final parting scene thematizes her lack of power in the circumstances: although she has always been the one to insist on caution, it is Alec who finally breaks off the relationship by going to Africa. Even to the last, Laura hopes he has not taken his train.

Mildred Pierce's dramatic appearance—her huge fur shoulders, and lowering hat on Joan Crawford's powerful body—her enormous success as a businesswoman, and her obsession with awful Veda make her an exaggerated, larger-than-life character, consonant with Crawford's star image. By contrast, Laura is unexciting: in her appearance, in repeatedly wearing the same clothes, in her routine life, and in her vulnerability and fragility, expressed formally through her confessional voice-over and her meticulous acting style. Such contrasts are at the root of one American critic's remark of *Brief Encounter* that "the British apparently do not know how to turn their heroines—and thus their plots—into something more gor-

---

[86] John Mason Brown, "Seeing Things," p. 37.
[87] Farber, "Middle-Aged Fling."
[88] *Time*, 9 September 1946, p. 102.
[89] John Mason Brown, "Seeing Things," p. 37.

geous than life.''[90] From an American perspective, this constraint in female representation held no patriotic charge, only one of reduced visual pleasure.

Because of her honesty of expression and appearance, her lack of a made-up face—in effect the removal of the support of paint and costume—Celia Johnson's Laura forms the most effective part of *Brief Encounter*'s ''mask'' of realism. The film can turn and depend on this absence of glamor for a morally secure outcome. Laura's looks circumscribe her actions and make it inconceivable that she should leave her post of wife and mother, make it impossible for her to live out a fantasy, a Hollywood-style ending. She is the quintessential realist woman, providing a counterpoint to dominant Hollywood constructions of femininity. As an anti-Crawford figure, Laura is part of the general British cinematic attempt to define not only moral and social codes, but also the national cinema style, through the image of woman. Woman could represent both past ways and values, in the traditional role of mother, but also change and new values, in the mobile woman and sexual mother. As Gledhill and Swanson remark, ''There is a desire to keep the stability of the past, and a need to respond to changes and shifts in experiences and values. The problem is how to secure continuity with change.''[91] The shifting temporalities of *Brief Encounter* are an attempt to solve this problem, by establishing distance with a link, peacetime seen through the lens of war. Being able to make the resolution of *Brief Encounter*, that is, Laura's return to Fred, appear natural, through a multitude of devices including these oscillations of temporality, was a very powerful way of controlling female sexual desire in general, both within and beyond the context of the film.

All these realist tropes accompany Laura's encounter with emotional desire, rallying together to resolved the dilemma of the married mother's affair in a way that naturalizes its demise and the repression of female agency, and makes the outcome of the film appear inevitable and logical. The grossly manipulated temporality and extreme references to blackouts, barred cages, blowing rubbish, and train symbolism could all be incorporated into the logic of realism. In *Brief Encounter* a woman's dilemma is aired within the terms of realism, subtly suggesting that women are naturally ineffective, remote from history and politics, and unable to control either shifts in *mise-en-scène*, genres, or their own destinies, while it ostensibly gives them a choice, held out by Laura's voice-over.

[90] *Time*, 9 September 1946, p. 102.
[91] Gledhill and Swanson, ''Gender and Sexuality in Second World War Films—A Feminist Approach,'' p. 62.

TO CLOSE we must return once more to the question of temporality. *Brief Encounter* proposes two temporally-defined options for Laura, and it is the tension between them that creates the possibility for drama and desire. The clockwork, chronological time of the external world—L.M.S. railway timetables and dependable, regular Fred—is pitted against the convoluted and chaotic time of the film's structure, organized as Laura's remembrance. By exorcising her guilt through a private confession, the tension between these temporalities is dispersed and the present of "normal" life resurfaces. The stability of a future with Fred ultimately displaces the torrid disorder of a remembered past with Alec. These two forms of time— linear and non-linear—are presented through the film as gendered realms, conforming to stereotypes of the patterns of masculine and feminine thinking. This classification is even buttressed by Dorothy Richardson, who in the early thirties described men as "occidental," "straight-line thinkers" who as directors consequently limited film's potential, while women were nonlinear thinkers who "excel in memory" and for whom film offered a unique outlet for expression, as yet unrealized.[92]

The diegetic train perfectly encapsulates Laura's temporal choices. It comprises elements of both alternatives; in fact, it occupies the interface between them. It stands for regular temporality, masculinity, and nittygritty realism on the one hand, and the power of passion and illicit longing on the other. Schivelbusch points out that it was the introduction of railways that first standardized time in Europe: small differences between local times were no longer tolerable if timetables were to be readable and workable.[93] In terms of the cinema, the train was one of realism's most powerful icons, established with 1930s documentary filmmaking, particularly through *Night Mail*, and rife with connotations of working-class male labor, industrialization, and specifically British invention.[94] On the other hand, the steam locomotive as a symbol of sexual passion had become an increasingly familiar idea as Freudian psychoanalysis was popularized, in part through use in the treatment of war derangements. Coward makes the

[92] Dorothy M. Richardson, "Continuous Performance: The Film Gone Male," *Close Up* 9, no. 1 (March 1932): 36. I am grateful to Catherine Benamou for this reference.

[93] Wolfgang Schivelbusch, *The Railway Journey: The Industrialization of Time and Space in the Nineteenth Century* (Berkeley: University of California Press, 1986), pp. 43– 44. This took place from the early nineteenth century onward and was fully accomplished by 1880.

[94] *Night Mail* (1936, G.P.O. Film Unit), a film about the journey of the mail train from London to Glasgow at night, was one of the best known, most influential works of the British documentary film movement. Representations of trains and stations have often been fraught with dire moods and consequences: witness Anna Karenina's suicide, the flight and pursuit along the railway in Dickens's *Little Dorrit*, the denouement of *It Always Rains on Sundays*.

train/sex metaphor laughably explicit in the scene near the station entrance where Alec and Laura kiss, rubbish blowing around their feet. The brief cutaway during the embrace to a screaming express train demands to be read as a symbol of active sexuality since it is not narratively motivated in any other way. *Brief Encounter*'s emphasis on the train's symbolic association with sex over its literal or political function, or its aesthetic link to new realism, further contributes to the over-fictionalization of Laura's account, marking hers again as an unrealizable desire.

In the closing moments of the film, Laura contemplates committing suicide by throwing herself in front of this train. The camera angle cants, and bright staccato lights flash across her face. The stroboscopic effect—the compression of a middle-class lifetime of days and nights—replays the terror of bombings and explosions of wartime. Her voice murmurs: "I meant to do it, Fred. . . . I should like to be able to say that it was the thought of you and the children—but it wasn't—I had no thoughts at all." For Laura there was no choice at all: by opting for life she had said "no" to desire and "yes" to the predictability of middle-class marriage. Because the phallic train is structurally dominant in the film, opening and closing it and marking off its stages, the whole film, including Laura's choice, is circumscribed by male norms: the "problem" of female desire is placed within male parameters. But there *is* one narrative space for Laura alone—on the train itself, rather than under it. The space of the railway carriage marks the distance between Laura's two alternatives, Milford/Alec and Ketchworth/Fred, but also represents a place that escapes the film's temporal system: the only points of temporal significance in the railway system are the times of departure and arrival. It is for this reason that the carriage scenes are the only sites of full-blown reverie, fantasy, and reflection for Laura—she never enjoys the movies—and also the reason why the two men are never shown within the train compartment. These men belong to the filmic world's fixed points; they form its temporal grid. It is Laura who must travel between them, as all wartime women must, emotionally and literally, trying to place themselves within this scheme.

If the moving train in *Brief Encounter* escapes temporal regimentation, it remains the quintessential location of another organizing system of difference: that of class. The British class structure finds one of its most literal and trenchant manifestations on the railway. While the American train was never class-stratified, the British one was from the start.[95] The class significance of the train kicks in with *Brief Encounter*'s opening moments, as Mr. Godby describes a recent infringement of class law to Myrtle: he has found a third-class passenger traveling first class and has handed the

[95] See Schivelbusch, *The Railway Journey*, pp. 89–112.

matter over to his superior, who will give the passenger a fine and a drub-bing. This early dialogue snatch initiates the film's efforts to keep class difference intact, and is also another clue to the film's prewar diegesis, since films with a wartime setting tended to stress the flexibility of class boundaries, as I have discussed earlier.

The class rift is highly conscpicuous throughout *Brief Encounter*; in fact, the film's investigation of the sexual mother is made at the price of keeping class difference intact. Alec and Laura's most lighthearted mo-ments are taken at the expense of Myrtle and Albert, against whom they are paired. The clichéd working-class couple has an earthier, more animal, and less rule-bound sexuality. Myrtle has, as Laura mocks, a "refined" accent, a high-class veneer superimposed on a working-class base, which ridicules her character for Laura. Myrtle and Albert never appear without either Alec or Laura being nearby, and their scenes together are usually presented from Laura and Alec's point of view, for whom they serve as the butt of several jokes. The irony is that Laura's predicament overlaps with Myrtle's experience: Myrtle has left her first husband, as she tells Albert Godby near the beginning of the film. Further, Myrtle's ebullient presence reminds Laura, and the audience, of the sexual desires she wishes to express.

It is easy to imagine how this kind of representation might alienate the largely working-class wartime audience, especially at a moment when the new Labour government was promising a fresh egalitarianism. This audi-ence recognized the attempt to represent a working-class environment, set vaguely in the North, and recognized peacetime class dynamics at work, but rejected both, bursting out with laughter at the conservative, guilt-rid-den couple: "What few people know is that even in 1945 the story proved too much for some. When the film was previewed in Rochester, it was laughed off the screen."[96] David Lean was reported as saying, "A woman in the front row began laughing and pretty soon the entire audience was hysterical. I wanted to burn the print, I was so humiliated."[97] Raymond Durgnat describes a frustrated 1965 audience at the Baker Street Classic that "couldn't restrain its derision and repeatedly burst into angry, exas-perated laughter," and Isabel Quigly recalls the headline "Laura a eu tort!" above the results of a poll of French women who were far from compelled by the moral imperative of the film.[98]

---

[96] See Richard Kayne, "In Defence of the Critics," in *This Year of Films*, comp. Ion Hammond (London: British Film Institute Library), p. 9. Kayne writes, "Noel Coward's *Brief Encounter* was a financial flop . . . yet the critics are agreed that it was one of the best films ever to come out of any British studio." See also *Sunday Express*, 3 November 1968.

[97] *Sunday Express*, 3 November 1968.

[98] Raymond Durgnat, *A Mirror For England: British Movies from Austerity to Affluence*

Clearly audiences did not identify solely with their own class, just as they did not identify solely with their own gender, or even nationality: how else can we explain the popularity of Lockwood's aristocratic mobility in *The Wicked Lady* over Laura's fixity in *Brief Encounter* in 1945? But to many audiences, the sexual constraints on Laura must have seemed ridiculous this side of war, while the setting in prewar life was too close for full-throttled fantasy, as compared with that of the Age of Charles II in *The Wicked Lady*. Identifying with Laura in 1945 would have meant rejecting that hat on the cover of *Picture Post* (Figure 2.2), and for what patriotic reason, now that the war was over? While *Brief Encounter* was formally advanced, its themes were received by these audiences as reactionary and middle-class: indeed, *Brief Encounter* belonged to exactly that kind of cinema that irked the young Lindsay Anderson as he set up a new journal, *Sequence*, in Oxford in 1946, to debate the break from precisely such films that only wore a mask of realism.[99]

(London: Faber and Faber, 1970), p. 180; Isabel Quigly, "*Brief Encounter* Programme Notes," microjacket, British Film Institute Library.

[99] See, for example, Lindsay Anderson, "Angles of Approach," *Sequence* 2 (Winter 1947): 6 and elsewhere.

From Mufti to Civvies:
A Canterbury Tale

Typical British life has been said to be too
uneventful and emotionally dull to make exciting
cinema . . . it is, of course, a fallacy to think
that we are slow or dull compared with
French or American people.

Roger Manvell, *Britain Today*, July 1945

THE CULTURAL, economic, and political turmoil of World War II precipitated massive changes in the use, and imagery, of all representational media in Britain. The cinematic apparatus was up against particular pressure in its duty of formulating coherent representations of masculinity and femininity. While all films made in Britain in wartime reveal the strains of this mission, none focus so obsessively or exclusively on the problem than the films of Michael Powell and Emeric Pressburger. Consider *The Life and Death of Colonel Blimp* (1943), with its *tour de force* of male aging in the character of Clive Candy (Roger Livesey), who lives from the Boer to the Second World War, and its splitting of his love interest into three women—three Deborah Kerr's—who, escaping history as it were, never age. Consider the fragmentation of femininity again in *The Spy in Black* (1939), in which the audience eventually discovers that there have been three female spies and counterspies, changing nationality and allegiance as they jostle around Captain Hardt (Conrad Veidt). The loss of nationality (Theo [Anton Walbrook] in *Blimp*), the masquerade of nationality (through spying in *The Spy in Black* and *Contraband*), and the difficulties of being alien but not enemy, of being non-national (Bob in *A Canterbury Tale*, and Theo again in *Blimp*) are themes that dominate Powell and Pressburger's work. These themes pertain certainly to the international nature of the Archers: Junge (German), Gray (Polish), Pressburger (Hungarian), Walbrook (Austrian), and Powell (English). But they are also a mark of wartime's pressures on definitions and differences of nationality—topographical, political, and personal.

197

The foregoing chapters have focused on crucial areas of difficulty in wartime's complex representational history: the making of the feminine, the imaging of the blackout, the manufacture of history through the erection of temporal distance, and the establishment of national identity. Powell and Pressburger's 1944 version of *A Canterbury Tale* is exemplary in tackling all these areas: it consistently works away at those nodal points— representations of the past, of blackouts, of mobile women, of G.I.'s—at which differences of sexuality, nationality, and temporality are established and eroded. The film functions as a limit text, a text that proves the centrality of these areas for British wartime cinema as a whole. By focusing excessively on them, the 1944 version of the film points to essential problems in the processes of wartime representation, and at times even parodies British realism itself. It at once embraces *and* critiques the idea of a genuine national cinema: it invokes a British cultural heritage, but moves away from recently established, realist filmic conventions, in its pace, themes, imagery, and unfamiliar narrative turns; for example, it combines location shooting with period costume in its opening sequence, and so dislocates the established "logical" connection between cinema and reality, that founding principle of British wartime cinema and criticism alike, illustrated so well by Manvell in the epigraph to this chapter.

In the 1949 version of *A Canterbury Tale*, these wayward, contentious points have been edited away, or reshot and reframed—some altered entirely—producing a different, though Powell-authorized, product, an emissary of British cinema for the postwar American audience. The differences between the two texts (1944 and 1949) point to the centrality of the viewer, of an address to a particular audience, in holding together the identity of a national cinema. When that audience shifts by changing nationality, as in the case of the reception of the 1949 version, not only different meanings but also a different film text may emerge, one exhibiting crucial rearrangements of gender and national relations. Because the two versions of the film differ in precisely the areas on which the rest of this book has been focused, a comparison of the two films forms an appropriate conclusion to the book.

THE PUBLICITY sheet advertised *A Canterbury Tale* (1944) as "a new story about an old custom." In this "modern" version of Chaucer's poem, G.I. Sergeant Bob Johnson of Johnson County, Oregon (Sgt. John Sweet), makes a pilgrimage to the Kentish countryside. His two fellow "pilgrims" are British Army Sergeant Peter Gibb (Dennis Price) and Land Army girl Allison Smith (Sheila Sim). In peacetime Bob Johnson works as a lumberjack, Peter Gibb as a cinema organist, and Allison Smith as a sales assistant in the garden-furniture section of a London department store. They converge on Chillingbourne, Kent, near Canterbury, in the wartime black-out, just prior to the D-Day landings of 1944. They are introduced to the spectator as they alight from a train in an excessively dark and lengthy blackout scene—a scene that is marked by all the undecidability of the blackout trope encountered in the analyses of Chapter 3.[1]

The opening blackout frames *A Canterbury Tale* and threads instability and uncertainty through its plot, particularly through its representations of sexual relations. As Allison emerges from the Chillingbourne blackout her gender is signaled initially by her voice in the darkness, and then by her striking silhouette as she stands in the gloomy station passageway wreathed in steam (Figure 5.1). She stamps out her cigarette and moves to join her co-travelers in the film, Bob and Peter, while protesting that she does not need an escort in the dark. Before long she has been attacked with "sticky stuff" and has to spend the rest of the film tracking down the culprit.

Allison has been sent by the War Agricultural Committee to work on Thomas Culpepper's farm, although he refuses to employ her early on in the film because she is a woman. Culpepper (Eric Portman) is the pilgrims' "guide." A local magistrate and country squire, he runs the Chilling-bourne historical society, lives with his mother, and contributes to the war effort by participating in the village's fire-watch and Home Guard rotas. This last fact holds the key to solving the film's very weak narrative enigma: the need to identify the "glueman" who attacks women in the blackout by throwing glue in their hair. Allison is the village's most recent victim. The crimes are finally pinned on Culpepper when Sergeant Gibb notices a correlation between the dates of the attacks and Culpepper's nighttime war duties. A shaft of light escaping from his ineffective office blackout at the town hall alerts the British Sergeant to the correspondence: the "clue" to the glue—that is, the light—indicates that the magistrate had returned to his office hurriedly, carelessly omitting to check his blackout. Showing a light—in wartime a carelessness tantamount to enemy action—identifies the culprit.

Through his association with the blackout, and other textual markers that contribute to his menacing aspect such as austere facial lighting, strict-ness of character, and misogyny, Culpepper is coded as questionable, strangely magical, and perhaps even evil, a quality enhanced through as-sociation with Portman's previous appearance in a Powell and Pressburger film, the *49th Parallel*, as an ardent Nazi (Figure 5.2). However, despite

[1] See Roland Barthes, "Textual analysis of Poe's 'Valdemar,' " in Robert Young, ed., *Untying the Text: A Post-Structuralist Reader* (London: Routledge and Kegan Paul, 1981), p. 158, on undecidability as a condition of expression.

Figure 5.1. Allison's dramatic emergence from the
station blackout. Frame enlargement from
A Canterbury Tale.

his demeanor and behavior, the publicity material described Culpepper
only as the "apparent malefactor" or "alleged miscreant."[2] His crime was
only minor because, as he ultimately explains, he throws glue in women's
hair to keep them inside, away from the local army base, in order to as-
suage the fears of their absent menfolk and preserve the women's virtues
for their fighting partners' returns. It is in keeping with the argument of the
film's status as a limit text that a sexualized action—glue in hair—is ironically employed to prevent sexual activity in women.

When, at the National Film Theatre's "Guardian Lecture" in 1985,
Emeric Pressburger was asked why he chose glue-throwing for the plot of
A Canterbury Tale he gave two replies: that he wanted to give the sense

[2] *The Cinema*, 10 May 1944, and 15 September 1948, on the film's re-release.

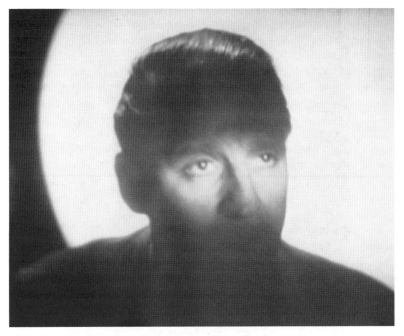

Figure 5.2. The mysterious Culpepper, caught in the beam of his
magic lantern. Frame enlargement from *A Canterbury Tale*.

that "at any moment strange things might happen," and that "nothing
better occurred to me." He denied that glue-throwing had any sexual connotations, quipping, "Doesn't it happen nowadays?" He then added,
"Anything odd in England has a sexual connotation." Powell himself
gives a different account, isolating the glueman as box office poison for *A
Canterbury Tale*, for it was not well received by contemporary critics.
Powell recalls that Emeric thought up "this almost sexual idea of a man
pursuing girls in the black-out and dropping glue on them. . . . It's a very
simple Freudian idea."[3] Sixteen years later, reviewers of Powell's *Peeping
Tom* named Culpepper, the glueman, as the forerunner of scopophiliac
Mark, noting a history of morbid, misogynist representation in Powell and
Pressburger's work.[4] In the film's weak resolution Culpepper is never pun-
ished for all the anxiety and fear he provokes in village women. Instead
he is transformed into a mystical overseer who ensures that each of the
pilgrims receives a blessing on reaching Canterbury (Figure 5.3):

[3] Michael Powell, in an unpublished interview with Graham Fuller, 1986. I thank Graham
Fuller for giving me access to his interview notes.
[4] See for example the *Sunday Times*, 4. 10. 60., and *The New Statesman*, 4. 9. 60.

Figure 5.3. The uniformed Allison and Bob arrive in
Canterbury Cathedral. *A Canterbury Tale*, production still.

Gibb has a chance to play on the Cathedral organ, Allison hears that her
boyfriend has not been shot down after all, but is alive and well in Gibral-
tar, and Johnson receives long-awaited mail from his American girlfriend
who has joined the W.A.C.'s in Australia.

Chapter 2 described the impossibility of preserving traditional femininity within wartime realist cinema. Powell and Pressburger's film confronted the problem head on through their choice of profession for Allison—a member of the Women's Land Army—a choice that skewed her
status as heroine, almost disqualifying her from that status altogether. Each
of the women's wartime services had its own particular reputation, often
based on its uniform's appearance, the class of woman that was liable to
join up, or the type of work involved. Princess Elizabeth was in the
A.T.S., and the Wrens also had an upper-class aura in their "neat dark

" Well, well, well! If it isn't Mary Jenkins home on leave from the farm ! "

Figure 5.4. Mary Jenkins's rural methods of portage impress the neighbors. *Punch*, 26 August 1942, p. 163.

blue."[5] By contrast, the women's Land Army had only one compulsory piece of uniform—jodhpur-like breeches—while any kind of blouse or headgear could usually be worn. This combination gave the women a distinctive and far from sleek silhouette. One visiting G.I. remembered that in Piccadilly "uniforms of all the Allied services abounded, a good many new to me, but I was really captivated by the get-up of the Women's Land Army."[6] Contemporary cartoons, which frequently explored the cultural significance of women's wartime dress, as discussed in Chapter 2, were fascinated with the W.L.A. uniform, particularly the pants, which supported many *Punch* jokes (Figures 5.4, 5.5, and 5.6).

The Women's Land Army was the most anomalous and ambiguous of women's wartime service, hardly existing as an "army" at all—especially not according to the *Encyclopedia Britannica* definition given in the opening minutes of *The Way Ahead*: "An army—a considerable body of men, armed, organized, and disciplined, to act together for purposes of warfare." W.L.A. women did not work in units, but instead were billeted,

---

[5] Priestley, *British Women Go to War*, p. 49.
[6] Moseley, *Backs to the Wall*, p. 332.

Figure 5.5. Little Bo Peep mobilized.
Punch, 18 July 1945, p. 51.

often singly, on individual farms. In both operations and representations, they lacked the panache of the other, fully uniformed forces, but also the community spirit emphasized in patriotic images of factory work. Their labor was arduous and they were quickly stereotyped as lesbian, perhaps because their work so resembled men's work and because jobs such as plowing, seeding, and dung-spreading represented the antithesis of femininity (Figure 5.7). In Priestley's terms, the women lost their "daintiness" and began to look "like the chorus in a rustic musical show."[7]

The mobile woman, that newly established phenomenon emerging to encapsulate the new social and economic roles that actual women were asked to take up in wartime, was a highly unstable category, as explained in Chapter 2. The meanings of flightiness, strength, lesbianism, separation, and patriotism that clustered about her could barely be held together. It is consistent with the precariousness with which Powell and Pressburger's films fit any nomenclature—realist, fantasist, British, or otherwise—that they would choose to represent the mobile woman in their film as a W.L.A. girl, rather than as a member of any one of the other female

[7] Priestley, *British Women Go to War*, p. 49.

"I've just had a most harrowing experience."

Figure 5.6. The harrowing experience of the Women's
Land Army. *Punch*, 13 August 1941, p. 139.

Forces, for these were the hardest of all mobile women to categorize, even though their title, Women's Land Army, literalized the gendered land/air division introduced in Chapter 1.

The representation of gender in *A Canterbury Tale* is intriguingly linked to the representation of historical and temporal change, particularly through the characters of Allison and Culpepper. These changes are initiated through a sort of cinematic prologue, wherein many of the differences from the 1949 American-release version lie. In the 1944 version, the opening credits are superimposed over an intricate moving shot of chiming steeple bells. Eventually the camera cranes toward an opening in the Gothic tracery through which the roof and twin towers of a grand cathedral appear. The sacred image fades to an image of a sheet of parchment inscribed with the opening lines of Chaucer's ''Prologue,'' recited in a mixture of modern and medieval pronunciation by a narrator's voice (that of Raymond Massey), a recital without the irony that went with Howard's rendering of Keats in *The Gentle Sex*. While the voice continues the shot fades to a woodcut print of three Chaucerian pilgrims on horseback, which then dissolves to a scene of ''real'' costumed pilgrims—that is, actors—riding on horseback through the English countryside; the jangling of reins, the clip-clopping of hooves, and the tinkling of a falcon's jesses enhance the fifteenth-century

Figure 5.7. Prudence Honeywood and a W.L.A. worker muck-spreading. Frame enlargement from *A Canterbury Tale*.

atmosphere. The Wife of Bath is even identifiable as she jovially pushes a fellow traveler from his horse.

This imagery and the recited Prologue automatically tie the ensuing story to the most famous pre-Shakespearian English narrative, Chaucer's *The Canterbury Tales*. But the grammatical change in Powell and Pressburger's title from a plural definitive (*The Canterbury Tales*) to an indefinite single (*A Canterbury Tale*) is effectively a shift from an official, authoritative, historically canonized account to an individual and private one—one version of a G.I.'s experience of Europe, or even a pilgrimage for Powell back to his birthplace and school days in Canterbury, or Pressburger's experience as a visiting alien in Britain during the war. Indeed, every audience member had made his or her pilgrimage for the war.

In this opening sequence, as in *The Gentle Sex*, history is represented visually by means of craft and aurally by means of poetry, but in The Archers' film calligraphy has displaced embroidery and Chaucer has displaced Keats. In contrast to *The Gentle Sex*, no superior, ironizing audience position is offered through the male voice: the Chaucerian script, the primitive map of Kent, falconry, the pilgrimage, and the modern soldier who follows them on the image track are carefully edited together to make an overlapping "picture," a skein of multiple references. While *The Gentle Sex* presents crude and amusing disjunctions between Victorian and 1940s conceptions of femininity, the opening sequence of *A Canterbury Tale* sets up the jarring complexities, bizarre coincidences, and strange discontinuities of English history. The medieval map and pageant situate the spectator *in* English history, journeying through it with the slowly tracking camera.

The transition to the present, to 1944—the most massive historical, six-hundred year jump cut—is effected through two well-established metaphors: bird/plane and horse/train.[8] An image of a soaring kestrel is revealed to be the point-of-view shot of a man in medieval dress, but after the kestrel shot is repeated it is edited to a shot of a biplane, soaring in the opposite direction. This is then revealed to be the point-of-view shot of a helmeted soldier who looks up from the same position as his ancestor, in an identical landscape, but this time not soothed by sweet, nondiegetic medieval music, but deafened by the roar of modern weaponry—a tank is pounding through the pastoral. When the plane's engine noise subsides the voice-over lyric begins: "Six hundred years have passed. . . . What would they see, Dan [*sic*] Chaucer and his goodly company today?" The voice recalls that the sounds of hooves and creaking wheels have been replaced by those of "roads of steel" as a train chuffs through the valley.

Tradition, repetition, and continuity are proposed and then questioned, for one of the main tasks of the 1944 version of *A Canterbury Tale* is to ask whether Sergeant Johnson's visit to the south of England merely repeats a pilgrimage of 600 years previously, or whether, as the male voice-over suggests, this is an entirely different phenomenon: "But though so little has changed since Chaucer's day, another kind of pilgrim walks the Pilgrim's Way." The film questions whether the "invasion" of G.I.'s, and wartime changes in general, can be incorporated into the "rich pageant" of English history, or whether perhaps this break with the past cannot be sewn in. Will the history of England continue to be linked to Chaucer, be seamless, or must it record ruptures, massive jump cuts, under the extreme conditions of war?

Although the question is never answered, the film suggests that any hope of continuity, and thus coherent national identity, is rooted in the British countryside. The land is foregrounded as a special repository of historical meaning, literally the ground in which history makes its marks. It even

---

[8] As Doug Riblet pointed out to me, this opening prefigures Kubrick's jump cut over two millenia in *2001*, between a spinning bone in the air and a spaceship.

holds the potential for international understanding, in that it is the cross-national language of lumber that Bob can speak with the wheelwright of Chillingbourne as they swap knowledge of seasoning cycles and felly joints, while the old men standing around them can only laugh at Allison in her jodhpur pants, excluding her from the tradition. Culpepper and Allison hold very different relations to this history of the land. It is as if history is divided along gender lines, Culpepper's history pertaining to love of country, to patriotism, Allison's to romantic love.[9]

Culpepper's access to history is patrilineal and displayed through knowledge. He welcomes soldiers (but not female soldiers or other womenfolk) to his lantern slide lectures at the Chillingbourne Historical Society. He explains how the ''fathers, and fathers' fathers'' of the village have used and walked the local part of the Pilgrim's Way, back to Chaucer's time and beyond: an archaeologist has even found Roman coins on the way, he adds, but they have since been lost. Allison, the only woman in the audience, is witness to this speech, listening closely. Symmetrical patterns of light fall on her face and Culpepper's, as the shots cut between them (compare Figure 5.2 with Figure 5.8). Her sense of place, her love of country, consists far more in private recollection than Culpepper's. She lost her virginity on the Pilgrim's Way, and her understanding of the route is inextricably linked to her lost lover, the archaeologist who had found the Roman coins, now apparently shot down over France.

Allison owns the coins, but decides at the lecture to donate them to the local Historical Society, thus converting them from private memory to public knowledge. They become the point of exchange, of currency, between the two histories, the two genders, as they are articulated in the film. *A Canterbury Tale* serves to make history natural, presents history as embedded in nature: in roads, in cathedrals, in coins buried underground, in weathering customs and felly joints. But it also intimates that woman is too close to the land to fully understand that history, to make it function publicly in the interests of patriotism. Powell and Pressburger's film repeats the schema of gendered labeling of air and land, identified in Chapter 1, in their pilot/Land Army girl couple, but, as with other textual elements of this film, the schema is pushed to its limits—the pilot character is entirely absent, and the *Land* Army girl's closeness to the land is finally imaged as something unhealthy and inappropriate. Later, when Allison hears that her archaeologist is alive and well after all, she desperately throws open the windows of their once-shared, now disused caravan. It has become redundant, immobilized. The tires have been requisitioned and moths have eaten the curtains and her lover's hat. Light now streams in

---

[9] I am indebted to Ingrid Periz's comments in my 1988 Powell and Pressburger seminar for this insight and for substantive contributions in the following two paragraphs.

Figure 5.8. Allison listens to Culpepper's local history lecture.
Frame enlargement from *A Canterbury Tale*.

through the dust. But the dust, the moths, the rust, the marooned, wheel-less vehicle present her harboring of this relic of her personal past as some-thing unwholesome, constricting, even rotten, outmoded. The caravan must be discarded and replaced by a public and exterior history, displayed in the form of coins in the museum.

The film marks female sexuality as strange and insalubrious, somehow activated by the blackout, emerging from it, through both the noirish intro-ductory shot of Allison as femme fatale, silhouetted and wreathed in smoke, stamping out her cigarette, and through the "glueman" plot. Al-lison's metamorphosis into rural worker and detective produces further strangeness, given the prognosis of her opening screen moments. The loss of clear and familiar gender boundaries which Allison and the blackout embody are compensated in the film's more confident presentation of national difference, conveyed through the figure of the G.I. Sergeant Johnson's nationality is immediately identifiable, even in the dark, since accent is signaled through sound track rather than image.[10] On his arrival

[10] The way language difference organizes national boundaries is neatly expressed in that

at Chillingbourne, Johnson initiates the film's dialogue with his intrusive twang, inquiring loudly into the blackness as the engine chuffs out, abandoning him at the wrong station. He boastfully displays his "flashlight," as he calls it, only to be reprimanded with a "Put that light out!" by the stationmaster. Both his actions and vocabulary distinguish his nationality: he is someone who does not blend in.

References to American accents in British wartime films are not uncommon, especially after 1943. The difference they signify is often narrativized through a character's linguistic difficulties or misunderstandings, as in Johnson's case, an emphasis consistent with the general importance of language, dialect, and accent, both in British cinema and British daily life.[11] When Americans take over the air base in *The Way to the Stars* (1945) the old-timers jibe at words such as "bombadier," "zonk," and "spud." When the family in *This Happy Breed* (1944) watches the "first" musical (*Broadway Melody*) they complain that they cannot understand the singer's words. In *Waterloo Road* Doctor Montgomery raises his eyebrows at a passing G.I.'s accent before he effects the flashback to the Blitz, that period now being defined as one before G.I.'s arrived in Britain. In a related example, Doctor Reeves (Roger Livesey), the British defending council in *A Matter of Life and Death*, cannot understand wartime American song—particularly the phrase "Shoo Shoo Baby"—but then neither can the American prosecutor opposing him (Raymond Massey), for he is an American of a different period, of the Revolution.

The G.I. was an historically "late" development of the war in Britain. Although the Japanese invasion of Pearl Harbor had brought America into the war as early as 7 December 1941, the British public became particularly aware of their new allies after their victories in North Africa, especially after the German surrender to Montgomery at Tunis on 11 May 1943. During 1943 it became necessary to billet U.S. troops on householders, and by 1944 one and a half million Americans were stationed in the country.[12] The G.I. as a cinematic figure began to displace other tropes of national specificity—the mobile woman and the blackout itself—because he more easily, indeed literally stood for the difference. While in Ameri-

---

familiar aphoristic description of Anglo-American relations, "two nations divided by a common language."

[11] I would suspect that further examination of the use of the voice in wartime British cinema would reveal that an increased emphasis on the voice coincided with the attenuation of the representability of sexual difference through the image track.

[12] These included 130,000 black G.I.'s. However, races were kept strictly segregated, leading to high-level Cabinet debates. See Graham Smith's Ph.D. dissertation on black G.I.'s in Britain, reviewed in Lotte Hughes, "How Racism Came to Britain with the American Army," *The Guardian*, 5 May 1984, p. 11.

can films the British accent had tended to be "absorbed" without comment, in wartime British films foreigners always became thematically significant, and particularly Americans, whose citizenship was associated both with potent sexuality and powerful cinema. Both these meanings were mobilized through the screen G.I., but they are present too in the welcoming British government pamphlet issued to smooth relations with the natives.

The document explained quirky aspects of British life to G.I.'s and included a vocabulary list to obviate offense or embarrassment—one that Sergeant Johnson apparently had not read.[13] The pamphlet's opening illustration was of two floating barrage balloons—phallic guardians of England—captioned, "You are about to land." The orientation material focused on the legacy of America's cultural hegemony and the myths that might accompany unwitting G.I.'s to Britain: "Most of the films we see are made in Hollywood. Many of the magazines we read are household names to you. You have a glamorous background for British people. . . ."[14] This admission of dominant cinema's ideological power was counterbalanced by the following caution:

> A word or two about conditions here. Nearly three years of war have made us pretty realistic in our outlook. The gayer side of British life has been subordinated to the grim business of war. . . . The streets are black at night and it is very difficult for a stranger to find his way about. Food is plentiful, up to a point, but there are few luxuries. Cinemas and theaters are open, of course, and indeed they flourish, but they open and close early.[15]

The gap between cultures is expressed in equivalent terms to those found in British cinema and criticism: in references to blackness, to realism, to the subordination of gaiety and luxury, and even to the fact that cinema thrives, but within strictly marked parameters, of time and of illumination.

The G.I. character in wartime film often ignored these privations, but this was ideologically advantageous in that he then both embodied national difference and bolstered the representation of sexual difference through his prowess in that department: he became exaggeratedly a man. The American military's reputation for potent sexuality, jealously recorded in the First World War saying "overpaid, oversexed and over here!" was inflected in a *Punch* cartoon captioned, "American girls can now get nylon

[13] Public Record Office, Leaflet INF 2/1, 1942, quoted in Marion Yass, *This Is Your War: Home Front Propaganda in the Second World War* (London: Public Record Office/Her Majesty's Stationery Office, 1983).
[14] Public Record Office, Leaflet INF 2/1, 1942, p. 3.
[15] Ibid.

stockings from slot machines. Ours will depend on transatlantic pilots as usual'' (Figure 5.9). The joke speculates on Britain's dependency on American masculinity in producing and maintaining her womanhood. It also attributes a relative remoteness of American women from the war, and from the problem. In film, the G.I.'s lively sexuality was thematized through his gifts of the coveted nylons, and also through his knowledge of energetic modern dances such as jitterbug and boogie-woogie, generously taught to British women. Flashing a light, like Sergeant Johnson, was also a well-used cinematic metaphor for the G.I.'s libidinal ability, also used in American films, including *Tonight and Every Night* and *To Each His Own*, as mentioned in Chapter 3.[16]

As the welcoming pamphlet suggested, as well as the social worker quoted in Chapter 2, the British audience was quick to associate the G.I. with Hollywood cinema. The main recreational base for G.I.'s in Britain

Figure 5.9. America demobilizes before Britain.
Punch, 14 November 1945, p. 409.

[16] One English woman in her early twenties who lived through World War II remembers the G.I.'s particularly for their flashlights, and for their frightening habit of training them on women's legs.

was the Rainbow Club in Piccadilly, but, set within the West End, the district was also understood to be the British equivalent of Hollywood, since most new films premiered there; this furthered the cultural link between the G.I. and his native cinema for Britons.[17] It is in keeping with the probing nature of their films that Powell and Pressburger should dwell on this connection in *A Canterbury Tale*, so that Bob Johnson mentions his love of cinema more than once, and would prefer an afternoon at Canterbury cinema to one at Canterbury Cathedral. Paradoxically, Powell and Pressburger use cinema, and particularly the figure of Culpepper, to open the G.I.'s eyes to a more expanded sense of history, and present the Cathedral as its own reward, thereby elevating the power of the cinema too.

That the American film character remains foreign in the last analysis, despite the rhetoric of alliance, is evidenced in an interesting dimorphism among the British films in which he or she is present. *Way to the Stars, I Live in Grosvenor Square* (U.S. title *A Yank in London*), *A Matter of Life and Death*, and *Piccadilly Incident* are among the many other films besides *A Canterbury Tale* that explore the figure of the American as ally but alien. In these films, however, a liaison between an American and a British subject is permanent and happy only if the American is female, as in *Piccadilly Incident* and *A Matter of Life and Death*. International romantic liaisons between an American man and a British woman usually end in the man's death or a distant posting, as in the plots of *I Live in Grosvenor Square*, *The Way to the Stars*, and also *Piccadilly Incident*, in which Diana turns down the Canadian soldier Bill. This narrative pattern reverses the trend of actual war bride marriages in which a British bride would usually sail to America to join her American husband. Ideologically speaking, the "capture" of an American female by a British male was a narrative "victory," while an American male's "capture" of a British woman was a loss. In other words, relations between subjects of the two nations could be represented cordially as long as certain national identities and boundaries—which had everything to do with gender—were maintained. A foreign woman could be absorbed into the British nation, but a native man could not be lost from it. Shifting the terms to those of filmmaking, the co-option of a G.I./Hollywood into the British system was a triumph; the loss of a British woman/the British industry to America was more than Britain could sustain in wartime. In multiple ways, the complex cultural, economic, and political relations between Britain and America in wartime were thematized in home front films through the figure of the G.I., who inevitably recalled the position of Hollywood cinema in Britain. Powell

[17] See for example, C. A. Lejeune, "Can Piccadilly Do Without Hollywood?" *New York Times Magazine*, 24 August 1947, p. 16.

and Pressburger acknowledge this in one further way: in a gesture magnified manyfold in American distributors' treatment of the British exhibitors' market, Bob Johnson pays off the schoolchildren in *A Canterbury Tale* after they have brought him information. Not surprisingly, these bribery scenes were cut from the 1949 American release version, albeit as part of a larger piece that was removed.

LIKE ALL too many Powell and Pressburger films, *A Canterbury Tale* had a checkered career in terms of release prints and popularity. Its two main versions span the transition from war to peace. The original 124-minute 1944 picture was recut for release in the United States in 1949, and while it gained a frame narrative its overall length was reduced by between 20 and 30 minutes. Although the re-editing was not extensive enough to constitute a remake, the changes blunted all those points in the text that evidence the peculiarities, struggles, and difficulties of wartime filmmaking. In the later American version the Chaucerian parchment is gone, replaced by statistical, cartoon illustrations in a modern style and an American voice-over that lists the number of G.I.'s who went to Britain during the war, the number who found brides there, the number who returned to America with them, and so on. Eventually the statistics are reduced to one couple, *ex*-G.I. Sergeant Bob Johnson and his war bride of one day, who are shown on top of the New York Rockefeller Center. They debate where to go for their honeymoon: either Sydney, where she has served in the W.A.C.s, or Canterbury, where he has been a pilgrim. The war bride is played by Kim Hunter, June in *A Matter of Life and Death*, which Powell and Pressburger had made in the interim between the two versions of *A Canterbury Tale*.

This frame addition in the American print precedes a flashback that is triggered by Bob's reminiscence of his army experience as he looks down at St. Patrick's Cathedral on Fifth Avenue, rather than Canterbury. In this 1949 version it is a flash*back*, as opposed to a flashforward, which occurs through the fade to chiming bells in the crossing of Canterbury cathedral, the same image that had appeared behind the 1944 titles. Johnson's explanation to his new wife becomes a voice-over as he describes the chuffing train and "arriving at one of those dark stations, not even knowing the language yet." The original 1944 flashlight scene follows, in which the three original pilgrims converge on the platform in the blackout.

Through this and other cuts and changes, the American print emphasizes different aspects of the plot, enclosing the original tale with a newlyweds framing story and quickening the pace of the rest of the film. It now privileges *one* couple's formation, rather than producing a "miracle" for three pilgrims. Bob recounts his travels to his wife, who becomes the crucial link to the new American audience, inscribed through her in the film. She replaces the local British audience anticipated by the voice-over of the 1944 print debating the old and new pilgrims of Kent. The introduction of a war bride in the frame narrative also reduces the romantic potential between Allison and Bob, who in 1944 had behaved as a possible ''pair'' of outsiders, helping each other in the glueman investigation. However, it is the characters of Allison and Culpepper, and their relation to the land, that are most thoroughly transformed in the American release print. While in the 1944 version Allison investigates the crime that has been perpetrated against her, enlisting the help of Sergeants Johnson and Gibb, in the 1949 version she is no longer the detective. All the interrogative scenes in which she questions villagers, friends, other W.L.A. workers, and Culpepper about who might have thrown glue at her in the blackout have been edited out, and the discovery of Culpepper's culpability is left mainly to Gibb (Figure 5.10). Such changes lessen the autonomy of the Land Army girl and suggest that the range of available representations of femininity and female behavior had shifted radically and constricted over the intervening five years and in the passage across the Atlan-

Figure 5.10. Allison investigates the crime, by interviewing a fellow W.L.A. worker. Frame enlargement from *A Canterbury Tale*.

tic Ocean. Postwar circumstances and a change of audience had removed or relieved old pressures that acted on the production of the earlier text, and had installed new ones, ones that produced a more confined space of female agency. The overall effect of the re-editing is an immense displacement of war and its attendant problems. Where the 1944 film looked to the future by literally flashing forward in the opening moments—"We don't know where our journey will end," announces the opening narration—the 1949 version carefully consigns the war period to the past, sealing it off in a flashback. In 1944 *A Canterbury Tale* directly confronted *the* problem that wartime cinema could not solve: it could not make history of pressing contemporary issues; it could not answer the question of who would win the war, or what form the postwar world would take. Powell has even recalled that the film's unpopularity and economic failure, in 1944, was due in part to bad timing: when the film was released, the soldiers amassing in east Kent had already left for D-Day—history had moved on from the film without him.

The 1944 version of the film cannot readily integrate G.I.'s or W.L.A. members into the rich pageant of British history, articulated by Culpepper, wherein already resides "Dan Chaucer and his goodly company." While films like *Perfect Strangers* and *Brief Encounter* attempted, with various degrees of success, to displace their diegeses onto the early war or prewar period, thus securing a stable point of view for their audience, *A Canterbury Tale* states explicitly that clear historical, national, and gendered boundaries are impossible to maintain in wartime when the physical threat of bombing, and new economic and ideological needs, are straining the cinematic apparatus to its limits. This fracturing effect of war can be repaired only with historical distance, as in the 1949 remake. But this version of the film, in combination with a new exhibition circuit and a new national audience, provokes such far-reaching changes in the organization, rhythm, and meaning of the narrative, that we are left in 1949 with a transatlantic text that is even less identifiable as the product of a national cinema than the original ever was.

This book began, as so many books on British cinema have, with a return to an old chestnut—to the question of the relations between a cinema and the nation that has produced it, a question hotly debated during World War II because the stakes of defining national identity were intensified to a matter of life and death. By focusing on the home front genre—which I have referred to as the genre of the national subject—and "new British realism," a central category in film critics' vocabulary during the crisis, I have looked to precisely the place where contemporary life and contemporary film imagery and narratives might be expected to line up. But it has become apparent that very different films, from a Woman's Film (*Brief Encounter*) to an omnibus training film (such as *The Gentle Sex* and *The Way Ahead*), were classified as purveying Britishness and falling under the realist rubric. The connection between these wartime films and the reality from which they grew was conceptualized by critics in terms of reflection, as indicated in Vesselo's 1938 comment that the films of a country "in some way reflect that country's national characteristics," and Manvell's insistence in 1945 that since the British are not dull, their cinema will not be either. However, closer examination of these films has revealed the limitations of that formulation, in that *In Which We Serve, Brief Encounter, Waterloo Road*, and *Perfect Strangers*, all films which took home front life as their subject matter, address contemporary issues through fantasy sequences and complicated temporal structures rather than through linearly presented stories shot on location. Powell and Pressburger's wartime films, with their weak plot lines and frayed representations of recurring wartime motifs, are merely the most truculent group in resisting easy classification. In retrospect we must say that realist rhetoric drew a veil over the evident diversity of British wartime production, even among home front films, and obscured the fluidity and complexity of contemporary filmmaking styles for which strict categories such as realist or fantasist, costume melodrama or historical picture, are inadequate. The litany on realism also obscured the important place that representations of gender, and an address to both the female and the national audiences, have had in shaping wartime cinema. It is as if the ideological need for a coherent national identity in cinema compelled writers too into producing that identity writ large, and as realism above all else.

Catherine de la Roche was among the critics who articulated the nationality/cinema relation in her essays. After reading Siegfried Kracauer's and Parker Tyler's film analyses in 1948, she came to reject their "premise that motion pictures reflect the dominant spirit of the times."[18] Instead she proposed that "the cinema is a phenomenon, rather than an interpreter, of the age which produced it." This theory was "as valid as ever" she argued, despite the extreme conditions of war that had forced cinema into a propagandist role. In fact, for her, the war had highlighted the distance between reality and cinema—in putting together series of British films for foreign (probably Soviet) presentation, de la Roche could not find films "typifying a nation's way of life." Instead she found only proximal references, "omissions and evasions, half-truths and distortions," a list of nouns prefiguring those of later ideological criticism.[19]

[18] de la Roche, "The Mask of Realism," p. 35.
[19] Ibid.

CONCLUSION

De la Roche's distinction between reflection and phenomenon is a productive one in conceptualizing how British wartime cinema functioned. I have argued that there *are* shared characteristics coursing through British wartime films, although these are not the reflection of some national essence or national psyche. Central are two motifs—the mobile woman and the blackout—but arguing that British wartime cinema simply reflected their physical facts flattens out the form and effect they had as part of cinematic representation. These were very literal instantiations of wartime—phenomena daily encountered on the home front, in the lives of audiences. They were national phenomena in being part and parcel of the material fabric of the country at war. However, what the cinema made possible was the conversion of these concrete peculiarities of wartime Britain into rich textual figures, mushrooming on the landscape, which in turn were connected to further representations of the blackout and mobile woman in magazines, posters, and government pamphlets. Wartime cinema lived epiphytically, taking its material support from the facts of home front existence, using it as a holdfast would (a cinema as kelp bed), and mobilizing its audience through the contact, but enabling vast and spreading networks of (often contradictory) meaning to grow from relatively circumscribed beginnings—the blackout and the mobile woman both began as inventions of government ordination. It is this style of fastening of wartime British cinema to its surroundings that could be said to distinguish it from other national cinemas, from Weimar cinema for example.

The blackout and the mobile woman, beyond being phenomena peculiar to war and thereby containing the promise of historical, if not always national, distinction, provided a rich substrate for cinema because they also exemplified the crisis of perceptual and cultural transformation that the social relations of war produced, and further because of their extraordinary kinship to established paradigms of narrative cinema. The blackout literalized both the space of war and the space of the cinema, but it also came to symbolize the new sensibilities demanded by war. The blackout could never be fully represented on the screen—without killing off the cinema in toto—even though it promised to convey the national predicament so definitively. In a parallel way, the mobile woman crystallized both the new social pressures and the now revealed inadequacies of past habits of representation. While representations of women had been central to narrative cinema, this one, from her oxymoronic name onwards, could not be pinned down, captured, essentialized on screen. Instead, upon her flourished a multitude of wartime femininities—her "double life," her uniform, her overall, her pitchfork, and other accessories of her new socioeconomic place—so that the fetishized facts of her patriotism came to overshadow her material contribution.

218

The blackout and the mobile woman were the basis of new dramatic forms precisely because they comprised chameleonic elements, were inherently unstable, and embodied the perceptual and ideological reinventions of wartime. (The prevalence of the train, the plane, and character memory in wartime films are then powerful supplementary figures of this challenge to established perceptual and material boundaries.) The blackout and the mobile woman became switching points for the articulation of social change, expressed in specific spatial and temporal relations with the cinema audience. I have referred, for example, to the wartime film's anticipation of a local audience, knowledgeable about the events of the recent past, precisely because cinema was unable to make full sense of the present—the outcome mattered too much, and yet was also obscure. The cinema could not provide dramatic closure for war because the plot was still unfolding, so wartime films juggled multiple temporalities, placing the present and past in insoluble tension for their audiences, and producing a plethora of references to the past which collided with preoccupations of the present. I have also referred to the way gender relations are rearticulated spatially in wartime cinema, according to a precarious vertical stratification which sexes the sky as male and the land as female. The blackout and the mobile woman were the most powerful figures in building these kinds of spatial and temporal patterns, to the point that they eventually intersected with one another—in wartime the blackout became a sexualized space, itself a metaphor for the transformation of women within it.

Bogart or Bacon: The British
Film Industry during
World War II

On 3 September 1939, as the British film world contemplated the prospect of new hostilities, the memory of World War I loomed large.[1] Its ruinous effect on domestic operations had been less a result of physical damage and slowed production than of the alacrity with which Hollywood had "moved in . . . seized the market, and . . . never . . . loosened its grip."[2] With the largest home audience of any national film industry, American producers had usually been able to cover production costs at home, so that practically all earnings made abroad were profits.[3] This had given American distributors the flexibility to undercut their competitors in foreign markets, so that even the strongest non-American circuits were unable to overcome the American business techniques of price-undercutting, block-booking, and blind-bidding.[4] European cutbacks in World War

[1] American infiltration into the British market actually began long before World War I. Vitagraph (later merged into Warner Brothers) opened its own office in Britain in 1912, followed shortly by Fox in 1916 and Famous Lasky Film Service (later Paramount) in 1919. For an extensive account see Michael Chanan, "The Emergence of an Industry," in Curran and Porter, *British Cinema History*, pp. 39–58.

[2] Ralph Bond, *Monopoly: The Future of British Films* (London: Association of Ciné-Technicians, 1946), p. 6. See also Michael Balcon, *Michael Balcon Presents: A Lifetime of Films* (London: Hutchinson, 1969), pp. 12–13; and the contributors' essay, "Newsreel," *Sight and Sound* 10, no. 37 (Spring 1941): 1.

[3] In America there was an average of 50 million weekly attendances by 1926, rising to an all-time peak of 95 million in 1929 before dropping off and rising again back to 90 million in 1945. The average British weekly attendance during these years was 19 million in 1917, 16 million in 1935, 19 million in 1940, and 30 million in 1945. These British figures are derived from Patricia Perilli, "Statistical Survey of the British Film Industry," in Curran and Porter, *British Cinema History*, p. 372. The American figures are taken from Cobbett S. Steinberg, *Reel Facts: The Movie Book of Records* (New York: Vintage Books, 1982; 1st ed., 1978), p. 46.

[4] Block-booking required an exhibitor to hire several films in addition to the first choice,

221

I had left a vacuum readily filled by American films, while the greater profits to be made from American pictures led British exhibitors to be increasingly reluctant to book homegrown films. The shared English language was merely the icing on the cake, making Britain the world site of easiest American infiltration. By November 1924, dubbed "Black November," American films had such a stranglehold on British screens that every studio was dark.

The unanimous opinion in 1939 was that at all costs history must not be allowed to repeat itself.[5] In the Great War "all the men were taken from the industry but the industry was then not so important."[6] Alan Page now suggested that Hollywood be prevented from providing any entertainment at all because "if the fullest possible use is not now made of the trained personnel of our industry, . . . the end of the war will see us back in the 1919 position."[7] Such a proposal could be implemented only through direct government intervention, and this had been a highly controversial matter ever since its beginnings in Stanley Baldwin's Conservative government response to "Black November."

Baldwin had passed *The Cinematograph Films Act, 1927*, or "Quota Act," to ban, at least in theory, the restrictive practices of block-booking and blind-bidding. Americans would now have to pay for their predominant position within the British home market by financing the production of a quota of British films while also taking some back to the States.[8] The "Britishness" of these quota films was to be secured in a rather literal fashion, requiring that seventy-five percent of the wages paid went to Brit-

---

while blind-bidding made exhibitors take films sight unseen, sometimes because they were not yet made!

[5] Ezra Goodman, reporting from the other side of the Atlantic, consoled British readers with the news that the American studios were "experiencing a local war of nerves" over the potential loss of their largest overseas market, but he conceded that the Americans "may yet emerge gainfully from the international holocaust" since the last world war had given them a "head start" that had "enabled them to outdistance other countries for many years." Ezra Goodman, "Hollywood Is Worried," *Sight and Sound* 8, no. 31 (Autumn 1939): 106.

[6] Lord Stragboli, *Parliamentary Debates* (Lords), vol. 114, col. 1219, 3 October 1939, quoted in Dickinson and Street, *Cinema and State*, p. 104.

[7] Alan Page, "Art Suspended," *Sight and Sound* 8, no. 31 (Autumn 1939): 100.

[8] This legislation is the subject of a comprehensive article by Simon Hartog, "State Protection of a Beleaguered Industry," in Curran and Porter, *British Cinema History*, pp. 60–73. The Act made it compulsory for distributors of foreign (i.e., mainly American) films to acquire a percentage of British films while it simultaneously obligated exhibitors to show a proportion of British pictures every year. Quotas were enforced for both renters and exhibitors, starting at low levels increased each year. The Act required that for 1928 a minimum of seven and a half percent of all films distributed, and five percent of all films exhibited, be of British manufacture. These percentages were to rise by increments of two and a half percent until they both reached twenty percent by 1936.

ish citizens, thus limiting the use of American stars and technicians. In addition, the author of the film's scenario had to be British, a condition far harder to enforce than to decree.

With the 1927 Act a film boom had begun, fueled by a misguided British optimism about sound: after all, it was thought, who would want to hear the American accent? The number of film stages quadrupled in the decade from 1927 to 1938, and the amount of studio floor space multiplied sevenfold. Under the same momentum the British Film Institute was founded, whose objectives were to "develop the use of cinema as a means of entertainment and instruction."[9] Protected by the quota system, British output rose each year, until by the early 1930s Britain had become the most important center of European production.[10] The worldwide success in 1933 of Korda's London Films' Prestige Production, *The Private Life of Henry VIII*, backed by United Artists and specifically designed for distribution in America, indicated that Britain might now challenge Hollywood directly.

In essence, the 1927 Quota Act had been introduced to preserve Britain's film industry in a hostile, competitive climate. In 1946 Ralph Bond remarked thankfully that without it "there would, in all probability, never again have been a [British] film producing industry."[11] However, the Act did not kill off American predominance.[12] Impressive production statistics disguised the fact that many—though not all—films were "quota quickies," made merely to satisfy the letter of the law and often financed at a rate per foot and never screened.[13] While they provided a training ground for some British directors such as Michael Powell, British quota films rapidly gained an appalling reputation, tainting the box office value of "Britishness" altogether and paradoxically strengthening exhibitors' preferences for the rival, stateside product.

When the 1927 Act expired in 1937 it was overhauled and some loopholes were closed. In the reconstituted *Cinematograph Films Act, 1938*, the seventy-five percent British labor rule was retained, though the British

---

[9] Oliver Bell, "The First Ten Years," *Sight and Sound* 12, no. 47 (October 1943): 56. The Institute was founded on 1 October 1933. Oliver Bell was its director in 1943.

[10] Output in 1936 was 212 films.

[11] Ralph Bond, *Monopoly*, p. 7.

[12] See the report of F. D. Klingender and S. Legg, *Money Behind the Screen: A Report Prepared on Behalf of the Film Council* (London: Lawrence and Wishart, 1937), described and quoted in Hartog, "State Protection of a Beleaguered Industry," p. 73.

[13] Only two American companies, Warner Brothers and Paramount, had set up and maintained production subsidiaries of any size in Great Britain to fulfill their quota requirements; Twentieth Century-Fox and Metro had only minor operations. The 1929 Wall Street crash had weakened all the majors, but most of them continued to exploit Britain by sponsoring cheap, bad films that were just long enough to qualify as features but dodged the main aims of the Act. See Hartog, "State Protection of a Beleaguered Industry."

scenario clause was relaxed. Films with a labor cost of under £7,500 would now no longer qualify for quota, a statute designed to maintain a certain level of quality. It encouraged some American majors to invest in film-making in Britain more seriously, a trend that was to pave the way for Korda's MGM–London Films deal, whose first release was *Perfect Strangers* in 1945, the central film discussed in Chapter 3.[14]

Despite government protection, another British film industry slump was around the corner. The City of London had been eager to support a repetition of Korda's *Henry VIII* triumph, but had lent British studios money in the form of loans, not capital. With insufficient profits, companies could not meet their payments and went bankrupt. The beginning of a series of closures and cutbacks in 1937 led to a fifty percent drop in output the following year, with only half the available studio space being utilized. The number of feature films made fell from 228 in 1937 to 116 in 1938, and the graph went downward for 1939. Korda ordered salary cuts at London Films, and Gaumont-British announced a loss of nearly £100,000 on the previous year's trading. It soon ceased production of its own films, closing down the Lime Grove studio. *Kinematograph Weekly* was able to summarize 1938 as "The Year of Disillusionment."

This was the sorry state of British cinema as war again was declared. Without government intervention in 1927, and then 1938, domestic studios would long since have expired, but even with it they were hardly in a position of strength. However, initial fears that World War II might affect the British film industry like the last proved unfounded. These were the most popular years of the British cinema ever, although not every participant in the industry benefitted from the attendance boom. Exhibitors mourned their lot, for costs had increased for almost everything from carbon supplies for projector arcs to wages and war bonuses.[15] In addition, the Home Office required exhibitors to show some government-produced documentaries and short propaganda films without remuneration, although they counted toward the quota of British films an exhibitor had to show.

[14] Metro-Goldwyn-Meyer (with Michael Balcon, now dissociated from Gaumont-British, as their British production manager) planned to make expensive feature films at Denham, which included *Goodbye Mr Chips* (1939), *Busman's Honeymoon* (1940), U.S. title *The Haunted Honeymoon*, *The Citadel* (1938), *A Yank at Oxford* (1937), and *Adventures of Tartu* (1943). Twentieth Century-Fox had similar plans for Pinewood, as had Warner Brothers for their newly extended studios at Teddington. Radio-Keith-Orpheum appointed Herbert Wilcox as their British production chief.

[15] *The Sunday Cinematograph Entertainments (Polls) Order* had legislated that a charity contribution could be levied by local licensing authorities on cinemas that opened on Sundays. Five percent of this was payable to the British Film Institute. See Oliver Bell, "The First Ten Years." The Order was made under the *Sunday Entertainments Act* (1932). Fuller also protested this new tax.

Entertainment Duty on sold tickets was levied three times during the conflict at an increasing rate, so that by 1945 the government was taking thirty-six percent of the price of every seat. Distributors were hiking their prices too. MGM tried to force the *Gone with the Wind* rental up from fifty percent of gross box office takings (which was then the average percentage) to seventy percent.[16] All these factors caused Fuller to write, with Eeyore-like melancholy, that "the average exhibitor, who provides trained A.R.P. workers, first aid staff, fire watchers, revenue to the Exchequer, distribution of official information, employment for many thousands and cheap recreation in luxurious surroundings to millions, and does not always get a bare living out of doing all these things, goes cheerfully on his way, conscious that he is in the most essential sense 'doing his bit.' "[17]

The question was, as it had been since the 1920s, "Was the government 'doing its bit'?" or, indeed, "What should its 'bit' be?" Parliamentary behavior provided no clear answer. Too many different government departments had jurisdiction over film, and the administration of the Ministry of Information's Films Division was frequently changing. During 1940 and 1941, *Sight and Sound* contributors complained of Minnie's (as it was jocularly known) lack of any "planned or coherent programme for film production," and described the British film industry as already being "partially wrecked" and in need of "salvage" because of this inaction.[18] Films lay "coiled in tins, unreleased. The industry lurk[ed], uncertain, behind sandbags."[19]

This state of uncertainty was understandable. The initial closure of cinemas had been read as a signal that officials considered mass entertainment a dispensable frippery in the crisis—that, in their view, the risk to life far outweighed the advantages of public pleasure, or the potential of cinema to galvanize war support. Further, during the exhibition blackout the House had mooted that British studios should follow suit. The option of a direct limitation on American imports was also explored as part of the

---

[16] The Macclesfield Majestic Cinema paid fifty-six percent of gross takings for this film. See Julian Poole, "British Cinema Attendance in Wartime: Audience Preference at the Majestic, Macclesfield, 1939–1946," *Historical Journal of Film, Radio and Television*, vol. 7, no. 1 (March 1987), p. 17. This trend provoked Charlie Chaplin to insist that no more than fifty percent was to be asked in England for the showing of *The Great Dictator*.

[17] Fuller "The Exhibitor's Part," p. 11. Fuller adds: "Voluntarily, the exhibitors have given five minutes a performance to the showing of Ministry of Information films, and the total value of this expressed in money would be enormous if the screen time had to be bought like newspaper advertising space." In fact, the time given could range from a 30-second food flash to a two-reeler.

[18] Contributors, "Newsreel," *Sight and Sound* 9, no. 36 (Winter 1940–41): 57; and Contributors, "Newsreel," *Sight and Sound* 10, no. 37 (Spring 1941): 1.

[19] Andrew Buchanan, "Let the Screen Help!" p. 87.

drive for dollar savings. It was a matter of deciding between "Bogart and Bacon," in M. P. Robert Boothby's vivid phrase.[20] Next there was talk that the Quota Act might be suspended during the emergency, and that the entire market would be handed over to the Amercians. This provoked a rash of anti-American feeling, especially among film personnel, an emotion uncomfortably at odds with the ideal of Allied solidarity.[21]

By December 1939, a delicate balance had been reached whereby the major Hollywood companies would agree to repatriate only up to $17.5 million, or a third of their British income; the rest would be blocked, but these funds could be reinvested in British production. In theory, the pact was to be renegotiated annually, but once America entered the war all her funds were released, all limits were lifted, and her film remittances soared. Britain could ill afford to offend the powerful Motion Picture Association of America by withdrawing its most profitable overseas market if she also wished to maintain America's friendship. As Margaret Dickinson has noted, it was the matter of such large-scale international relations as much as concern for the domestic film industry's cultural power that dictated intercourse between government and cinema during the war.[22]

The publication of two opposing articles by Brian Smith and Michael Balcon in the Winter 1940 issue of *Sight and Sound* marked a crucial stage in the debate over the extent to which the government should intervene to preserve home production.[23] Smith argued for nationalization because, in his view, all other measures taken in the past twenty years to ensure steady domestic output had failed. Quota protection did not serve the public well because it checked "the progress of the entertainment film" and arrested "the natural development of the industry." He argued that big business

---

[20] Robert Boothby, quoted in Karol Kulik, *Alexander Korda: The Man Who Could Work Miracles* (London: W. H. Allen, 1975), p. 278.

[21] Michael Balcon wrote, in 1940, "When, at the outbreak of war, and in the strangest circumstances, the Quota Act was almost done away with unknown to British producers, whose interests it was designed to protect, I, with others, fought for its maintenance." Balcon, "Rationalise!" p. 62.

[22] The Board of Trade figures for American remittances show a jump from a low of £4.8 million in 1940, through £8.5 million in 1942, to £26.3 million in 1943, after the end of restrictions. These figures are quoted in Margaret Dickinson, "The State and the Consolidation of Monopoly," in Curran and Porter, *British Cinema History*, p. 76. See also p. 75.

[23] Brian Smith, "Nationalise!" *Sight and Sound* 9, no. 36 (Winter 1940–41): 60–61, and Balcon, "Rationalise!" pp. 62–63. Balcon had become the mouthpiece for various critics' and producers' interests through his position (from 1938) as head of Ealing Studios and as producers' representative on the Cinematograph Films Council. Korda was away in America from 1940 to 1942, John Maxwell died in October 1940, and Rank was not yet highly visible: his combine was still in the making. This left the role of spokesperson to Balcon, until Fall 1944 when neither Michael Balcon nor the other producers' representative was reappointed at the end of their term of office; they were replaced by Rank and Korda.

investment had failed in the late 1930s, and that reducing production costs while returning more box office revenue to the producer would not have enough effect. He proposed that the film industry be nationalized along the lines of the G.P.O. and B.B.C. His logic ran thus: since radio had been improved by such measures, it was in the public interest that cinema should be also. Smith concluded, dramatically, that "without Government protection, the entertainment production section of the British film industry will die instantly."[24]

Michael Balcon agreed with Smith's conclusion, but was violently opposed to nationalization. Such a step was appropriate for the steel, railway, and coal industries, he argued, but not for the arts. He pointed to the decline in Soviet cinema after nationalization to support his view.[25] His most serious and perceptive charge was that nationalization was currently underway, "under the unimpeachable banner of 'national effort,' " in that Minnie's Film Division was not cooperating with the commercial industry, but competing with it—and unfairly—since the Division had Treasury backing and could call on skilled film workers in the Services now unavailable to commercial producers. The lack of expertise in the Division's administration merely made matters worse. Balcon called his solution "Rationalisation," or getting rational government support for the industry: "Let the Government sufficiently recognize the potential value of the film as a weapon of war . . . let it have proper war insurance risks, a credit bank to draw on, and it will flourish. But let it be controlled by free individuals and not by Government memoranda." Balcon was to be disappointed both in the matter of a film bank and on the question of full-blooded government support of cinema.

The main beneficiary of the wartime film industry, besides the documentary units, was J. Arthur Rank. Yorkshireman, millionaire, and Methodist, Rank first encountered film production in 1934 through Lady Yule, with whose help he founded British National Films, *Turn of the Tide* being his first film with British National. He also made short religious pictures. Fifteen years later, having lost large amounts of her jute fortune in his film ventures, Yule's quoted opinion was that film people were "over-paid, lazy, incompetent, extravagant—and incorrigible."[26] But that was all with hindsight, standing amidst yet another British film industry crisis in the late 1940s. Until that point, Rank's record had been impressive: by 1943

[24] Smith, "Nationalise!" p. 61.
[25] Balcon, "Rationalise!" p. 62. Balcon seems to be referring to Soviet film of the 1930s here, since he writes, "We used to see some very interesting productions from the Russian studios. But instead of flowering under nationalization, the industry declined."
[26] Nigel Davenport, "Common Sense on the Film Crisis," *Sight and Sound* 18, no. 72 (January 1950): 12.

he had amassed assets equivalent to that of an American major. Associated British Picture Corporation was the only other vertically integrated group anywhere near equivalent in size to Rank's, having production facilities, studios, and its own ABC cinema circuit.[27] The existence of these two combines by the early forties simplified transatlantic transactions enormously, at least when looking eastward. In the first instance it meant that American majors needed to deal with only two British groups in order to ensure a fairly wide distribution of their product in England. On top of this, both ABPC and Rank had inherited ties with American companies.[28] Fifty-six percent of studio space in Britain was now owned by Rank, and a booking with one of the three major exhibition circuits—Gaumont, Odeon, or ABC—was essential for the "successful exploitation of a British (or American) feature in the United Kingdom."[29] As the duopoly developed American companies gained an even larger say in British home bookings, so that while the wartime swell of audiences on both sides of the Atlantic, Rank's backing, and the overall shortage of films produced a temporarily favorable climate for independent production—and with it a chance to avoid "imitation" American films—the atmosphere for independent producers became increasingly hostile. Domestic duopoly was the bedfellow of American competition.[30]

The smell of monopoly was sufficiently offensive for the government to set up a committee of investigation in 1943. Headed by Albert Palache, with Michael Balcon as one of the two producers' representatives, the committee recommended the establishment of a film bank, and supervision of the industry by independent tribunals to arbitrate in cases of trade disputes. However, Hugh Dalton, president of the Board of Trade, only obtained personal commitments from Rank and ABPC not to expand further without his consent, and his Board prevaricated about the various specific recommendations so that no decisions were taken in wartime.

After commissioning the Palache report, the government did not intervene directly in film industry matters again until June 1947, when the seventy-five percent "Dalton Tax" was imposed on all earnings in Britain of

---

[27] For more details on the pre-1940s emergence of monopolies see Chanan, "The Emergence of an Industry," p. 57.

[28] Warners owned a large share of ABPC, and Rank was heir to Gaumont-British's connection with Twentieth Century-Fox, which he later supplemented on his own with bonds to Universal and United Artists.

[29] These conclusions were arrived at by Albert Palache's Cinematograph Films Council Committee. See Board of Trade, *Tendencies to Monopoly in the Cinematograph Industry: Report of a Committee appointed by the Cinematograph Films Council* (London: H.M.S.O., 1944), quoted in Dickinson, "The State and the Consolidation of Monopoly," p. 81.

[30] See Dickinson, "The State and the Consolidation of Monopoly," p. 78, on this point.

foreign films.[31] This draconian measure was intended to stem the worsening postwar economic crisis, under way despite a $3,750 million Marshall loan from Congress in 1946. Hollywood responded to the tax with an unexpected six-month boycott of the British market, a boycott that paradoxically hit British films the hardest. Stocks of American films in Britain were sufficient for six months—if exhibitors scraped the barrel in giving circuit-bookings to weaker new films—so there was no immediate gap to be filled, and anyway, reissues of old films were exempt from the tax.

Samuel Goldwyn described what the loss of the overseas market would mean to Hollywood, not only in dollars, but in terms of representing America abroad. ''The film has come to be not just another export, like tractors or cotton or coal, but perhaps the most important medium for expressing America to the world.''[32] He defended the industry against accusations of distortion and invention by disclaiming film noir—''America is not a land composed almost exclusively of neurotics and psychoanalysts, as a recent cycle of pictures might lead one to believe''—and latching onto his own production, *The Best Years of Our Lives*, as a picture in ''honest American terms, without any attempts to gloss over the deficiencies.''[33] The very existence of the article underscores Hollywood's persistent and deep-seated fear of losing the British market.

The American embargo renewed temptation among British producers to beat Hollywood at its own game: Rank's reaction was to step up production in the absence of U.S. films, with disastrous results. In March 1948 Hollywood lifted its ban on the signing of a new four-year pact.[34] The pact's provisions favored American interests: the seventy-five percent tax was eliminated, and Americans could withdraw up to $17 million of their annual earnings from films in Britain. They could also invest up to $10 million of their blocked sterling in *non-film* British enterprises during the first two years of the agreement. Any income from such investments could be remitted to the U.S. in dollars. As Woodrow Wyatt wrote, ''By this clause Britain realistically surrenders hope of her film industry being a dollar earner in the next four years, and, instead, buys valuable good will for the future.''[35]

---

[31] The Government also placed a restriction on the number of dupes of a film that could be made, to save on dollar-imported film base. See Duncan Crow, ''Days of Reckoning,'' *Sight and Sound* 18 (January 1950): 10.

[32] Samuel Goldwyn, ''World Challenge to Hollywood,'' *New York Times Magazine*, 31 August 1947, p. 8.

[33] Ibid.

[34] This was between Harold Wilson (successor to Dalton at the Board of Trade) and Eric Johnston, head of the Motion Picture Producers and Directors Association, replacing Will Hays in 1945.

[35] Woodrow Wyatt, ''Champagne for Hollywood,'' *The New Statesman and the Nation*,

When the tax was lifted the market was flooded and all British films lost heavily, particularly because many of them had been rushed through production and were of poor quality. A renewal of the ever paltry British distribution agreements in the United States could do little to redress the imbalance. By mid-1948 Korda's company, British Lion, was on the verge of bankruptcy, and the Rank organization was also suffering. Its annual budget statement "could not have been more gloomy than the prognostications."[36] *Sight and Sound* predicted that the output of British films would now be greatly curtailed, that "the present degree of unemployment" would continue, and that "the much hoped-for Renaissance of our cinema will be further postponed under conditions that inevitably encourage the independent producer to play very safe."[37]

The April 1950 transcript of a roundtable discussion on economic and creative problems in the British film industry makes equally depressing reading. Henry Cornelius pointed out that "the post-war mood in this country is merely symptomatic of general apathy and staleness"; Thorold Dickinson pronounced "British films are in the doldrums"; Anthony Havelock-Allen felt "that picture-makers are in need of some emotional mainspring"; and Frank Launder found the situation all too familiar in that "exactly the same things [are] happening today that I saw happening in the crisis of 1937—all of the major companies are doing the same thing as they did then."[38] The optimism of the mid and late war period had declined by the end of the decade to a dire mood of retrenchment, pessimism, and conservatism. The "much hoped-for Renaissance" of the film industry had evaporated and the relative, short-term success of wartime output, both economic and aesthetic, had already been eclipsed in Launder's retrospective assessment.

---

20 Mar 1948, p. 231. See also Woodrow Wyatt, "Dollars and Films," *The New Statesman and the Nation*, 8 May 1948, p. 368. Wyatt also disclosed that the real explanation for the Johnston "victory" was that Washington had indictated that, failing agreement, over $60 million worth of American films would be included in the package of commodities allocated to Britain under the Economic Recovery Program. The specter of such an avalanche had driven Wilson back to the bargaining table.

[36] Anonymous, "Points of View," *Sight and Sound* 18, no. 71 (Autumn 1949): 5.

[37] Ibid.

[38] "Round Table on British Films," *Sight and Sound* 19, no. 3 (April 1950): 114–22. Basil Wright, Anthony Havelock-Allen, Frank Launder, and Rachel Low, among others, were in attendance.

British Box Office Information, 1940–1950

As Julian Poole has pointed out, precise attendance figures for wartime British cinema are hard to come by.[1] The list below is taken from *Kinematograph Weekly*'s somewhat impressionistic annual survey, compiled mainly by R. H. "Josh" Billings.

1940   Biggest Winner: *Rebecca*
        Best British Film: *Convoy*
        Runners Up: *Foreign Correspondent, Ninotchka*

1941   Biggest Winner: *49th Parallel*
        Best British Film: *49th Parallel*
        Runners Up: *The Great Dictator, Pimpernel Smith, All This and Heaven Too, Lady Hamilton*
        British Runners Up: *Pimpernel Smith, Major Barbara*

1942   Biggest Winner: *Mrs. Miniver*
        Best British Film: *The First of the Few*
        Runners Up: *The First of the Few, How Green Was My Valley, Reap the Wild Wind, Holiday Inn, Captain of the Clouds, Sergeant York, One of Our Aircraft Is Missing, Hatter's Castle, Young Mr. Pitt*

1943   Biggest Winners: *In Which We Serve, Casablanca, The Life and Death of Colonel Blimp, Hello Frisco Hello, The Black Swan, The Man in Grey*
        Best British Film: *In Which We Serve*
        Runners Up: *The Gentle Sex, The Lamp Still Burns, Dear Octopus, The Adventures of Tartu*
        Best Documentary: *Desert Victory*

1944   Biggest Winners: *For Whom the Bell Tolls, This Happy Breed, Song of Bernadette, Going My Way, This Is the Army, Jane Eyre, The Story of Dr. Wassell, Cover Girl, White Cliffs of Dover, Sweet Rosie O'Grady, The Sullivans, Fanny by Gaslight*

[1] Julian Poole, "British Cinema Attendance in Wartime," p. 15.

231

Best British Film: *This Happy Breed*
British Runners Up: *Fanny by Gaslight, The Way Ahead, Love Story*

1945   Biggest Winner: *The Seventh Veil*
Best British Film: *The Seventh Veil*
Runners Up: (in release order) *Madonna of the Seven Moons, Old Acquaintance, Frenchman's Creek, Mrs. Parkington, Arsenic and Old Lace, Meet Me in Saint Louis, A Song to Remember, Since You Went Away, Here Come the Waves, Tonight and Every Night, Hollywood Canteen, They Were Sisters, The Princess and the Pirate, The Affairs of Susan, National Velvet, Mr. Skeffington, I Live in Grosvenor Square, Nob Hill, Perfect Strangers, Valley of Decision, Conflict, Duffy's Tavern*
British Runners Up: *They Were Sisters, I Live in Grosvenor Square, Perfect Strangers, Madonna of the Seven Moons, Waterloo Road, Blithe Spirit, The Way to the Stars, I'll Be Your Sweetheart, Dead of Night, Waltz Time, Henry V*

1946   Biggest Winner: *The Wicked Lady*
Best British Film: *The Wicked Lady*
Runners Up: *The Bells of Saint Mary's, Piccadilly Incident, The Road to Utopia, Tomorrow Is Forever, Brief Encounter, Wonder Man, Anchors Aweigh!, Kitty, The Captive Heart, The Corn Is Green, Spanish Main, Leave Her to Heaven, Gilda, Caravan, Mildred Pierce, Blue Dahlia, The Years Between, O.S.S., Spellbound, Courage of Lassie, My Reputation, London Town, Caesar and Cleopatra, Meet the Navy, Men of Two Worlds, Theirs Is the Glory, The Overlanders, Bedelia*

1947   Biggest Winner: *The Courtneys of Curzon Street*
Best British Film: *The Courtneys of Curzon Street*
Runners Up: *The Jolson Story, Great Expectations, Odd Man Out, Frieda, Holiday Camp, Duel in the Sun*

1948   Biggest Winner: *The Best Years of Our Lives*
Best British Film: *Spring in Park Lane*
Runners Up: *It Always Rains on Sunday, My Brother Jonathan, Road to Rio, Miranda, An Ideal Husband, Naked City, The Red Shoes, Green Dolphin Street, Forever Amber, Life with Father, The Weaker Sex, Oliver Twist, The Fallen Idol, The Winslow Boy*

1949   Biggest Winner: *The Third Man*
Best British Film: *The Third Man*
Runners Up: *Johnny Belinda, The Secret Life of Walter Mitty, Paleface, Scott of the Antarctic, The Blue Lagoon, Maytime in Mayfair, Easter Parade, Red River, You Can't Sleep Here*

1950   Biggest Winners: *The Blue Lamp, The Happiest Days of Your Life, Annie Get Your Gun, The Wooden Horse, Treasure Island, Odette*
Biggest British Film: *The Blue Lamp*
Runners Up: *Stage Fright, White Heat, Trio, They Were Not Divided, Morning Departure, Destination Moon, Sands of Iwo Jima, Little Women, The Forsythe Saga, Father of the Bride, Neptune's Daughter, The Dancing Years, The Red Light, Rogues of Sherwood Forest, Fancy Pants, Copper Canyon, State Secret, The Cure for Love, My Foolish Heart, Stromboli, Cheaper by the Dozen, Pinky, Three Came Home, Broken Arrow, The Black Rose*

SELECT FILMOGRAPHY

ABBREVIATIONS:
pc—production company   d—director
dist—original distributor   sc—screenplay
rel—release date   r—running time
p—producer

Brief Encounter

pc—Cineguild. dist—General Film. rel—December 1945 (reissued in 1948; distributed by A.B.F.D.). p—Anthony Havelock-Allan and Ronald Neame. d—David Lean. sc—David Lean, Noel Coward, and Ronald Neame, based on Noel Coward's play *Still Life*. r—86 minutes.

PLAYERS AND CHARACTERS: Celia Johnson (Laura Jesson), Trevor Howard (Dr. Alec Harvey), Stanley Holloway (Albert Godby), Joyce Carey (Myrtle Bagot), Cyril Raymond (Fred Jesson), Everley Gregg (Dolly Messiter), Margaret Barton (Beryl Waters), Valentine Dyall (Stephen Lynn), Marjorie Mars (Mary Norton), Irene Handel (Organist).

A Canterbury Tale

pc—The Archers. dist—Eagle Lion (G.B.); Eros Films (U.S.). Trade show—9 May 1944. rel—21 August 1944 (G.B.); 21 January 1949 (U.S.). p/d/sc—Michael Powell and Emeric Pressburger. r—124 minutes (G.B.); 95 minutes (U.S.).

PLAYERS AND CHARACTERS: Eric Portman (Thomas Culpepper, J.P.), Sheila Sim (Allison Smith), Dennis Price (Sgt. Peter Gibbs), John Sweet (Sgt. Bob Johnson), Esmond Knight (Narrator/Seven-Sisters Soldier/Village Idiot), Charles Hawtrey (Thomas Duckett), Hay Petrie (Woodcock), George Merritt (Ned Horton), Edward Rigby (Jim Horton), Freda Jackson (Prudence Honeywood), Betty Jardine (Fee Baker), Eliot Makeham (Organist), Harvey Golden (Sgt. Roczinsky).

The Foreman Went to France
(U.S. title: Somewhere in France)

pc—Ealing Studios. dist—United Artists. rel—April 1942. p—Michael Balcon. Associate producer—Alberto Cavalcanti. d—Charles Frend. sc—John Dighton, Angus Macphail, and Leslie Arliss, based on a story by J. B. Priestley, taken from the experience of Melbourne Johns, to whom the film is dedicated. r—87 minutes.

235

PLAYERS AND CHARACTERS: Tommy Trinder (Tommy), Clifford Evans (Fred Carrick), Constance Cummings (American Girl), Gordon Jackson (Jock), Robert Morley (French Major), Paul Bonifas (Prefect), Ernest Milton (Stationmaster), Francis L. Sullivan (Skipper), Ronald Adam (Sir Charles Fawcett), Anita Palacine and Thora Hird (Barmaids).

The Gentle Sex

pc—Two Cities-Concanen. dist—General Film. rel—April 1943 (reissued in 1948, 620 feet cut). p—Derek de Marney and Leslie Howard. d—Leslie Howard and Maurice Elvey. sc—Moie Charles, Aimee Stuart, Roland Pertwee, and Phyllis Rose, based on a script by Moie Charles. r—93 minutes.

PLAYERS AND CHARACTERS: Meredith Baker (Maggie Fraser), Joan Gates (Gwen), Jean Gillie (Good-time Dot), Joan Greenwood (Betty), Joyce Howard (Anne Lawrence), Rosamund John (Maggie Frazer), Lilli Palmer (Erna), Barbara Waring (Joan), John Justin (Flying Officer David Sheridan), Frederick Leister (Col. Lawrence), Mary Jerrold (Mrs. Sheridan), Everley Gregg (Mrs. Simpson), Anthony Bazell (Ted), John Laurie (Corporal), Rosalyn Boulter (Sally), Meriel Forbes (Commander), Harry Welchman (Captain), Ronald Shiner (Racegoer), Jimmy Hanley (Soldier), Miles Malleson (Guard), Peter Cotes (Taffy).

Great Day

pc—RKO-Radio. rel—April 1945. p—Victor Hanbury. d—Lance Comfort. sc—Wolfgang Wilhelm and John Davenport, based on a play by Lesley Storm. r—79 minutes.

PLAYERS AND CHARACTERS: Eric Portman (Captain Ellis), Flora Robson (Mrs. Ellis), Sheila Sim (Margaret Ellis), Isabel Jeans (Lady Mott), Walter Fitzgerald (John Tyndale), Philip Friend (Geoffrey Winthrop), Marjorie Rhodes (Mrs. Mumford), Margaret Withers (Mrs. Tyndale), Maire O'Neill (Mrs. Walsh), Beatrice Varley (Miss Tracy).

I See A Dark Stranger
(U.S. title: *The Adventuress*)

pc—Individual Pictures. dist—General Film. Trade show—3 July 1946. rel—5 August 1946 (G.B.). p—Frank Launder and Sidney Gilliat. d—Frank Launder. sc—Frank Launder and Sidney Gilliat, based on a story by Frank Launder, Sidney Gilliat, and Wolfgang Wilhelm. r—112 minutes (cut to 98 minutes for U.S. release).

PLAYERS AND CHARACTERS: Deborah Kerr (Bridie Quilty), Trevor Howard (Lt. David Baynes), Raymond Huntley (Miller), Michael Howard (Hawkings), Liam Redmond (Timothy), William O'Gorman (Danny Quilty), Eddie Golden (Terence Delaney), Brefni O'Rorke (Michael O'Callaghan), David Ward (Oscar Pryce), James

Harcourt (Grandfather), Garry Marsh (Capt. Goodhusband), Tom Macaulay (Lt. Spanswick), Olga Lindo (Mrs. Edwards).

In Which We Serve

pc—Two Cities. dist—British Lion. rel—October 1942. p—Noel Coward. d—Noel Coward and David Lean. sc—Noel Coward. r—114 minutes.

PLAYERS AND CHARACTERS: Noel Coward (Capt. Kinross), Celia Johnson (Alix Kinross), John Mills (Shorty Blake), Bernard Miles (Walter Hardy), Joyce Carey (Kath Hardy), Kay Walsh (Freda Lewis), Michael Wilding (Flags), George Carney (Mr. Blake), Kathleen Harrison (Mrs. Blake), Derek Elphinstone (No. 1), Philip Friend (Torps), Frederick Piper (Edgecombe), Wally Patch (Uncle Fred), Richard Attenborough (Young Stoker), Daniel Massey (Bobby Kinross), Ann Stephens (Lavinia Kinross).

It Always Rains on Sunday

pc—Ealing Studios. dist—General Film. rel—November 1947. p—Michael Balcon. Associate producer—Henry Cornelius. d—Robert Hamer. sc—Angus Macphail, Robert Hamer, and Henry Cornelius, based on the novel by Arthur La Bern. r—92 minutes.

PLAYERS AND CHARACTERS: Googie Withers (Rose Sandigate), Susan Shaw (Vi Sandigate), Edward Chapman (George Sandigate), Patricia Plunkett (Doris Sandigate), David Lines (Alfie Sandigate), Jack Warner (Detective Sgt. Fothergill), John McCallum (Tommy Swann), Jimmy Hanley (Whitey Williams), John Carol (Freddie Price), Alfie Bass (Dicey Perkins).

Love Story
(U.S. title: *A Lady Surrenders*)

pc—Gainsborough Pictures. dist—Eagle Lion. rel—October 1944. p—Harold Huth. d—Leslie Arliss. sc—Leslie Arliss, Doreen Montgomery, and Rodney Ackland, based on a short story by J. W. Drawbell. r—113 minutes.

PLAYERS AND CHARACTERS: Margaret Lockwood (Lissa Campbell), Stewart Granger (Kit Firth), Patricia Roc (Judy Martin), Tom Walls (Tom Tanner), Reginald Purdell (Albert), Moira Lister (Carol), Dorothy Bramhall (Susie), Vincent Holman (Prospero), Joan Rees (Ariel), Walter Hudd (Ray), A. E. Matthews (Col. Pitt Smith), Josephine Middleton (Mrs. Pitt Smith), Laurence Hanray (Angus Rossiter), Beatrice Varley (Mrs. Rossiter), Harriet Cohen (Pianist).

The Man in Grey

pc—Gainsborough Pictures. dist—General Film. rel—July 1943. p—Edward Black. d—Leslie Arliss. sc—Margaret Kennedy, Leslie Arliss, and Doreen Montgomery, based on a novel by Lady Eleanor Smith. r—116 minutes.

PLAYERS AND CHARACTERS: Margaret Lockwood (Hester Shaw), James Mason (Marquis of Rohan), Phyllis Calvert (Clarissa Rohan), Stewart Granger (Peter Rokeby), Helen Haye (Lady Rohan), Raymond Lovell (Prince Regent), Nora Swinburne (Mrs. Fitzherbert), Martita Hunt (Miss Patchett), A. E. Matthews (Auctioneer), Roy Emerton (Game Keeper), Amy Veness (Mrs. Armstrong), Diana King (Jane Seymour), Beatrice Varley (Gipsy).

Millions Like Us

pc—Gainsborough Pictures. dist—General Film. Trade show—2 September 1943. rel—15 November 1943. p—Edward Black. d—Frank Launder and Sidney Gilliat. sc—Frank Launder and Sidney Gilliat. r—103 minutes.

PLAYERS AND CHARACTERS: Patricia Roc (Celia Crowson), Eric Portman (Charlie Forbes), Gordon Jackson (Fred Blake), Anne Crawford (Jennifer Knowles), Joy Shelton (Phyllis Crowson), Megs Jenkins (Gwen Price), Moore Marriot (Jim Crowson), John Boxer (Tom Crowson), Hilda Davies (Labour Officer), Terry Randall (Annie Earnshaw).

The Next of Kin

pc—Ealing Studios. dist—United Artists. rel—May 1942. p—Michael Balcon. d—Thorold Dickinson. sc—Thorold Dickinson, Sir Basil Bartlett (Military Supervisor), Angus Macphail, and John Dighton. r—102 minutes.

PLAYERS AND CHARACTERS: Mervyn Johns (no. 23, Mr. Arthur Davis), John Chandos (no. 16, his contact), Nova Pilbeam (Beppie Leemans), Stephen Murray (Ned Barratt), Reginald Tate (Major Richards), Geoffrey Hibbert (Pte. John), Philip Friend (Lt. Cummins), Phyllis Stanley (Miss Clare), Mary Clare (Miss Webster), Joss Ambler (Mr. Vernon), Brefni O'Rorke (Brigadier), Jack Hawkins (Major Harcourt), Thora Hird (A.T.S. girl).

Perfect Strangers
(U.S. title: Vacation from Marriage)

pc—MGM-London Films. rel—August 1945 (G.B.): December 1945 (U.S.) (reissued in 1948). p/d—Alexander Korda. sc—Clemence Dane and Anthony Pelissier, based on a script by Clemence Dane, and others. r—102 minutes. Academy Award 1946: Best Original Story.

PLAYERS AND CHARACTERS: Robert Donat (Robert Wilson), Deborah Kerr (Catherine Wilson), Glynis Johns (Dizzy Clayton), Ann Todd (Elena), Roland Culver (Richard), Elliot Mason (Mrs. Hemmings), Eliot Makeham (Mr. Staines), Brefni O'Rorke (Mr. Hargrove), Edward Rigby (Charlie), Muriel George (Minnie).

238

Piccadilly Incident

pc—Associated British Picture Corporation. dist—Pathé. rel—August 1946. p/d—Herbert Wilcox. sc—Nicholas Phipps, based on a story by Florence Tranter. r—102 minutes.

PLAYERS AND CHARACTERS: Anna Neagle (Diana Fraser), Michael Wilding (Capt. Alan Pearson), Michael Laurence (Bill Weston), Frances Mercer (Joan Draper), Coral Browne (Virginia Pearson), A. E. Matthews (Sir Charles Pearson), Edward Rigby (Judd), Brenda Bruce (Sally Benton).

Tawny Pipit

pc—Two Cities. dist—General Film. rel—May 1944. d—Bernard Miles and Charles Saunders. sc—Bernard Miles and Charles Saunders, based on a story by Bernard Miles. r—85 minutes.

PLAYERS AND CHARACTERS: Bernard Miles (Col. Barton-Barrington), Rosamund John (Hazel Brooke), Niall MacGinnis (Jimmy Bancroft), Jean Gillie (Nancy Forrester), Christopher Steele (Rev. Kingsley), Lucie Mannheim (Russian Sniper), Brefni O'Rorke (Uncle Arthur), George Carney (Whimbrel), Wylie Watson (Croaker), John Salew (Pickering), Marjorie Rhodes (Mrs. Pickering), Ernest Butcher (Tommy Fairchild), Grey Blake (Capt. Dawson), Joan Sterndale-Bennett (Rose).

This Happy Breed

pc—Two Cities-Cineguild. dist—Eagle Lion. rel—May 1944. p—Noel Coward and Anthony Havelock-Allan. d—David Lean. sc—David Lean, Ronald Neame, and Anthony Havelock-Allan, based on a play by Noel Coward.

PLAYERS AND CHARACTERS: Robert Newton (Frank Gibbons), Celia Johnson (Ethel Gibbons), John Mills (Billy Mitchell), Kay Walsh (Queenie Gibbons), Stanley Holloway (Bob Mitchell), Amy Veness (Mrs. Flint), Alison Leggatt (Aunt Sylvia), Eileen Erskine (Vi), John Blythe (Reg), Guy Verney (Sam Leadbitter), Merle Tottenham (Edie).

Two Thousand Women

pc—Gainsborough Pictures. dist—General Film. Trade show—22 August 1944. rel—6 November 1944. p—Edward Black. d—Frank Launder. sc—Frank Launder. r—97 minutes.

PLAYERS AND CHARACTERS: Phyllis Calvert (Freda Thompson), Flora Robson (Mrs. Manningford), Patricia Roc (Rosemary Brown), Renée Houston (Maud Wright), Reginald Purdell (Alec Harvey), Anne Crawford (Margaret Long), Jean Kent (Bridie Johnson), James McKechnie (Jimmy Moore), Bob Arden (Dave Kennedy), Carl Jaffe (Sgt. Hentzner), Muriel Aked (Miss Meredith), Kathleen Boutall (Mrs. Hatfield),

Hilda Cambell-Russell (Mrs. Hope Latimer), Christina Forbes (Frau Holweg), Thora Hird (Mrs. Buttshaw), Dulcie Gray (Nellie Skinner).

Victory Wedding

pc—Gainsborough Pictures. rel—May 1944. d—Jessie Matthews. r—20 minutes.

PLAYERS AND CHARACTERS: John Mills (Soldier Bill), Dulcie Gray (Mary), Beatrice Varley (Mother), Vincent Holman (Father).

Waterloo Road

pc—Gainsborough Pictures. dist—General Film. Trade show—12 January 1945. rel—5 February 1945. p—Edward Black. d—Sidney Gilliat. sc—Sidney Gilliat, based on a story by Val Valentine. r—76 minutes.

PLAYERS AND CHARACTERS: John Mills (Jim Colter), Stewart Granger (Ted Purvis), Alastair Sim (Dr. Montgomery), Joy Shelton (Tillie Colter), Beatrice Varley (Mrs. Colter), Alison Leggatt (Ruby), Arthur Denton (Fred), Ben Williams (Corporal Lewis), George Carney (Tom Mason), Johnny Schofield (Landlord), Frank Atkinson (Barman), Wylie Watson (Tattooist), John Boxer (Policeman).

The Way Ahead

pc—Two Cities. dist—Eagle Lion. rel—June 1944. p—John Sutro and Norman Walker. d—Carol Reed. sc—Eric Ambler and Peter Ustinov, based on a story by Eric Ambler. r—115 minutes.

PLAYERS AND CHARACTERS: David Niven (Lt. Jim Perry), Raymond Huntley (Davenport), Billy Hartnell (Sgt. Fletcher), Stanley Holloway (Brewer), James Donald (Lloyd), John Laurie (Luke), Leslie Dwyer (Beck), Hugh Burden (Parsons), Jimmy Hanley (Stainer), Renee Asherson (Marjorie Gillingham), Penelope Dudley Ward (Mrs. Perry), Reginald Tate (CO), Leo Glenn (Commander), Mary Jerrold (Mrs. Gillingham), Raymond Lovell (Garage Proprietor), Alf Goddard (Instructor), A. E. Matthews (Col. Walmsley), Peter Ustinov (Rispoli), Tessie O'Shea (Herself).

The Way to the Stars
(U.S. title: Johnny in the Clouds)

pc—Two Cities. dist—United Artists. rel—June 1945. p—Anatole Grunwald. d—Anthony Asquith. sc—Terence Rattigan, from a script by Terence Rattigan and Anatole Grunwald, based on a story by Terence Rattigan and Richard Sherman. r—109 minutes.

PLAYERS AND CHARACTERS: Michael Redgrave (David Archdale), John Mills (Peter Penrose), Rosamund John (Toddy Todd), Douglass Montgomery (Johnny Hollis), Renee Asherton (Iris Winterton), Stanley Holloway (Mr. Palmer), Felix Aylmer (Rev. Charles Moss), Basil Radford (Tiny Williams), Bonar Colleano Junior (Joe Friselli), Trevor Howard (Squadron Leader Carter), Joyce Carey (Miss Winterton).

The Wicked Lady

pc—Gainsborough Pictures. dist—Eagle Lion. rel—December 1945. p—R. J. Minney. d—Leslie Arliss. sc—Leslie Arliss, Aimee Stuart, and Gordon Glennon, based on *The Life and Death of the Wicked Lady Skelton* by Magdalen King-Hall. r—103 minutes.

PLAYERS AND CHARACTERS: Margaret Lockwood (Barbara Worth), James Mason (Captain Jerry Jackson), Patricia Roc (Caroline), Griffith Jones (Sir Ralph Skelton), Michael Rennie (Kit Locksby), Felix Aylmer (Hogarth), Enid Stamp Taylor (Henrietta Kingsclere), Francis Lister (Lord Kingsclere), Jean Kent (Captain Jackson's Doxy), Emrys Jones (Ned Cottrell), Martita Hunt (Agatha Trimble).

SELECT BIBLIOGRAPHY

THIS LIST is arranged under two headings: general references and film references. For an extensive bibliography on the British cinema, see James Curran and Vincent Porter, eds., *British Cinema History* (London: Weidenfeld and Nicholson, 1983).

GENERAL REFERENCES

Barthes, Roland. *Mythologies*. New York: Hill and Wang, 1972.

Beauman, Nicola. *A Very Great Profession: The Woman's Novel, 1914–1939*. London: Virago, 1983.

Bell, Robert. *History of the British Railways during the War, 1939–1945*. London: The Railway Gazette, 1946.

Belsey, Catherine. *Critical Practice*. London: Methuen, 1980.

Briggs, Asa. *The History of Broadcasting in the UK*. 3 vols. New York: Oxford University Press, 1970.

————. *The BBC: The First Fifty Years*. New York: Oxford University Press, 1985.

Broad, Richard, and Fleming, Suzie. *Nella Last's War: A Mother's Diary, 1939–1945*. London: Falling Wall Press, 1981.

Calder, Angus. *The People's War: Britain 1939–1945*. London: Jonathan Cape, 1969, Granada, 1971.

Calder, Angus, and Sheridan, Dorothy, eds. *Speak for Yourself: A Mass-Observation Anthology, 1937–1949*. London: Jonathan Cape, 1983.

Clark, T. J. *The Painting of Modern Life: The Art of Manet and His Followers*. New York: Knopf, 1985.

Cleveland, Les. "When They Send the Last Yank Home: Wartime Images of Popular Culture." *Journal of Popular Culture* 18, no. 3 (Winter 1984): 31–36.

Costello, John. *Love, Sex and War: Changing Values, 1939–1945*. London: Collins, 1985.

Darracott, Joseph, and Loftus, Belinda. *Second World War Posters*. London: Imperial War Museum, 1972.

Davies, Andrew. *Where Did the Forties Go?: A Popular History*. London: Pluto Press, 1984.

Douie, Vera. *The Lesser Half: A Survey of the Laws, Regulations and Practices Introduced during the Present War Which Embody Discrimination against Women*. London: Women's Publicity Planning Association, 1943.

Eagleton, Terry. "Pierre Macherey and the Theory of Literary Production." *Minnesota Review* 5 (Fall 1975): 134–44.

————. *Criticism and Ideology: A Study in Marxist Literary Theory*. London: New Left Books, 1976.

————. *Literary Theory: An Introduction*. Minneapolis: University of Minnesota Press, 1983.

Ferguson, Sheila, and Fitzgerald, Hilde. *Studies in the Social Services*. History of the Second World War, United Kingdom Civil Series. London: H.M.S.O., 1954.

Fussell, Paul. *Wartime: Understanding and Behavior in the Second World War*. London: Oxford University Press, 1989.

Harrisson, Tom. "Article for *Polemic*." Sussex Mass Observation Archives. File Report no. 2465. Subject index: "Sexual Behavior."

Higonnet, Margaret Randolph; Jenson, Jane; Michel, Sonya; and Weitz, Margaret Collins, eds. *Behind the Lines: Gender and the Two World Wars*. New Haven: Yale University Press, 1987.

Jameson, Fredric. "Reification and Utopia in Mass Culture." *Social Text* 1 (Winter 1979): 130–48.

Leitch, Michael, ed. *Great Songs of World War II*. London: Wise Publications, 1982.

Lock, Stephen, ed. *As You Were: VE Day—A Medical Retrospective*. London: British Medical Association, 1984.

Longmate, Norman. *How We Lived Then: A History of Everyday Life during the Second World War*. London: Hutchinson, 1971.

Macherey, Pierre. Interview with Pierre Macherey. *Red Letters* 5 (Summer 1977).

Marwick, Arthur. *The Home Front: The British and the Second World War*. London: Thames and Hudson, 1976.

Mass-Observation. *War Begins at Home*, edited and arranged by Tom Harrisson and Charles Madge. London: Chatto and Windus, 1940.

Minns, Raynes. *Bombers and Mash: The Domestic Front, 1939–1945*. London: Virago, 1980.

Moseley, Leonard. *Backs to the Wall: London under Fire, 1939–1945*. London: Weidenfeld and Nicholson, 1971.

Ourselves in Wartime: An Illustrated Survey of the Home Front in the Second World War. London: Odhams Press Ltd., 1944.

Parker, Rozsika. *The Subversive Stitch: Embroidery and the Making of the Feminine*. London: The Women's Press, 1984.

Perkins, Teresa. "Re-thinking Stereotypes." Pages 135–59 in Barrett, Michèle; Corrigan, Philip; Kuhn, Annette; and Wolff, Janet, eds. *Ideology and Cultural Production*. London: Croon Helm, 1979.

Priestley, J. B. *Black-out in Gretley: A Story of—and for—Wartime*. London: Heinemann, 1942.

———. *British Women Go to War*. London: Collins, n.d. (1944?).

Reilly, Catherine, ed. *Chaos of the Night: Women's Poetry and Verse of the Second World War*. London: Virago, 1984.

Riley, Denise. " 'The Free Mothers': Pronatalism and Working Women in Industry at the End of the Last War in Britain." *History Workshop Journal* 11 (Spring 1981).

———. *War in the Nursery: Theories of the Child and the Mother*. London: Virago, 1983.

Roosevelt, Eleanor. "British Women's War Work." *Ladies' Home Journal* 60 (April 1943): 22–25 + .

Root, Jane. *Pictures of Women: Sexuality*. London: Pandora, 1985.

Rowbottom, Sheila, and McCrindle, Jean, eds. *Dutiful Daughters: Women Talk about Their Lives*. London: Allen Lane, 1977.

Sackville-West, Vita. *The Women's Land Army*. London: Michael Joseph, 1944.

Schivelbusch, Wolfgang. *The Railway Journey: The Industrialization of Time and Space in the Nineteenth Century*. Berkeley: University of California Press, 1986.

Settle, Mary Lee. *All the Brave Promises: Memories of Aircraft Woman 2nd Class 2146391* [1966]. London: Pandora, 1984.

Summerfield, Penelope. "Women Workers in Wartime." *Capital and Class* 1 (1977).

————. "Women, Work and Welfare: A Study of Childcare and Shopping in Britain in World War II." *Journal of Social History* 17, no. 2 (Winter 1983).

————. *Women Workers in the Second World War*. London: Croon Helm, 1984.

Thomas, S. Evelyn. *Everyman's Guide to the War Regulations: An ABC of Essential Information for the Ordinary Citizen*. St. Albans: Donnington Press, November 1939.

"Wartime Corsets." *Picture Post*, 2 March 1940, vol. 6–7, pp. 26–27 + .

Westall, Robert, comp. *Children of the Blitz: Memories of Wartime Childhood*. Harmondsworth: Penguin, 1987.

Williamson, Judith. "Woman Is An Island: Femininity and Colonization." In Tania Modleski, ed. *Studies in Entertainment: Critical Approaches to Mass Culture*. Bloomington: Indiana University Press, 1986.

Yass, Marion. *This Is Your War: Home Front Propaganda in the Second World War*. London: Public Record Office/H.M.S.O., 1983.

Young, Robert, ed. *Untying the Text: A Post-Structuralist Reader*. London: Routledge and Kegan Paul, 1981.

FILM REFERENCES

Abrams, Mark. "The British Cinema Audience." *Hollywood Quarterly* 3 (1947–48).

————. "The British Cinema Audience, 1949." *Hollywood Quarterly* 4 (1949–50).

Agee, James. "Vacation from Marriage." *The Nation*, 23 March 1946.

————. "Brief Encounter." *The Nation*, 31 October 1946.

Aldgate, Anthony. "Ideological Consensus in British Feature Films, 1935–1947." Pages 94–112 in Short, K.R.M., ed. *Feature Films as History*. Knoxville: Tennessee University Press, 1981.

Aldgate, Anthony, and Richards, Jeffrey. *Best of British: Cinema and Society, 1930–1970*. Oxford: Blackwell, 1983.

————. *Britain Can Take It: The British Cinema in the Second World War*. Oxford: Blackwell, 1986.

Anderson, Lindsay. "Angles of Approach." *Sequence* 2 (Winter 1947): 5–8.

Anstey, Edgar. "Brief Encounter." *The Spectator*, 7 December 1945.

Armes, Roy. *A Critical History of the British Cinema*. London: Cinema Two Series, Secker and Warburg, 1978.

The Arts Council of Great Britain. *The Art of the Film*. Catalogue by Roger Manvell, accompanying exhibition in London and at the Museum of Modern Art, New York. London: Arts Council, 1945.

245

Aspinall, Sue. "Women, Realism and Reality in British Films, 1943–1953." In Curran, James, and Porter, Vincent, eds. *British Cinema History*. London: Weidenfeld and Nicholson, 1983.

Aspinall, Sue, and Murphy, Robert, eds. *Gainsborough Melodrama: BFI Dossier 18*. London: British Film Institute Publishing, 1983.

Atwell, David. *Cathedrals of the Movies: A History of British Cinemas and Their Audiences*. London: Architectural Press, 1981.

Balcon, Michael. "Rationalise!" *Sight and Sound* 9, no. 36 (Winter 1940–41): 62–63.

———. *Michael Balcon Presents: A Lifetime of Films*. London: Hutchinson, 1969.

Balcon, Michael; Lindgren, Ernest; Hardy, Forsyth; and Manvell, Roger. *Twenty Years of British Film, 1925–1945*. London: Falcon, 1947; reprint ed., New York, Literature of Cinema Series, Arno Press, 1972.

Barker, Felix. "Programme Notes for *Brief Encounter*." Microjacket, British Film Institute Library.

Barr, Charles. "Projecting Britain and the British Character: Ealing Studios." Part I: *Screen* 15, no. 1 (Spring 1974): 87–121; part II: *Screen* 15, no. 2 (Summer 1974): 129–63.

———. *Ealing Studios*. London: Cameron and Tayleur, David and Charles, 1977.

———, ed. *All Our Yesterdays: Ninety Years of British Cinema*. London: British Film Institute Publishing, 1986.

Barthes, Roland. "Upon Leaving the Movie Theater." Trans. Bertrand Augst and Susan White in *Apparatus: Cinematographic Apparatus, Selected Writings*. Ed. Theresa Hak Kyung Cha. New York: Tanam Press, 1980.

Basinger, Jeanine. *The World War Two Combat Film: Anatomy of a Genre*. New York: Columbia University Press, 1986.

Baudry, Jean-Louis. "The Apparatus." Trans. Bertrand Augst and Jean Andrews. *Camera Obscura* 1, no. 1 (Fall 1976): 104–26.

Bazin, André. *What Is Cinema?* vols. 1 and 2. Translated by Hugh Gray. Los Angeles: University of California Press, 1967.

Bean, K. F. "Letter to Oliver Bell." *Sight and Sound* 12, no. 46 (September 1943): 35–38.

Bell, Oliver. "The First Ten Years." *Sight and Sound* 12, no. 47 (October 1943): 56–58.

Bennett, Tony. "Text and Social Process: The Case of James Bond." *Screen Education* 41 (Winter/Spring 1982): 3–14.

Betts, Ernest. *The Film Business: A History of British Cinema, 1896–1972*. London: Allen and Unwin, 1973.

Bhabha, Homi K. "The Other Question . . . the Stereotype and Colonial Discourse." *Screen* 24, no. 6 (November/December 1983): 18–36.

Billings, R. H. "Josh." "Box Office Stakes Results." *Kinematograph Weekly*, 8 January 1942.

———. "Good News for Britain." *Kinematograph Weekly*, 20 December 1945.

————. "These Were the Box Office Hits of the Year." *Kinematograph Weekly*, 19 December 1946, pp. 46–47.

Bond, Ralph. "What Is the Future of British Films?" *Picture Post*, 6 January 1945, pp. 11–13 +.

————. *Monopoly: The Future of British Films* (pamphlet). London: Association of Ciné-Technicians, 1946.

Box, Kathleen. *The Cinema and the Public*. Social Survey Report no. 106. London: Central Office of Information, 1947.

Brief Encounter. Anonymous reviews: *Today's Cinema*, 14 November 1945; *Kinematograph Weekly*, 15 November 1945; *Daily Telegraph*, 22 November 1945; *Manchester Guardian*, 22 November 1945, and 19 February 1946; *Daily Mirror*, 23 November 1945; *Chronicle*, "Grown-up Love," 24 November 1945; *Motion Picture Herald*, 15 December 1945; *Time*, 9 September 1946; *Theater Arts*, October 1946, no. 30, p. 596; *Documentary News Letter*, eds., "The Films of 1945" (1946/1947), p. 10; *Sunday Express*, 3 November 1968.

Brown, Geoff. *Launder and Gilliat*. London: British Film Institute Publishing, 1977.

Brown, John Mason. "Seeing Things: The Midas Touch." *Saturday Review of Literature*, 12 October 1946, pp. 36–38.

Buchanan, Andrew. "Ships and Sealing Wax." *Sight and Sound* 7, no. 26 (Summer (1938): 80–81.

————. "Let the Screen Help!" *Sight and Sound* 8, no. 31 (Autumn 1939): 87–88.

Carew, Dudley. "Hollywood Indicted: A British Viewpoint." *New York Times Magazine*, 23 September 1945, pp. 22–23.

Chanan, Michael. "The Emergence of an Industry." Pages 39–58 in Curran, James, and Porter, Vincent, eds. *British Cinema History*. London: Weidenfeld and Nicholson, 1983.

Christie, Ian, ed. *Powell, Pressburger and Others*. London: British Film Institute Publishing, 1978.

————. *Arrows of Desire: The Films of Michael Powell and Emeric Pressburger*. London: Waterstone, 1985.

Collier, Lionel. "Brief Encounter." *The Picturegoer*, 2 February 1946.

"Competition from London." *Time*, 11 June 1945, pp. 84–85.

Curran, James, and Porter, Vincent, eds. *British Cinema History*. London: Weidenfeld and Nicholson, 1983.

Dickinson, Margaret. "The State and the Consolidation of Monopoly." Pages 74–95 in Curran, James, and Porter, Vincent, eds. *British Cinema History*. London: Weidenfeld and Nicholson, 1983.

Dickinson, Margaret, and Street, Sarah. *Cinema and State: The Film Industry and the British Government 1927–1984*. London: British Film Institute Publishing, 1985.

Dickinson, Thorold. "Why Not a National Film Society?" *Sight and Sound* 7, no. 26 (Summer 1938): 75.

Dixon, Campbell. "Pathos of Frustrated Love." *The Daily Telegraph*, 26 November 1945.

Doane, Mary Ann. "The Voice in the Cinema: The Articulation of Body and Space." *Cinema/Sound*. New Haven: Yale French Studies no. 60 (1980), pp. 33–50.

———. "Possession and Address: The 'Woman's Film.' " Pages 67–82 in Doane, Mary Ann; Mellencamp, Patricia; and Williams, Linda, eds. *Re-vision: Essays in Feminist Film Criticism*. Frederick, Md.: University Publications of America/ American Film Institute, 1984.

———. *The Desire to Desire: The Woman's Film of the 1940s*. Bloomington: Indiana University Press, 1987.

Doane, Mary Ann; Mellencamp, Patricia; and Williams, Linda, eds. *Re-vision: Essays in Feminist Film Criticism*. Frederick, Md.: University Publications of America/ American Film Institute, 1984.

Durgnat, Raymond. *A Mirror for England: British Movies from Austerity to Affluence*. New York: Praeger, 1971.

Edwards, Tudor. "Film and Unreality." *Sight and Sound* 15, no. 58 (Summer 1946): 59–61.

Ellis, John. "Art, Culture and Quality: Terms for a Cinema in the Forties and Seventies." *Screen* 19, no. 3 (Autumn 1978): 9–49.

———. "Victory of the Voice?" *Screen* 22, no. 2 (1981): 69–72.

———. *Visible Fictions*. London: Routledge and Kegan Paul, 1982.

Elvin, George. "British Labour Problems." *Sight and Sound* 10, no. 40 (Spring 1942): 79–81.

"England, Their England." *Time*, 10 November 1947, p. 103.

Farber, Manny. "Middle-Aged Fling." *The New Republic* , 21 October 1946.

"The Film and the Young Person." *Sight and Sound* 7, no. 25 (Spring 1938).

Fletcher, Helen. "Films in Review." *Time and Tide*, 7 April 1945, p. 290.

Fuller, W. R. "The Exhibitor's Part." *Sight and Sound* 10, no. 37 (Spring 1941): 10–11.

The Gentle Sex. Anonymous reviews: *Kinematograph Weekly*, 8 April 1943, p. 24; *Sunday Times*, 11 April 1943; *Monthly Film Bulletin*, 30 April 1943, p. 37; *Daily Telegraph*, 2 May 1943.

Gifford, Dennis. *The British Film Catalogue, 1895–1970: A Guide to Entertainment Films*. Newton Abbott: David and Charles, 1973.

"Glad Hands Across the Sea." *Time*, 10 December 1945, p. 82 + .

Gledhill, Christine. "Recent Developments in Feminist Film Criticism." *Quarterly Review of Film Studies* 3, no. 4: 458–93; reprint ed. in Doane, Mary Ann; Mellencamp, Patricia; and Williams, Linda, eds. *Re-vision: Essays in Feminist Film Criticism*. Frederick, Md.: University Publications of America/American Film Institute, 1984.

Gledhill, Christine, and Swanson, Gillian. "Gender and Sexuality in Second World War Films—A Feminist Approach." In Hurd, Geoff, ed. *National Fictions: World War Two in British Films and Television*. London: British Film Institute Publishing, 1984.

Goldwyn, Samuel. "World Challenge to Hollywood." *New York Times Magazine*, 31 August 1947, p. 8 + .

SELECT BIBLIOGRAPHY

Goodman, Ezra. "Hollywood Is Worried." *Sight and Sound* 8, no. 31 (Autumn 1939): 106.

Grant, Elspeth. "From Pearl White to Pearl Harbour." *Sight and Sound* 11, no. 43 (Winter 1942): 61–62.

Gray, J. C. "The Outlook for British Films." *Political Quarterly* (October/December 1940): 384–94.

Hammond, Ion, comp. *This Year of Films: What the Critics Said.* London: British Film Institute Library, 1948.

Hardy, Forsyth. "An Open Letter to the Film Societies." *Sight and Sound* 10, no. 38 (Summer 1941): 29–30.

Harman, Jympson. "Film to Have First Radio Preview." *Evening News*, 20 July 1946.

Harper, Sue. "Historical Pleasures: Gainsborough Costume Melodrama." Pages 167–96 in Gledhill, Christine, ed. *Home Is Where the Heart Is: Studies in Melodrama and the Woman's Film.* London: British Film Institute Publishing, 1987.

Hartog, Simon. "State Protection of a Beleaguered Industry." Pages 60–73 in Curran, James, and Vincent Porter, eds. *British Cinema History.* London: Weidenfeld and Nicholson, 1983.

Higson, Andrew. "Addressing the Nation: Five Films." Pages 22–26 in Hurd, Geoff, ed. *National Fictions: World War Two in British Films and Television.* London: British Film Institute Publishing, 1984.

Hill, John. "Ideology, Economy and the British Cinema." Pages 115–34 in Barrett, Michèle; Corrigan, Philip; Kuhn, Annette; and Wolff, Janet, eds. *Ideology and Cultural Production.* London: Croon Helm, 1979.

Houston, Penelope. *The Contemporary Cinema, 1945–1963.* London: Pelican, 1963.

Howard, Ronald. *In Search of My Father: A Portrait of Leslie Howard.* London: Kimber, 1981.

Hurd, Geoff, ed. *National Fictions: World War Two in British Films and Television.* London: British Film Institute Publishing, 1984.

Kaplan, E. Ann. *Women and Film: Both Sides of the Camera.* New York: Methuen, 1983.

Kardish, Larry, ed. *Michael Balcon: The Pursuit of British Cinema.* New York: Museum of Modern Art, 1984.

Kirwan, Patrick. "Star . . ." *Evening Standard*, 23 November 1945.

Kracauer, Siegfried. "The Mass Ornament." Trans. Barbara Correll and Jack Zipes. *New German Critique* 5 (Spring 1975): 67–76.

Kuhn, Annette. "*Desert Victory* and the People's War." *Screen* 22, no. 2 (1981): 45–68.

———. *The Power of the Image: Essays on Representation and Sexuality.* London: Routledge and Kegan Paul, 1985.

Kulik, Karol. *Alexander Korda: The Man Who Could Work Miracles.* London: W. H. Allen, 1975.

Lean, David. "*Brief Encounter.*" *Penguin Film Review* 4: 27–35. Harmondsworth: Penguin, October 1947.

Lejeune, Caroline Alice. "The Gentle Sex." *The Observer*, 11 April 1943.

———. "The Films." *The Observer*, 25 November 1945.

Lejeune, Caroline Alice. "Can Piccadilly Do Without Hollywood?" *New York Times Magazine*, 24 August 1947, p. 16 +.

———. *Chestnuts in Her Lap, 1936–1946*. London: Phoenix House, 1947.

Lester, Joan. "New Coward Film Is Good." *Reynolds Weekly*, 25 November 1945.

McArthur, Colin. "National Identities." In Hurd, Geoff, ed. *National Fictions: World War Two in British Films and Television*. London: British Film Institute, 1984.

McGarry, Eileen. "Documentary, Realism and Women's Cinema." *Women and Film* 2, no. 7 (Summer 1975): 50–59.

MacPherson, Don, ed. *British Cinema: Traditions of Independence*. London: British Film Institute Publishing, 1980.

Manvell, Roger. "Brief Encounter Review Notes." British Film Institute Library, microjacket.

———. "Recent Films." *Britain Today*, February 1945, p. 36.

———. "Recent Films." *Britain Today*, May 1945, p. 36.

———. "Recent Films." *Britain Today*, July 1945, p. 36.

———. "Clearing the Air." *Hollywood Quarterly* 2 (1946–47): 176–78.

———. "The Cinema and the State: England." *Hollywood Quarterly* 2 (1946–47): 289–93.

———. *The Film and the Public*. Harmondsworth: Penguin, 1955.

Mayer, Jacob Peter. *British Cinema and Their Audiences: Sociological Studies*. London: Dobson, 1948.

Morgan, Guy. *Red Roses Every Night: An Account of London Cinemas Under Fire*. London: Quality Press, 1948.

"Movie Missionary: Britain's J. Arthur Rank." *Fortune* 23, no. 4 (October 1945): 149–51 +.

Mulvey, Laura. "Visual Pleasure and Narrative Cinema." *Screen* 16, no. 3 (Autumn 1975): 6–18.

———. "Notes on Sirk and Melodrama." *Movie* 25 (1977–78): 53–56.

Murphy, Robert. "Rank's Attempt on the American Market." Pages 164–78 in Curran, James, and Porter, Vincent, eds. *British Cinema History*. London: Weidenfeld and Nicholson, 1983.

"New British Film Pact Cheers Hollywood." *Business Week*, 20 March 1948, p. 100.

Noble, Peter, comp. *The British Film Yearbook*. Foreword by Sir Alexander Korda; introduction by J. Arthur Rank, London: British Yearbooks, 1946.

Oakley, Charles. *Where We Came In: Seventy Years of the British Film Industry*. London: Allen and Unwin, 1964.

Page, Alan. "Art Suspended." *Sight and Sound* 8, no. 31 (Autumn 1939): 99–100.

Perfect Strangers. Anonymous reviews: *Monthly Film Bulletin* 12, no. 141 (30 September 1945): 106; *Motion Picture Herald*, 1 December 1945, p. 2733.

Perry, George. *The Great British Picture Show: From the Nineties to the Seventies*. London: Hart-Davis MacGibbon, 1974.

Piccadilly Incident. Anonymous Review: *Reynolds Weekly*, 25 August 1946.

Piccadilly Incident. London: Book-of-the-Film Series, in World Film Series, 1946.

Pihodna, Joe. "Vacation from Marriage." *Herald Tribune*, 15 March 1946.

Powell, Dilys. *The Film since 1939*. London: British Council Series no. 3, "The Arts in Britain," 1947.

Pronay, Nicholas, and Thorpe, Frances. *British Official Films in the Second World War: A Descriptive Catalogue*. London: Clio Press, 1980.

Quigly, Isabel. "*Brief Encounter* Programme Notes." Microjacket, British Film Institute Library.

Ray, Cyril. "These British Movies." *Harper's Magazine*, June 1947, pp. 516–23.

Robertson, E. Arnott. "Woman and the Film." *Penguin Film Review* 3: 31–35. Harmondsworth: Penguin, August 1947.

de la Roche, Catherine. "A Director's Approach to Filmmaking: David Lean," unpublished script of interview, broadcast on BBC Radio 3, 18 August 1947. Script at British Film Institute Library.

———. "The Mask of Realism." *Penguin Film Review* 7: 35–43. Harmondsworth: Penguin, September 1948.

———. "That 'Feminine Angle'." *Penguin Film Review* 8: 25–34. Harmondsworth: Penguin, January 1949.

"Round Table on British Films." Editors of *Sight and Sound*. *Sight and Sound* 19, no. 3 (May 1950): 114–22.

Russell, Evelyn. "Why Not a School of British Film-making?" *Sight and Sound* 10, no. 37 (Spring 1941): 12–13.

———. "Films of 1942." *Sight and Sound* 11, no. 44 (Spring 1943): 99.

Silverman, Kaja. *The Acoustic Mirror: The Female Voice in Psychoanalysis and Cinema*. Bloomington: Indiana University Press, 1988.

Sklar, Robert. *Movie-Made America: A Social History of the American Movies*. New York: Random House, 1975.

Sklar, Robert and Musser, Charles, eds. *Resisting Images: Essays on Film and History*. Philadelphia: Temple University Press, 1990.

Smith, Brian. "Nationalise!" *Sight and Sound* 9, no. 36 (Winter 1940–41): 60–61.

Taylor, Philip, ed. *Britain and the Cinema in the Second World War*. London: Macmillan, 1988.

Thomas, F. L. "Whither Our Business?" *Sight and Sound* 10, no. 40 (Spring 1942): 64–67.

"U.S. Exports: End of a Boom—Hollywood Hits Back—and Hits Rank." *Business Week*, 16 August 1947, p. 15.

"U.S. Films Face Fight Abroad." *Business Week*, 29 December 1945, pp. 109–10.

Vargas, A. L. "British Films and Their Audience." *Penguin Film Review* 8: 71–76. Harmondsworth: Penguin, January 1949.

Vermilye, Jerry. *The Great British Films, 1933–1971*. Secaucus, N.J.: Citadel Press, 1978.

Watts, Stephen. "A Seat in the . . ." *Sunday Express*, 25 January 1946.

Weinberg, Herman G. "News from New York." *Sight and Sound* 10, no. 40 (Spring 1942): 73.

Whitman, Howard. "What Hollywood Doesn't Know about Women." *Colliers*, 5 March 1949.

Wickware, Francis Sill. "J. Arthur Rank." *Life*, 8 October 1945, pp. 106–8 +.

Winnington, Richard. *Film Criticism and Caricatures, 1943–53*. New York: Harper and Row, 1976.

Wollenberg, H. H. *Anatomy of the Film*. London: Marshland, 1947.

Wright, Basil. "Realist Review." *Sight and Sound* 10, no. 38 (Summer 1941): 20–21.

Wyatt, Woodrow. "Champagne for Hollywood." *The New Statesman and the Nation*, 20 March 1948, p. 231.

―――. "Dollars and Films." *The Statesman and the Nation*, 8 May 1948, p. 368.

INDEX

Academy Award, 30, 165
adultery, 17, 155, 159, 175, 187
Adventures of Tartu, The (1943), 9, 231
Adventuress, The. See I See a Dark Stranger
advertising, 49–50, 53–55, 56, 61, 63; address of, 61, 155; of beauty products, 79–83; and the blackout, 130, 148
Agate, James, 217
Agee, James, 122, 126, 184
Air Raid Patrol, 24
Air Raid Precaution, 44, 50, 52, 61, 225
Air Transport Auxiliary, 65
Aked, Muriel, 138
Akerman, Chantal, 4
American Army Filmmaking Unit, 8
American cinema. *See* Hollywood cinema
American Red Cross, 136
American Revolution, 210
Amies, Hardy, 68
Anderson, Lindsay, 196
androgyny, 8. *See also* uniforms, cross-dressing
Anstey, Edgar, 185
Archers, The, 13, 28, 206
Army and Navy Camp Film Societies, 4
Arnheim, Rudolf, 113
A.R.P. *See* Air Raid Precaution
Arthur, Jean, 57
Asquith, Anthony, 13
Associated British Picture Corporation, 228
Association of Ciné-Technicians, 25
A.T.S. *See* Auxiliary Territorial Service
Attlee, Clement, 160
audience, wartime, 4–5, 7, 21, 24, 29, 31, 33, 149–52, 167, 170–71, 196, 198, 224; address to, 62–63, 65, 72, 89–91, 93, 111–12, 113, 118, 134–35, 138, 163, 173, 180, 216; American, 21, 32, 33, 34, 198, 216; and the blackout, 115, 122; character of, 20, 164; female, 11, 20, 23, 24, 25, 48, 59, 75, 84, 85, 89–

91, 93, 111, 181, 184, 194; fragmentation of, 5–6, 113; male, 9, 90, 103; mobilization of, 11, 32, 35, 36–37, 44, 48, 61, 127, 151, 152; opinions of, 11, 23, 24, 25, 38–39, 73–74, 83, 169
Austerity Regulations, 96
Auxiliary Territorial Service, 47, 65, 66, 76, 84, 89, 91, 93, 94, 97, 98, 104, 108, 111, 113, 129, 202

Bakhtin, Mikhail, 116
Balázs, Béla, 23
Balcon, Michael, 21, 31, 32, 226, 227, 228
Baldwin, Stanley, 222
Balloon Goes Up, The (1942), 65
Barker, Felix, 187
barrage balloon, 118, 119, 211; and sexual difference, 53–56
Barthes, Roland, 115, 145
Battle of Britain, 53, 119
Baudry, Jean-Louis, 151–52
Bazin, André, 165
B.B.C. *See* British Broadcasting Corporation
Beethoven, Ludwig von, 40
Bells Go Down, The (1943), 118
Berger, John, 148
Berlei, Frederick R., 110
Bernstein, Sidney, 33
Best Years of Our Lives, The (1946), 166, 229, 232
Bevan, Aneurin, 63, 85, 88, 101
Bhabha, Homi K., 89
Biddle, Eric, 5
Big Sleep, The (1946), 65
Billings, R. H. "Josh," 231
"Black November," 222
Blackout. See Contraband
blackout, the, 158, 169, 218; and daily life, 128–29, 146; definitions of, 128; and femininity, 114–15, 116, 137, 144,

blackout (*cont.*)

146; in fiction film, 16, 31, 114, 115, 119, 121, 126, 133–42, 176, 187, 199, 209–10, 214; and film going, 115, 121–22, 127, 142, 144, 151; and film technology, 115, 121, 123; as military strategy, 24, 114, 116, 150; and sexual difference, 121, 144; and sexuality, 136–37, 144, 146; as symbol, 116, 123, 126, 128, 129, 130, 131, 134, 140, 141, 142, 144, 148

Blackout Stroll, the, 146

Black Swan, The (1942), 9, 231

Blitz, the, 17, 27, 46, 113, 119, 120, 123, 135, 137, 138, 147, 148, 210, 218

Board of Trade, 69, 70, 228

Boer War, 197

bombing, 37, 40, 46, 117, 154, 161, 163, 168; in fiction film, 31, 35, 38, 45–46, 47, 49, 65, 121, 134

Bond, Ralph, 21, 29, 32, 33, 223

Boothby, Robert, MP, 226

Box, Muriel, 26

Brains Trust, 111

Brief Encounter (1945), 16, 17, 28, 36, 47, 48, 85, 154–60, 161, 163–96, 216, 217, 232, 235

Britain at War (1945), 26

Britain Speaks, 93, 111

Britain Today, 158

British Broadcasting Corporation, 41, 111, 227; Home Service, 44–45

British cinema. *See* national cinema

British Film Institute, 27, 223

British Lion, 230

British National, 227

British National Services Acts, 85

Broadway Melody (1929), 48

Brown, John Mason, 184, 191

Buchanan, Andrew, 23, 33

Caesar and Cleopatra (1945), 60, 232

Canterbury Tale, A (1944), 17, 28, 29, 34, 47, 49, 60, 65, 108, 197–203, 205–16, 235

Canterbury Tales, The, 206

Carey, Joyce, 167

Casablanca (1943), 9, 49, 231

Caught (1949), 179

Cavalcanti, Alberto, 133

censorship, 22, 28, 161

Chamberlain, Nevil, 138

Charles II, King, 140, 161, 196

Charles, Moie, 90

Chaucer, Geoffrey, 34, 198, 205, 206, 207, 208, 214, 216

Chronicle, The, 186

Churchill, Winston, 44, 76, 87, 119, 160

Cineguild, 28, 168

Cinema Exhibitors' Association, 23

cinemas: alternative venues to, 27; effect of war on, 22, 24, 26, 28, 211, 225; representations of, 36, 40, 49, 179–80, 187–88, 213; wartime role of, 24–25, 127, 211

Cinematograph Films Act, 222–24, 226

Civilian Clothing Order, 68

class relations, 4, 6, 24, 48, 68, 87, 108, 111, 123, 127, 159, 202–3; in cinema audience, 20, 35, 36, 164, 195–96; and embroidery, 96, 98; in fiction film, 39, 41, 42–43, 63, 90, 91–92, 155–56, 166–67, 175, 191, 194–95; and sexual difference, 41–42

Cleopatra, 60

Cleveland, Les, 12

clothing, 150, 191–92. *See also* hats, uniforms, underwear

collaboration, 199; and femininity, 43, 48, 75–79, 148, 152; and film exhibition, 22, 152

Colliers, 57

Comolli, Jean-Louis, 116

conscription. *See* draft

Conservative Party, 222

Contraband (1940), 141, 197

Cook, Pam, 153, 154

Cornelius, Henry, 230

cosmetics. *See* makeup

costume melodrama, 4–5, 21, 24, 25, 34, 74, 139, 161–62

countryside, 31, 34, 48, 49–50, 160, 162–63, 198–99, 205–8. *See also* regionalism, geography

Coward, Noel, 13, 30, 47, 167, 168, 177, 188, 193

Craigie, Jill, 26

Crawford, Joan, 191, 192

critics: opinions of, 31, 32, 33, 161, 162,

163–64, 165–66, 169, 182–83, 184–87, 188–89, 190–92, 195; role of, 3, 164–67

Cromwell, Oliver, 48, 161

cross-dressing, 103, 106–7. *See also* uniforms, androgyny

Crown Film Unit, 26, 28

Curtis, Michael, 153

Dad's Army (1971), 52

Daily Mirror, 169

Daisy Kenyon (1947), 179

Dalton, Hugh, 228

Dalton Tax, 228

Darling (1965), 113

Darracott, Joseph, 84

Davis, Bette, 23, 72

D-Day, 45, 199, 216

de Havilland, Olivia, 141

de la Roche, Catherine, 165–67, 169, 217, 218

Delacroix, Eugène, 59

Del Guidice, Filippo, 21

Denham Studios, 26

Desert Victory (1943), 9, 49, 65, 86, 182, 231

Destination Moon (1950), 233

Diary for Timothy (1945), 34, 40, 41, 43, 45, 50

Dickinson, Margaret, 226

Dickinson, Thorold, 76, 230

Dieppe raid, 76, 135

Dietrich, Marlene, 57, 58

distribution: in Britain, 225; of British film in America, 29, 230

Dixon, Campbell, 188

Doane, Mary Ann, 72, 154

documentary film, 9, 27, 35, 36–38, 112, 113, 125, 193; relationship to fiction film of, 34–35

Documentary News Letter, 164

Domesday Book, 48, 162

domestic life: as a double life, 61, 103, 155; effect of war on, 4, 14, 36, 55, 94, 128, 147, 154–55; as subject matter, 33, 41, 47, 117–18, 119, 142, 166, 171, 185–86; and war work, 97–99

Donald Duck, 169

Donat, Robert, 117

Double Indemnity (1944), 182, 183

draft, 4, 25, 52, 85; of women, 13, 46, 63, 65, 85–89, 102

Dresden bombings (13/14 Feb. 1945), 163

Dunkirk, 119, 135

Durgnat, Raymond, 195

Eagleton, Terry, 17, 116

Ealing Studios, 13

Eddy, Nelson, 23

El Alamein, 144

Elgar, Sir Edward, 48

Elizabeth I, 60

Elizabeth II, 202

Elstree Studios, 26

Elvey, Maurice, 89

Elvin, George, 25

embroidery, 90, 93–98, 113, 180, 182

Embroidery Magazine, 96

enemy, representation of the, 38, 51, 76, 78, 90, 130–31, 141–42, 149, 150, 197, 199

English without Tears (1944), 65

Enoch Arden, 136

Enola Gay, 75

Entertainment Duty, 225

Eros, statue of, 135

Eve of St. Mark, The (1944), 46

Everybody's Weekly, 12, 41

exhibition: effect of war on, 24, 26, 28, 224–25, 229; by Rank Organization, 28; restrictions on, 22–23

exhibitors, opinions of, 21, 22, 225

Family Allowances Act (1945), 155

fantasy, 157, 159; representations of, 101, 168, 179, 181, 194

Farber, Manny, 181, 184, 186

femininity: and beauty products, 79–83; and the blackout, 116, 130, 146, 148, 176–77, 199, 209; classifications of, 72–74, 87–89, 179–80, 181–82, 215–16; and collaboration, 43, 48, 75–79, 148, 152; legislation of, 62, 109–10; and mobilization, 11, 14, 61–62, 79–83, 97–99; and national identity, 84–85, 197–98, 211–12, 217–19; and uniforms, 102–3, 107, 202–5; Victorian, 93–98

Fiddlers Three (1944), 65

Fighting Sullivans, The (1944), 46

film bank, 227

film noir style, 176–79, 229
Fire over England (1936), 60
Fire Watches, 24, 199
First of the Few, The (1942), 111, 231
flashbacks, 156, 162, 163, 168, 172–79,
    180–83, 210, 214, 216
Fletcher, Helen, 57
Foreign Affair, A (1948), 57
Foreman Went to France, The (1942), 38,
    43, 45, 47, 48, 49, 235
Formby, George, 21
49th Parallel (1941), 28, 111, 199, 231
Fougasse, 37, 76, 144
Four Jills in a Jeep (1944), 39, 101
France, 5; the Fall of, 139; and Free
    French, 6; Occupied, 138; representa-
    tions of, 38, 50
Frenchman's Creek (1944), 232
Freud, Sigmund, 181–82, 193, 201
Frieda (1947), 166, 232
Fuller, W. R., 23, 225

Gable, Clark, 124
Gainsborough Studios, 5, 9, 10, 13, 21,
    24, 25, 73, 74, 139. *See also* costume
    melodrama
Games, Abram, 84
Garbo, Greta, 23
Gaumont-British, 224
Gaumont Cinemas, 28, 228
gender: and genre, 10, 59, 63–65, 183–85;
    and ideology, 17, 75; and national iden-
    tity , 9, 15, 18, 31, 56–58, 71–73, 76,
    79, 80–81; and neutrality, 78–79; repre-
    sentation of, 6–7, 57–58, 62, 66, 126–
    27, 138, 144, 149, 183, 217–18; spatial-
    ization of, 32, 39, 46, 51–55, 65, 91,
    93, 100, 158, 204–5, 208; and temporal-
    ity, 171, 193–94, 205, 208–9. *See also*
    women, femininity
G.I., 129, 137, 141, 198, 203, 209, 216;
    in audience, 6, 21; in fiction film, 52,
    206–7; and national identity, 17, 48–49,
    210–14; and sexuality, 83–84, 211, 212
G.I. Movie Weekly, 8
General Post Office, 226
genre, 36, 44, 47, 71, 92, 113, 154, 157;
    and gender, 10, 59, 63–65, 183–85
Gentle Sex, The (1943), 9, 15, 16, 28, 29,
    37, 40, 41, 43, 45, 47, 60, 62, 63, 65,

73, 89–99, 103, 106, 107, 110, 112,
    113, 125, 150, 166, 182, 187, 205, 206–
    7, 231, 236
geography, 45, 207–8; and national iden-
    tity, 6, 32, 41, 48, 50, 51–52. *See also*
    countryside, maps, regionalism
Germany. *See* enemy
Ghilchik, 130
Gillen, Charles, 137
Gilliat, Sidney, 13, 28, 59, 79, 88, 184
glamour, 33, 125; and men, 120, 211; and
    patriotism, 56–57, 71–74, 81–83, 107,
    188; in posters, 84; and uniforms, 101;
    and women, 56–57, 79–83, 120, 179,
    189–92
Gledhill, Christine, 13, 89, 192
Goldwyn, Samuel, 229
Gone with the Wind (1939), 111, 225
Goodman, Ezra, 161
government: and the blackout, 114, 116,
    150; and daily life, 45, 62; debate on
    cinema in, 20, 225–26; and femininity,
    68–70, 86–89, 109; and film legislation,
    226–27, 228–30; filmmaking sponsored
    by, 26, 28; guidelines for cinema by, 21,
    25, 36, 224–25; in 1945, 30, 160, 195
G.P.O. *See* General Post Office
G.P.O. Film Unit, 26
Grable, Betty, 9, 10
Granger, Stewart, 39
Grant, Cary, 106
Grant, Elspeth, 14, 125
Gray, Allan, 197
Gray, Dulcie, 7
Great Day (1945), 47, 52, 60, 62, 65, 109,
    236
"Great Masculine Renunciation, The," 68
Grierson, John, 19
Guardian, The, 185, 188

hairstyles, 79–80, 104–5, 109, 120, 124
Hall, Jon, 39
Harlow, Jean, 75
Harman, Jympson, 135
Harrisson, Tom, 128, 138
Hartnell, Norman, 68
hats, 66, 67, 76, 191, 196
Havelock-Allan, Anthony, 28, 230
Hawks, Howard, 106
Hayworth, Rita, 75

Hello, Frisco, Hello (1943), 9, 231
Henry V (1944), 5, 232
Herald Tribune, 85
Higson, Andrew, 36, 44
Hird, Thora, 76
history: and countryside, 49, 207–8; as an escape from war, 23–24, 47, 71, 94, 166; representation of, 16, 24, 34, 46, 60, 94, 97, 118, 125, 126, 138, 140, 158–59, 161–63, 166, 168–70, 197, 205–8, 216
Hitler, Adolf, 87, 88
Holloway, Stanley, 171
Hollywood cinema, 126, 127, 211, 217, 218, 219, 221, 222, 223, 229; artificiality of, 25, 32, 33, 34, 38–39, 57, 83, 115, 188–89; and the blackout, 140–41; boycott of Britain by, 229; domination by, 4, 12, 19, 20, 84, 124, 212–13, 221–22, 226; and femininity, 56–58, 60, 81, 83, 84–85, 115, 127, 179, 187, 189–92, 217; and national identity, 10, 11, 22, 31, 33, 41, 84, 123, 125
home as symbol, 44–45, 88–89
Home Guard, 44, 48, 52, 199
Home Intelligence Unit, 44
Home Office, 26, 83, 224
Home Secretary, 44
Home Service. *See* British Broadcasting Corporation
House of Commons, 133, 225
House of Lords, 20
Howard, Leslie, 13, 16, 59, 89, 90, 91, 92, 93, 94, 104, 111, 112, 182, 184, 205
Hundred Pound Widow, The (1943), 65
Hunter, Kim, 214
Huston, Nancy, 104, 154, 158, 173

iconography, wartime, 41, 43–44, 46–47, 90, 117, 142, 157–58, 187. *See also* blackout, bombing, countryside, mobile women, pilots, singsongs
I Live in Grosvenor Square (1945), 45, 65, 213, 232
illegitimacy, 83, 137, 138, 155, 187–88
Independent Producers Limited, 28
Individual Pictures, 28
Inland Revenue, 25

I See A Dark Stranger (1946), 36, 45, 77, 78, 236
In Which We Serve (1942), 9, 25, 28, 29, 30, 36, 40, 45, 46, 48, 63, 65, 111, 133, 134, 167, 217, 231, 237
Islington Studios, 26
Italian Neorealism, 14
It Always Rains on Sunday (1947), 49, 133, 140, 232, 237
I Was a Male War Bride (1949), 106

Jameson, Fredric, 116
Jaws (1975), 116
Jazz Singer, The (1927), 210
Jeanne Dielman, 23 Quai du Commerce, 1080 Bruxelles (1979), 4
Jennings, Humphrey, 43, 50
Johnny in the Clouds. See Way to the Stars, The
Johnson, Celia, 165, 182, 183, 184, 189–90, 192. *See also* stardom
Junge, Alfred, 197

Kaplan, E. Ann, 157–58, 178
Keats, John, 97, 205, 206
Keep Your Powder Dry (1945), 57
Kerr, Deborah, 35, 77, 78, 117, 123, 197
Kinematograph Weekly, 13, 30, 164, 224, 231
King Arthur Was a Gentleman (1942), 65
Kirk, Norah, 96
Koch, Gertrud, 180
Korda, Alexander, 13, 21, 114, 117, 123, 124, 125, 144, 223, 224, 230
Kracauer, Siegfried, 217
Kristeva, Julia, 145

Labour Party, 30, 159, 160, 195. *See also* government, in 1945
Ladies' Home Journal, 184
Lady Surrenders, A. See Love Story
Lake, Veronica, 105
Lamp Still Burns, The (1943), 65, 231
Launder, Frank, 13, 28, 59, 79, 88, 115, 138, 184, 230
Lean, David, 13, 28, 47, 155, 168, 195
Lejeune, C. A., 33
lesbianism, 204; representations of, 93, 94, 107–9; and uniforms, 107–8

Letter from an Unknown Woman (1948), 181
Liberty Guiding the People (1830), 60
Lidell, Alvar, 45
Life, 12
Life and Death of Colonel Blimp, The (1943), 9, 29, 77, 197, 231
Life with Father (1947), 232
lighting, 4, 115, 121, 123, 127, 146, 150; in fiction film, 38, 41, 154, 157, 159, 176–77, 185, 194; neon, 24, 141; symbolism of, 130, 132–33, 138, 139, 145, 210, 212
Lillie, Bea, 8, 10
Lion Has Wings, The (1939), 49
Listen to Britain (1942), 43, 50
Livesey, Roger, 197, 210
Local Defence Volunteers, 44
Lockwood, Margaret, 39, 73, 74, 139, 196
Loftus, Belinda, 84
London Blackout Murders, The. See Secret Motive
London Can Take It (1940), 34, 36
London Films, 13, 223, 224
London Town (1946), 232
Longmate, Norman, 69
Love on the Dole (1941), 123
Love Story (1944), 39, 41, 43, 53, 54, 65, 73, 74, 75, 232, 237
Lynn, Vera, 43

Macherey, Pierre, 12
McLean, Alice, 129
Madge, Charles, 128
Maedchen in Uniform (1931), 93
"Mae Wests," 75
Major Barbara (1941), 231
makeup, 57, 68–72, 73, 76, 79, 81–83, 101, 103, 120, 126, 147–48, 190–92
Man in Grey, The (1943), 5, 9, 73, 74, 93, 133, 231, 237
Manvell, Roger, 21, 47, 124, 127, 198
maps, 50–51, 207. *See also* countryside, geography
Marshall Plan, 229
Mason, James, 140
Massey, Raymond, 205, 210
Mass-Observation, 112, 128, 129, 144
Mata Hari, 116
Matter of Life and Death, A (1946), 50, 51, 53, 65, 210, 213, 214

Matthews, Jessie, 7, 26
Mayer, J. P., 83
Maytime in Mayfair (1949), 232
melodrama, 44, 47–48, 164, 177, 179. *See also* costume melodrama
men: absence of, 23, 44, 52, 73, 92, 200; and cosmetics, 68–69; and glamour, 120, 123–24, 211; on the home front in film, 52–53, 60–61, 74, 162–63, 197
Metz, Christian, 158
MGM, 225
MGM-London Films, 117, 224
Mildred Pierce (1945), 153–54, 156, 159, 161, 181, 182, 185, 191, 232
Milland, Ray, 141
Millions Like Us (1943), 28, 29, 36, 37, 43, 44, 47, 50, 53, 63, 65, 72, 73, 88, 92, 99, 103, 133, 135, 238
Mills, John, 7
Mine Own Executioner (1947), 166
Ministry of Agriculture and Fisheries, 50
Ministry of Fear (1944), 141–42
Ministry of Food, 53
Ministry of Home Security, 44
Ministry of Information Films Division, 22, 27–28, 63, 65, 88, 91, 93, 225, 227
Ministry of Labour, 86, 100, 101
Miss London Ltd. (1943), 65
mobile woman. *See* women, mobile
mobilization, 5, 9, 11, 28, 32, 35, 36–37, 44, 48, 61, 127, 151, 152; of femininity, 11, 14, 61–62, 79–83, 97–99
Montez, Maria, 39
Montgomery, Sir Bernard Law, 210
Monthly Film Bulletin, 125
Morgan, Guy, 111
Mormont, Jean, 107–8
Morocco (1930), 49
motherhood, 154, 157–58, 172–73, 176, 178–79, 190, 192. *See also* femininity
Motion Picture Association of America, 226
Motion Picture Herald, 164
Mrs. Miniver (1942), 9, 21, 53, 231
Mulvey, Laura, 56, 124, 181
musicals, 23, 24, 48, 65, 210

narrative: recurrent themes in, 31–32, 35–53, 59, 71, 92, 125, 158–59, 213; women central to, 59, 63–65, 179–83
national cinema, 20; as affected by war, 4,

29–30, 226; as ambassador, 23, 29, 229; characterizations of, 3; compared to Hollywood, 4, 123, 157; and femininity, 56–58, 65, 71–79, 89–98, 103–13, 187–92; iconography of, 41, 46–47; and mobilization, 28, 36; and national identity, 31, 33, 34, 38, 157, 165, 188–92, 198, 217–19; and national morale, 23. *See also* iconography, wartime

national identity: and accent, 48–49, 111, 209–10; and allies, 8–9, 17, 48–49; and the blackout, 114, 117, 123, 142, 150; and British cinema, 23, 29, 31, 34, 57–58, 217–19; and the Civilian Clothing Order, 68; clichés of, 48, 197; formation of, 3, 5–6, 20, 31, 32, 35, 38, 40, 48, 84, 90, 222–23; and gender, 9, 15, 18, 57–58, 62, 63, 66, 75, 86, 94; and geography, 6, 41, 51–52, 150, 207; and Hollywood, 10–11, 31, 84, 125, 188–92; home and, 32, 44–45, 47–48, 52, 88–89. *See also* national cinema

National Register, 6

National Service, 19

natural beauty, 81–83. *See also* makeup

nature. *See* countryside

Neagle, Anna, 136

Neame, Ronald, 28

neutrality, 78–79

Newman, Rosie, 26

news: newsreel, 24, 27, 34, 36, 45. *See also* documentary

Newton, Eric, 84

New York Film Critics' Association, 30, 165

Next of Kin (1942), 36, 37, 43, 50, 65, 76, 238

Night Mail (1936), 193

Night Witches, 85

Noble, Peter, 111

nostalgia, 16, 170, 174

Notorious Gentleman. See Rake's Progress, The

Now, Voyager (1942), 23, 72, 74

O'Brien, Kate, 180

Odeon Cinemas, 28, 228

Of Great Events and Ordinary People (1979), 51

Old Mother Riley Joins Up (1941), 65

Olivier, Laurence, 5, 23

Pacific Blackout (1942), 141

Page, Alan, 222

Painted Boats (1945), 65

Palache, Albert, 228

Paramount Studios, London, 27

Parker, Rozsika, 94

Parliament, 28, 225

Pascal, Gabriel, 60

Pasolini, Pier Paolo, 145

Pearl Harbor, 210

Peeping Tom (1960), 201

People's War, The, 4

Perfect Strangers (1945), 16, 17, 35, 49, 54, 65, 73, 103, 114, 117–27, 129, 133, 134, 135, 142, 144, 162, 182, 216, 217, 224, 232, 238

phoney war, 118–19

Piccadilly, 135, 203, 213

"Piccadilly Flash," 138

Piccadilly Incident (1946), 43, 46, 65, 133, 135–38, 147, 162, 187, 213, 232, 239

Picture Post, 12, 36, 66, 110, 147, 148, 155, 159, 196

Pilgrim's Way, The, 207, 208

pilots, 34–35, 37, 38–39, 43, 46–47, 51–53, 85, 91, 100, 138, 162–63, 208

Pimpernel Smith (1941), 111, 231

Pinewood Studios, 26

Poole, Julian, 231

Portman, Eric, 199

posters, 31, 36–37, 70–71, 76–77, 84, 101

Powell, Michael, 9, 13, 17, 28, 34, 51, 77, 197, 198, 201, 202, 204, 206, 208, 213–17, 223

Prayer for the Wanderer (1939), 180

Pre-Raphaelites, 94

Pressburger, Emeric, 9, 13, 17, 28, 34, 51, 77, 197, 198, 200, 201, 202, 204, 206, 208, 213–17

Prestige Productions, 223

Price, Dennis, 198

Priestley, J. B., 59, 86, 87, 88, 184, 204

prisoners of war, 138

Private Life of Henry VIII, The (1933), 223, 224

producers, opinions of, 30, 32

production: effect of war on, 25–29, 34, 126, 227–28; independent, 28, 228; and military cooperation, 28, 34, 94, 113

Programme for Film Propaganda, 36

Public Health and Sanitary Services, 61
Punch, 12, 66, 69, 102, 103, 142, 203, 211
Pygmalion (1938), 111

Quigly, Isabel, 169, 195
Quo Vadis (1951), 123
"Quota Act." *See* Cinematograph Films Act

Rachmaninov, Sergei, 173, 174–75, 184
radio, 20, 36, 41, 45, 90, 93, 111, 173
R.A.F. *See* Royal Air Force
railways, 4, 37, 42, 47, 90, 92, 97, 157, 166, 168, 169, 171–72, 175, 177–78, 193–95, 199, 207
Rainbow Club, 213
Rake's Progress, The (1945), 166
Rank, Arthur J., 13, 21, 28, 29, 227
Rank Organization, 228, 229, 230
rationing, 4, 23, 24, 36, 60, 109, 154, 168–69; and embroidery, 96–97; and femininity, 56–57, 63, 66, 68–72, 74–75; of film stock, 28; of light, 115
Ray, Cyril, 30, 31
Raymond, Cyril, 182
realism, in British cinema, 124–25, 157, 159, 196; definitions of, 14, 33, 162, 163–65, 169, 185, 217–19; and femininity, 89–90, 123, 160–62, 172, 174, 184–85, 192; and national identity, 14, 31, 34, 106, 114, 198
Rebecca (1940), 179, 231
Redgrave, Michael, 40
Reed, Carol, 13
refugees, 21, 38, 50, 92
regionalism, in British cinema, 21, 34, 41, 45, 48, 49, 78, 92, 169
Revolt of Mamie Stover, The (1956), 46
Richardson, Dorothy, 193
Rigoletto, 87
Riley, Denise, 155
Robertson, E. Arnot, 164
Robson, Flora, 60, 138
Roc, Patricia, 73, 138
Rogers, Ginger, 101
Roosevelt, Eleanor, 109
Roosevelt, Franklin Delano, 87
Royal Air Force, 34, 47, 51, 75, 100, 141, 162, 163

Royal Society for the Prevention of Accidents, 144
Ruiz, Raoul, 51
Russell, Evelyn, 33
Russell, Rosalind, 83

Sally Gets a New Job (1943), 65
Sapphire (1959), 113
Schivelbusch, Wolfgang, 193
Secret Motive, 141
Selznick, David O., 46
Sequence, 196
Seventh Veil, The (1945), 165, 232
sexual difference, 7, 8, 53–56, 68–69, 94, 96–97, 124, 148, 189; and the blackout, 121, 122, 123, 126, 140, 142, 147; and class relations, 41–42, 63; and cross-dressing, 106–7, 140; and hairstyles, 104–6; and uniforms, 69, 102–3
sexuality: and the blackout, 144–45, 146; in film, 119, 120–21, 135, 139, 183, 193–94, 195, 200–201, 208–9; and G.I.'s, 83–84; in wartime, 129–30, 135, 137–38. *See also* lesbianism
Shakespeare, William, 48
Shepherd's Bush Studios, 26
Shepperton Studios, 26
shortages. *See* rationing
Sight and Sound, 225, 226, 230
Silverman, Kaja, 182
Sim, Alastair, 135, 182
Sim, Sheila, 198
Since You Went Away (1944), 46, 47, 65, 101, 232
Singing with the Stars (1943), 7–9, 10
singsongs, 43–44, 65
Small Back Room, The (1949), 65, 133
Smith, Brian, 226, 227
Some Like It Hot (1959), 107
Somewhere in France. See Foreman Went to France, The
Somewhere on Leave (1942), 65
soundtrack, 173, 175–76; recurrent themes in, 41, 43–44. *See also* voice-over.
Soviet cinema, 32, 35
Soviet Union: and femininity, 43, 53, 84–85; representation of, 43, 53
Spanish Civil War, 169–70
spectacle, 123–24; attenuation of, 15–16, 68–69, 72–73, 84–85, 103, 189–92; and

the blackout, 115; female, 16, 43, 57, 60–61, 66, 70–71, 75, 101; and postwar life, 123

spectatorship, 6, 48, 151–52, 158, 182, 207; female, 161, 179–80, 181; and temporality, 158–59, 170–71, 193

spies, 78–79, 197

Spy in Black, The (1939), 133, 197

Stage Door Canteen (1943), 85, 101

Stalin, Joseph, 87

stardom, 123, 141; of Celia Johnson, 183, 190–92; of Joan Crawford, 191–92; of Margaret Lockwood, 73–74

Stella Dallas (1937), 179

stereotypes, 89

Still Life (1936), 167

Stragboli, Lord, 20, 28

studios: effect of war on, 25–29, 30; prewar, 224

Subversive Stitch, The, 94

suffrage, 75

Sunday Express, 189

Swanson, Gillian, 13, 192

Sweet, Sgt. John, 198

Target for Tonight (1941), 34, 38, 50, 51

Tarr, Carrie, 113

Tartu. See Adventures of Tartu, The

Tawny Pipit (1944), 36, 37, 40, 43, 47, 48, 49, 50, 52–53, 60, 65, 85, 239

Technicolor, 24

television, 5

Tempest, The, 74

temporality, 158–63, 166, 168–69, 187, 206–8, 216; and gender, 171–72, 193–94, 205, 208–9; and spectatorship, 158–59, 170–71, 193

Tender Comrade (1943), 46, 47, 60, 63, 65, 101

theater, relationship of film to, 3, 167–68

Theater Arts, 168

They Flew Alone (1941), 65

They Met in the Dark (1943), 141

This Happy Breed (1944), 17, 37, 44, 47, 48, 50, 62, 210, 231, 232, 239

Time and Tide, 12, 61, 86, 87, 108

Tivoli Theatre, 26

Today's Cinema, 164, 181, 184

Todd, Ann, 120

To Each His Own (1946), 141, 212

Tonight and Every Night (1945), 101, 141, 212, 232

Tonight at 8:30 (1936), 167

Truffaut, François, 2

Turner, Lana, 57

Turn of the Tide, The (1935), 227

Two Thousand Women (1944), 43, 115, 116, 133, 138–39, 239

Two Cities, 13, 21

Tyler, Parker, 217

underwear, 104, 107, 109–10, 145

uniforms: and cross-dressing, 103, 107; and femininity, 102–3, 107, 202–5; and glamour, 99, 101, 202–5; and sexual difference, 69, 102; and undressing, 103–4

United Artists, 27, 223

United States Air Force, 162

Up with the Lark (1943), 65

U.S.A.F. *See* United States Air Force

utility measures, 68

Vacation from Marriage. See Perfect Strangers

V-E Day, 17, 132, 163

Veidt, Conrad, 197

Verdi, Guiseppe, 87, 88

Vesselo, Arthur, 22

veterans, in fiction film, 39, 52, 166

Victoria, Queen, 48

Victory Wedding (1944), 7, 9, 10, 26, 36, 240

Virilio, Paul, 16, 32, 55

voice-over: female, 156, 168, 174–78, 181–83; male, 34, 36, 86, 92, 111–12, 118, 135, 163, 182, 214

V-1 Aircraft, 129, 133

V-2 Rocket, 129, 133, 136

W.A.A.C. *See* Women's Auxiliary Air Corps

W.A.A.F. *See* Women's Auxiliary Air Force

W.A.C. *See* Women's Army Corps

Walbrook, Anton, 197

Walsh, Raoul, 46

War Agricultural Committee, 199

War Office, The, 84, 98, 109, 113, 154

Waterloo Road (1945), 36, 37, 40, 41, 46, 47, 48, 52, 62, 88, 118, 133, 135, 182, 210, 217, 232, 240

Watt, Harry, 34

Watts, Stephen, 189

Way Ahead, The (1944), 28, 29, 34, 36, 37, 39, 41, 42, 43, 48, 49, 52, 56, 60, 62, 63, 65, 91, 125, 162, 166, 187, 203, 232, 240

Way to the Stars, The (1945), 40, 47, 53, 57, 92, 160, 162–63, 165, 210, 213, 232, 240

We'll Meet Again (1942), 43

Weaker Sex, The (1948), 65, 232

Went the Day Well? (1942), 65, 133

Wessex, 28

West End, 26–27, 213

Wicked Lady, The (1945), 139–40, 161–62, 165, 168, 196, 232, 241

Wilcox, Herbert, 13

Wilder, Billy, 57

Wilding, Michael, 136

Williams, Linda, 154, 159

Williamson, Judith, 75

Wilson, Mervyn, 160, 162

Winchester .73 (1950), 233

Wings and the Woman. See They Flew Alone

Winslow Boy, The (1948), 232

W.L.A. *See* Women's Land Army

Woman and Beauty, 84

Woman's Film, the, 10, 63, 72, 73, 184

women: and advertising, 63–64; as allegorical figures, 87–88, 130–31; and the blackout, 128, 129–30; as central to narrative, 59, 63–65, 179–83; and cosmetics, 68–72; in Germany, 86; mobile, 85–89, 99, 204–5, 218; opinions of, 23, 61–62, 86; representations of, 66, 74, 76–77, 89, 93, 118, 139; representation of relationships between, 74, 93, 103–9, 156, 215; and representation of war work, 36, 60, 65, 89, 93, 101, 112, 134; and suffrage, 75; and war work, 4, 23, 25, 60, 61–62, 68, 75, 84, 88–89, 94, 96–97, 203–4. *See also* gender, femininity

Women Aren't Angels (1942), 65

Women's Army Corps, 106, 202, 214

Women's Auxiliary Air Force, 65, 74, 100

Women's Auxiliary Air Force, 65, 74, 10

women's fiction, 180–81, 184

Women's Land Army, 65, 74, 85, 101, 102, 198, 202–5, 208, 215, 216

Women's Royal Naval Service, 60, 65, 66, 110, 120, 126, 136, 145, 167, 202

World Film News, 19

World War I, 39, 44, 97, 128, 138, 178, 211, 221–22

Wrens. *See* Women's Royal Naval Service

W.R.N.S. *See* Women's Royal Naval Service

Wright, Basil, 35

Wyatt, Woodrow, 229

Yank in London, A. See I Live in Grosvenor Square

''You Made Me Love You'' (1913), 8

Yule, Lady, 227